COMPARING AND ASSESSING

PROGRAMMING LANGUAGES

Ada, C, and Pascal

ALAN R. FEUER   and   **NARAIN GEHANI, Editors**
Catalytix Corporation   *Bell Laboratories*

PRENTICE-HALL, INC.
Englewood Cliffs, New Jersey 07632

Library of Congress Cataloging in Publication Data

Main entry under title:

Comparing and assessing programming languages.

(Prentice-Hall software series)
Bibliography: p.
Includes index.
1. Ada (Computer program language)—Addresses, essays,
lectures.   2. C (Computer program language)—Addresses,
essays, lectures.   3. PASCAL (Computer program language)—
Addresses, essays, lectures.   I. Feuer, Alan R.
II. Gehani, Narain (date) III. Series.
QA76.73.A35C66   1984   001.64'24   83-26865
ISBN 0-13-154857-3
ISBN 0-13-154840-9 (pbk.)

Editorial/production supervision: Nancy Milnamow
Cover design: Photo Plus Art (Celine A. Brandes)
Manufacturing buyer: Gordon Osbourne

Printed in the United States of America

10 9 8 7 6 5 4 3 2 1

ISBN   0-13-154857-3
ISBN   0-13-154840-9 {PBK}

PRENTICE-HALL INTERNATIONAL, INC., *London*
PRENTICE-HALL OF AUSTRALIA PTY. LIMITED, *Sydney*
EDITORA PRENTICE-HALL DO BRASIL, LTDA., *Rio de Janeiro*
PRENTICE-HALL CANADA INC., *Toronto*
PRENTICE-HALL OF INDIA PRIVATE LIMITED, *New Delhi*
PRENTICE-HALL OF JAPAN, INC., *Tokyo*
PRENTICE-HALL OF SOUTHEAST ASIA PTE. LTD., *Singapore*
WHITEHALL BOOKS LIMITED, *Wellington, New Zealand*

COMPARING AND ASSESSING

PROGRAMMING LANGUAGES

Ada, C, and Pascal

PRENTICE-HALL SOFTWARE SERIES
Brian W. Kernighan, advisor

To Indu, Jeannette and Daniel

Contents

ASSESSING PROGRAMMING LANGUAGES

LANGUAGE CRITICISMS

METHODOLOGY FOR COMPARING AND ASSESSING LANGUAGES

Contents

Preface

Selecting a language appropriate for an application from the plethora of programming languages in use today can confuse not only the novice programmer but also the experienced computer scientist. Despite the current abundance of programming languages, new languages will continue to be designed and implemented as we extend the reach of computers and enhance our understanding of programming. The push for designing new languages comes not only from individual computer scientists wishing to improve on existing languages, but also from large organizations that realize the potential advantages of a programming language tailored to meet their needs.

And those advantages can be great. Many people have observed that the cost of developing and maintaining software can be far greater than the cost of procuring hardware. Choosing an appropriate language in which to write the software for a project is an important factor in minimizing its total cost.

But programming languages are complex. The criteria for evaluating them are ill defined and the impact of most language design decisions is not fully understood. The papers in this collection have been chosen because each illuminates some aspect of how to compare and assess a programming language.

WHY ADA*, C, AND PASCAL?

Programming languages are as diverse as they are complex. There are people who favor languages based on hardware architecture, on English, on algebra, on mathemati-

---

* Ada is a registered trademark of the U.S. Government, Ada Joint Program Office.

cal logic, and on less traditional foundations. Other texts describe the taxonomy of programming languages; this text concentrates on comparing and assessing programming languages.

Our focus is on three languages—Ada, C, and Pascal—that are important today and likely to become more important in the future. In the large view of programming languages, these three are similar in many ways: they are all procedural, they have similar control constructs, and have similar type constructors. They resemble other popular languages that, as a class, dominate industrial programming.

However, there are significant differences that distinguish C and Pascal from each other and from Ada. Although both Pascal and C were each designed primarily by one person at about the same time (in the late 1960s and early 1970s), they embody very different programming philosophies; Pascal emphasizes reliability while C stresses flexibility. In contrast, Ada was designed more than a decade later by a group of people; it reflects several years of widespread discussion among computer scientists about what a general-purpose programming language should look like. As a result, Ada represents a later point in the evolution of programming languages than either C or Pascal.

ORGANIZATION

The papers in this book are grouped into four sections:

- Programming language comparisons
- Programming language assessments
- Language criticisms
- Methodology for language comparison and assessment

The first section contains specific comparisons of Ada, C, and Pascal. These papers play the additional role of introducing the languages.

The second section contains papers assessing each of the languages individually. The assessments differ in one important respect. C and Pascal have been used widely for over a decade, whereas Ada has yet to be used in any real applications. Thus the assessments of C and Pascal are based on substantial programming experience, while the assessment of Ada is based partly on language analysis.

The third section contains papers criticizing Pascal and C. In contrast to the papers in the second section, where the authors attempt to view the languages as a whole, in these papers the authors highlight weak points of the languages and in some cases propose alternative designs.

The discussion in the final section steps back from the programming languages themselves and concentrates on the process of comparing and assessing languages.

HOW THE BOOK CAME TO BE

When Narain Gehani joined Bell Labs in 1978, he found C in wide use at Bell Labs, whereas Pascal was virtually ignored.[1] Being very familiar with Pascal and convinced that it had many points in its favor, Gehani suggested to his management that they encourage the use of Pascal. To support his suggestion, Gehani embarked on a comparison of C and Pascal. In order that the study be fair, Gehani asked Alan Feuer, who was not only very familiar with C but convinced that it had many advantages over Pascal, to join him in doing the comparison.

In 1982 the comparison of C and Pascal was published in the *ACM Computing Surveys*. The paper generated a considerable amount of interest. Not only were there requests for comparisons of other languages, but also requests to expand on the original work. This collection of papers is a direct result of these requests.

On a personal note, the process of performing the comparison lead us to view each language more objectively and to appreciate the strong points of each.

ACKNOWLEDGMENTS

We are grateful to our respective managements at Bell Labs for their support and encouragement in the compilation of these papers. Jim Fegen and Nancy Milnamow of Prentice-Hall were very helpful in the production of this book.

We are indebted to the authors and publishers for giving us permission to reprint their papers. The individual credits are given below.

- Feuer, A. R. and N. H. Gehani, "A Comparison of the Programming Languages C and Pascal," *ACM Computing Surveys,* Vol. 14, No. 1, March 1982. Copyright 1982, Association for Computing Machinery, Inc., reprinted by permission.
- Mateti, P., "Pascal versus C: A Subjective Comparison," *Proceedings of the Symposium on Language Design and Programming Methodology,* September 1979. Copyright 1979, Springer-Verlag, Inc., reprinted by permission.
- Wichmann, B. A., "A Comparison of Pascal and Ada," *The Computer Journal,* Vol. 25, No. 2, 1982. Copyright 1982, John Wiley & Sons, Inc., reprinted by permission.
- Evans, A., Jr., "A Comparison of Programming Languages: Ada, Pascal, C." Shortened version of "A Comparison of Programming Languages: Ada, Praxis, Pascal, C," Lawrence Livermore Laboratory Technical Report UCRL-15346, April 1981. Prepared under the auspices of University of California, Lawrence Livermore National Laboratory and the U.S. Department of Energy. Reprinted by permission.

[1] C was designed at Bell Labs by Dennis Ritchie; Pascal was designed by Niklaus Wirth of ETH in Switzerland.

- Wirth, N., "An Assessment of the Programming Language Pascal," *Proceedings of the International Conference on Reliable Software,* April 1975. Copyright 1975, IEEE, reprinted by permission.
- Ritchie, D. M., S. C. Johnson, M. E. Lesk, and B. W. Kernighan, "The C Programming Language," *Bell System Technical Journal,* Vol. 57, No. 6, July–August 1978. Copyright 1978, AT&T, reprinted by permission.
- Habermann, A. N., "Critical Comments on the Programming Language Pascal," *Acta Informatica,* Vol. 3, pp. 47–57, 1973. Copyright 1973, Springer-Verlag, Inc., reprinted by permission.
- Lecarme, O. and P. Desjardins, "More Comments on the Programming Language Pascal," *Acta Informatica,* Vol. 4, pp. 231–43, 1975. Copyright 1975, Springer-Verlag, Inc., reprinted by permission.
- Kernighan, B. W., "Why Pascal is Not My Favorite Programming Language," Computer Science Technical Report, No. 100, Bell Labs, Murray Hill, N.J., July 1981.
- Anderson, B., "Type Syntax in the Language C: An Object Lesson in Syntactic Innovation," *SIGPLAN Notices,* Vol. 15, No. 3, March 1980, reprinted by permission.
- Shaw, M., G. T. Almes, J. M. Newcomer, B. K. Reid, and W. A. Wulf, "A Comparison of Programming Languages for Software Engineering," *Software— Practice and Experience,* Vol. 11, pp. 1–52, 1981. Copyright 1981, John Wiley & Sons, Inc., reprinted by permission.
- Boom, H. J. and E. De Jong, "A Critical Comparison of Several Programming Language Implementations," *Software—Practice and Experience,* Vol. 10, pp. 435–73, 1980. Copyright 1981, John Wiley & Sons, Inc., reprinted by permission.
- Wirth, N., "Programming Languages: What to Demand and How to Assess Them," *Software Engineering,* Academic Press, 1977. Copyright 1977, Academic Press, Inc. (London) Ltd, reprinted by permission.

Alan Feuer
Narain Gehani

COMPARING AND ASSESSING

PROGRAMMING LANGUAGES

Ada, C, and Pascal

COMPARING PROGRAMMING LANGUAGES

Ada, C, and Pascal are representative of three different language design philosophies. C and Pascal are similar in that they are relatively small languages, but differ considerably in their treatment of data types. Pascal and Ada have a similar view of data types, but differ enormously in size and complexity. C is also smaller than Ada, although when it is considered in conjunction with the UNIX* operating system, C addresses many of the same issues as Ada.

Some people argue that because of these philosophical differences and because the languages were designed for different application areas, the languages are largely incomparable. We feel that it is precisely the philosophical differences that enliven (and sometimes heat) comparisons of Ada, C, and Pascal. And, although they may have been designed for different application areas, C and Pascal have been used in all application domains; undoubtedly, Ada will also be used in applications other than those for which it was designed.

The papers in this section introduce the three languages, present the design philosophies of each, and contrast them from a variety of academic and practical standpoints.

The first two papers compare C and Pascal. In their paper "A Comparison of the Programming Languages C and Pascal," Feuer and Gehani present an objective comparison of C and Pascal. They first compare the features and design philosophies of the two languages, and then discuss the relative suitability of each language for a variety of programming domains. The features of the languages are presented before they are discussed, so this paper is a good starting point for readers unfamiliar with either C or Pascal.

* UNIX is a trademark of Bell Laboratories.

Mateti, by contrast, does not believe that any comparison can be wholly objective and thus presents a more personal view. In his paper "Pascal versus C: A Subjective Comparison," he expresses unhappiness with the dangers resulting from the permissiveness of C and contrasts this permissiveness with the discipline enforced by Pascal. The brunt of his criticisms fall on C, partly because he feels it is so deserving and partly because he feels that the weaknesses of C have been largely ignored in the literature.

The next paper is a high-level comparison of Ada and Pascal. Wichmann, in "A Comparison of Pascal and Ada," shows how similar concepts are expressed in the two languages and points out that there are many facilities in Ada that have no counterparts in Pascal (e.g., concurrent programming, exception handling, and packages). He claims that some of the seeming simplicity of Pascal and complexity of Ada is actually a result of the completeness of the Ada language definition. When the cracks in the definition of Pascal are patched, it no longer looks like a "very simple language."

The last paper compares all three languages for use in a specific programming domain. In his paper "A Comparison of Programming Languages: Ada, Pascal, C," Evans evaluates each of the languages for their suitability for systems programming. He begins by listing characteristics of system programs and then compares the languages on a feature-by-feature basis. Although Evans is especially critical of C, he criticizes the other two languages as well. This paper is a revised version of a paper by Evans comparing Ada, C, Pascal, and Praxis. The language Praxis was designed by Evans. Accordingly, he acknowledges that he is not a wholly unbiased observer. It is therefore not surprising that he is critical of the other three languages. Nevertheless, his criticisms are by and large valid.

ALAN R. FEUER AND NARAIN H. GEHANI

Bell Laboratories, Murray Hill, New Jersey

A Comparison of the Programming Languages C and Pascal

The limits of my language mean the limits of my world.

Ludwig Wittgenstein

1 INTRODUCTION

The languages C and Pascal are growing in popularity. Although they were designed for different application areas, they are being used for similar kinds of programming. In this paper we summarize and compare the two languages and provide a basis on which to select between them for a particular programming application.

In comparing C and Pascal we were confronted with the problem of deciding what to compare since it is not clear what constitutes each language and what constitutes its environment. It is not sufficient to say that each language is specified by its reference manual since the designers of the two languages adopted different philosophies about what belongs in a language. For example, input/output is considered to be part of Pascal and is found in its reference manual, *The Pascal Report*.[1] But input/output is not considered to be part of C; instead, input/output comes with the standard library and is not included in *The C Reference Manual*.[2]

We resolved this problem by considering each language with its environment as described in the standard text for the language. For Pascal we used *The Pascal User Manual and Report* (Jensen and Wirth, 1974) and for C we used *The C Program-*

[1] *The Pascal Report* is part of *The Pascal User Manual and Report* by Jensen and Wirth (1974).

[2] *The C Reference Manual* is included as an appendix in *The C Programming Language* by Kernighan and Ritchie (1978).

ming Language (Kernighan and Ritchie, 1978). Occasionally, we point out features desirable for C or Pascal and changes that have taken place in the languages but that are not described in the respective texts.

This paper is organized as follows. First we discuss the history and design philosophies of these two languages. This is followed by a sample program from each language and a summary and comparison of the features in the two languages. Finally, we comment on the suitability of the languages for a variety of programming domains.

2 THESIS

Pascal programs tend to be more reliable than C programs primarily because of Pascal's strong typing. They also, because of Pascal's richer set of data types, tend to be more readable and portable than C programs. However, C, because of its flexibility and lack of restrictions, can be used in a larger variety of programming domains than Pascal.

The weaknesses of both languages have been recognized. Pascal has been adapted for wider use by extending it, and C has been moving toward better program reliability and error detection through stronger typing (as evidenced by the Portable C Compiler[3]).

3 LANGUAGE HISTORY AND DESIGN PHILOSOPHY

C and Pascal are both fairly small languages. Compared to other languages designed in the late 1960s such as PL/I and ALGOL 68, both C and Pascal have relatively few facilities and can easily be implemented on small machines.

The lineage for C includes BCPL (Richards, 1969) and B (Johnson and Kernighan, 1973). B and BCPL have typically been used for implementing operating systems and language processors. Because their underlying model closely resembles that of commonly used computing equipment, they provide the programmer with an efficient interface to computer hardware. The major advance of C was the addition of typed variables; both B and BCPL are typeless.

C was designed and implemented in 1972 by Dennis Ritchie. It has been used to implement a wide variety of applications, mostly under the UNIX[4] operating system running on the DEC PDP-11[5] series of computers. In 1977 development began on a machine-independent version of the C compiler, known as the Portable C Compiler (Johnson, 1978), to simplify the task of moving the C compiler to new environments. As a result, compatible versions of C now run on upward of 15 different machines from micro- to maxicomputers. This effort has led to modifications of C to allow easy portability of C programs.

---

[3] The Portable C Compiler (Johnson, 1978) implements a restricted version of C, particularly with respect to type coercions.

[4] UNIX is a trademark of Bell Laboratories.

[5] PDP is a trademark of Digital Equipment Corporation.

Pascal was influenced by ALGOL 60 (Naur, 1963), and ALGOL W (Wirth and Hoare, 1966). It was designed by Niklaus Wirth in 1969 as a direct response to the size and complexity of ALGOL 68. Pascal was to be a high-level language that would (Wirth, 1971a)

1. Allow the systematic and precise expression of programming concepts and structures.
2. Allow systematic program development.
3. Demonstrate that a language with a rich set of flexible data and program structuring facilities can be implemented efficiently.
4. Demonstrate that the use of a machine-independent language with flexible data and program structures for compiler writing leads to an increase in the compiler's readability, verifiability, and consequently its reliability, without loss of efficiency.
5. Help gain more insight into methods of organizing large programs and managing software projects.
6. Have extensive error checking facilities and thus be a good vehicle for teaching programming.

Pascal provides the user with a high-level machine, namely, Pascal. By strongly enforcing language restrictions, Pascal makes it difficult for the user to escape from the high-level machine into the underlying hardware.

The first Pascal compiler was written for the CDC 6000 series of computers. Early use was concentrated largely in the universities. As Pascal became available on more (currently over 75) machines, its usage spread dramatically. Extensions of Pascal, such as Concurrent Pascal (Brinch Hansen, 1975) for real-time programming and UCSD Pascal (Bowles, 1977) for programming microcomputers, have become very popular. An international standard for Pascal has been proposed ("Second Draft Proposal," 1981). Additionally, Pascal has been a strong influence on the design of several modern languages, the most notable being Ada (U.S. Department of Defense, 1980).

The design goals of Pascal and C were quite different. Pascal's restrictions were intended to encourage the development of reliable programs by enforcing a disciplined structure. By strongly enforcing these restrictions, Pascal helps the programmer detect programming errors and makes it difficult for a program, either by accident or design, to access memory locations outside its data area.

In contrast, C's permissiveness was intended to allow a wide range of applicability. The basic language has been kept small by omitting features such as input/output and string processing. Ideally, C was to be sufficiently flexible so that these facilities could be built as needed. In practice this philosophy has worked well. Most of the UNIX operating system and all of its system utilities (including several Pascal compilers) have been written in C.

A precise definition of a programming language is vital to users and implementors, and requisite to verifying program correctness. From the start, a precise specification of the Pascal syntax was available (Wirth, 1971b), and in 1973 Hoare and Wirth produced an axiomatic definition for most of the Pascal semantics (Hoare and Wirth, 1973). To date, a complete definition of the C syntax has not been published. Sethi, in 1980, published a denotational definition for the semantics of most of C (Sethi, 1980). Unlike axiomatic definitions, denotational definitions are not very useful in demonstrating program correctness. In addition, the programming style encouraged by C (e.g., side effects in expressions, use of pointers, interchangeable use of arrays and pointers) makes programs harder to verify.

3.1 Type Philosophy

C and Pascal differ most widely in their treatment of types. C descended from typeless languages, while the languages that influenced Pascal were typed. Before discussing the type philosophies of the two languages, let us define what we mean by a strongly typed language (Gehani and Wetherell, 1980).

A language is strongly typed if

1. Every object in the language belongs to exactly one type.
2. Type conversion occurs by converting a *value* from one type to another. Conversion does not occur by viewing the representation of a value as a different type. (In FORTRAN, by contrast, viewing the representation of a value as a different type is possible by means of the *equivalence* statement.)

Experiments have shown that strongly typed languages increase program clarity and reliability (Gannon, 1977). Representation viewing is a mechanism that allows the subversion of strong typing and, unless the programmer exercises great care, the resulting programs will be neither reliable nor portable.

When the above definition is used, Pascal comes very close to being a strongly typed language. It is not perfect in this regard because its strong typing can be breached, by means of the variant record mechanism, for example, and through routines passed as parameters. Although C is a typed language, it is not strongly typed. It was designed to give the programmer the ability to manipulate data type representations. It provides several ways for viewing the representation of an object as different types, as in the case of unions, pointers, parameter passing, and structure component names.

A provision to breach strong typing is necessary in any programming language used for systems programming. However, instead of including several different facilities that each allow bypassing of the strong typing mechanism, it would be better to provide one facility especially designed for this purpose. Then breaches of strong typing could be isolated and easily located. For example, Ada provides the user with a generic function UNCHECKED_CONVERSION for breaching strong typing. Unfortunately, in C, typing can be breached in several ways by means of representation viewing.

Another difference in the type philosophies of the two languages is their treatment of implicit conversions. The only implicit conversions allowed in Pascal are those that do not result in any loss of information, as in converting from subranges to their parent ranges and from integers to reals (the latter is not quite correct for on some machines not all integers can be represented as reals). For conversions between other types, Pascal provides type transfer functions that must be called explicitly. On the other hand, C allows implicit conversion between any of its basic types or pointers. The Portable C Compiler, however, does *warn* the user of implicit conversions involving pointers.

Pascal's handling of types allows mechanical detection of more errors than does C's, and also prevents certain security violations, one of the most important contributions of high-level languages (Horning, 1979). Additionally, Liskov (1976) advocates that implicit conversions should almost never be permitted even if we understand mathematically that the conversion makes sense, because conversions make programs more difficult to understand. On the other hand, Pascal's treatment of types can occasionally lead to problems, as in the case of arrays. Since Pascal considers the array size to be part of the type of the array, one cannot write a routine that accepts arrays with different numbers of elements. For example, one cannot write a routine *sort* to sort arrays of different sizes. This is a serious handicap.[6]

The value of strong typing is being increasingly appreciated by the C community. Implementations of C are becoming stricter in their treatment of types. In addition, a utility program *lint* is available that analyzes C programs to look for violations of strong typing and other potential sources of errors, such as using a variable before it is initialized.

Both languages allow the user to define new types. However, both C and Pascal have ignored the issue of type equivalence. This is a detriment to program portability since different implementations may use different type equivalence strategies (e.g., name versus structural type equivalence (Welsh et al., 1977)).

We conclude that Pascal, by being restrictive, emphasizes program reliability and readability, while C, by its absence of restrictions, emphasizes programmer flexibility.

4 SUMMARY AND COMPARISON OF FEATURES

This section contains a feature-by-feature comparison of C and Pascal. We assume that the reader is familiar with programming language concepts, but not necessarily with either C or Pascal. For this reason, we describe each language feature before discussing it. An informal syntax summary of the languages is given in Table 1, which presents how most of the similar facilities in C and Pascal are used. Items designating syntactic classes are in italics and items surrounded by oversized square brackets are optional. The italics convention is followed throughout the paper.

---

[6] Solutions to eliminate this problem have been proposed by Wirth (1975) and others ("Second Draft Proposal," 1981).

TABLE 1   SUMMARY OF SYNTAX

Facility	C	Pascal
Declarations		
constant	#define *name value*	**const** *name-value*
type	typedef *type name*;	**type** *name = type*
variable	[*storage-class*] [*type*] *names*;	**var** *variables: type*
array	[*storage-class*] *element-type name* [*size*] . . . ;	**var** *name:* **array** [*index-type*, . . .] **of** *element-type*
record	[*storage-class*] struct *name* {*fields*};	**var** *name:* **record** *fixed-part*; *variant-part* **end**
pointer	[*storage-class*] *type* *name*;	**var** *name:* ↑*type*
routine	[*storage-class*] *result-type name* ([*formal-parameters*]) [*parameter-declarations*] *compound-statement*	**function** *name* [(*formal-parameters*)]: *result-type*; *local-declarations*; *compound-statement* **procedure** *name* [(*formal-parameters*)]; *local-declarations*; *compound-statement*
Referencing		
array element	*array-name* [*i₁*] . . . [*iₙ*]	*array-name* [*i₁*, . . . , *iₙ*]
record field	*record-name.field-name*	*record-name.field-name*
pointer object	*p	p↑
Statements		
assignment	*variable = expression*;	*variable := expression*
compound	{*variable-declarations statements*}	**begin** *statements* **end**
conditional	if(*expression*) *statement₁* else *statement₂*	**if** *Boolean* **then** *statement₁* **else** *statement₂*
selection	switch(*expression*) { *labeled-statements* }	**case** *expression* **of** *labeled-statements* **end**
while loop	while(*expression*) *statement*	**while** *Boolean* **do** *statement*
repeat loop	do *statement* while (*expression*)	**repeat** *statements* **until** *Boolean*
for loop	for(*initialization*; *expression*; *reinitialization*) *statement*	**for** *variable := initial-value* **to** *final-value* **do** *statement* **for** *variable := initial-value* **downto** *final-value* **do** *statement*

4.1 Sample Programs

To illustrate the flavor of programs in the two languages, we begin the comparison by giving a binary search routine written in both. The routine takes an array of records sorted by key and searches for a specified value. It returns the index of the record if one is found with the specified key; otherwise, it returns failure. Assuming the records are in an array A and the key to be searched for is in k, the algorithm may be stated as

1. Set *low* to the lowest index and *high* to the highest index of A.
2. While *low* $\leq$ *high* repeat steps 3–5. If *low* $>$ *high* return failure.

3. Set *mid* to an index halfway between *low* and *high*.
4. If the key at $A_{mid} = k$ return *mid*.
5. If the key at $A_{mid} < k$ set *low* = *mid* + 1, otherwise set *high* = *mid* − 1.

The programming examples in this and following sections are presented in the style used by the corresponding standard texts (e.g., keywords are boldface in Pascal but not in C).

    C. The routine is coded in C as an integer function named *BinarySearch*. BinarySearch takes three arguments: an array *A* of items, the number of items *n*, and the key *k* to be searched for. It returns either the index of the item that matches the key or −1 if the key is not matched. The type *item* is defined to be a structure with two elements, *key* and *value*.

    Statements in C are terminated by semicolons, and blocks are surrounded by braces. Comments are surrounded by the pair "/* */". Lines beginning with "#" are C preprocessor instructions. "=" is the assignment operator, "[ ]" is the array indexing operator, and "." is the field selector for structures. In the example below, the *include* instruction is replaced by the contents of the file "stdio.h" and the *define* instruction defines the macro "FAILURE" to be the string "(−1)". The *typedef* statement defines the type "item." The *while* loop executes as long as the condition "low <= high" remains true. "A[mid].key" accesses the "key" field from the "mid" element of the array "A".

```
#include ⟨stdio.h⟩
#define FAILURE (−1)

typedef struct {
   int key;
   char *value;
} item;

int BinarySearch(A, n, k)
/* return index of item in A with key k, return FAILURE if k is not in A */
item A[ ];
int n, k;
{
   int low = 0, high = n − 1, mid;
   while(low <= high) {
      mid = (low + high)/2;
      if(k < A[mid].key) high = mid − 1;
      else if(k > A[mid].key) low = mid + 1;
      else return(mid);
   }
   return (FAILURE);
}
```

Pascal. The routine is implemented as an integer function in Pascal. As with the C implementation, the Pascal function accepts three arguments and returns either the index of the item that matches the key or failure.

Compound statements in Pascal are surrounded by the pair **"begin end"**. Comments are enclosed in braces. A semicolon is used as a statement separator. Declarations in a Pascal program always appear in the same order: labels, constants, types, variables, and then procedures and functions. ":=" is the assignment operator, "[ ]" is used to subscript arrays, and "." is the field selector for records. **"div"** is the division operator for integers. The following declarations are used by BinarySearch and are global to it:

```
const   max = 100;        {max size of the array}
        failure = −1;
type    index = 1..max;
        string = packed array[1..20] of char;
        item = record
          key: integer;
          value: string
        end;
        data = array[1..max] of item;
```

"max" is defined to be the constant 100 and "failure" to be −1. "index" is a type with values from 1 to 100, "data" is an array of 100 "items," and "item" is a record with two fields.

The function BinarySearch is

```
function BinarySearch (var A: data; n: index; k: integer): integer;
{return index of item in A with key k, return failure if k is not in A}
var     mid: index;
        low, high, result: integer;
begin
        low := 1;
        high := n;
        result := failure;
        while (low <= high) and (result = failure) do
        begin
          mid := (high + low) div 2;
          if k < A[mid].key then
            high := mid −1
          else if k > A[mid].key then
            low := mid + 1
          else
            result := mid
        end;
        BinarySearch := result
end
```

In the procedure header, **"var"** indicates that an argument is passed by reference; by default arguments are passed by value.

4.2 Data Types

Declaration of variables.   Declarations in C have the form

   storage-class data-type variable-list;

where either of *storage-class* or *data-type* may be omitted. The *data-type* is either a *type-identifier* or a specification of a structure or a union. For example, an integer array *v* with 50 elements is declared as

   int v[50];

   A *type-identifier* may either be predefined or user defined. The statement

   typedef int[50] vector;

creates a user-defined *type-identifier* named *vector* that is a 50-element integer array. The array *v* may now alternately be defined as

   vector v;

   The scope of a variable depends upon where the variable is declared and upon its *storage-class*. A variable may have the scope of a block, a function, a source file, or all source files. The lifetime of a variable depends on its *storage-class*; it may have the lifetime of the execution of a block, a function, or a program. Lifetime and scope are independent of each other. For example, a variable local to a block with the lifetime of the block is an *automatic* variable. A variable local to a block with the lifetime of a program is *static* (or *own* as in ALGOL 60).

   C also includes a *register* storage class to inform the compiler that a particular variable will be heavily used. If possible, the compiler will bind the variable to a machine register. On some machines this can lead to a savings in both space and time; on others it can actually slow down the program.

   Variables can be initialized along with their declarations. However, structured variables, such as arrays, can be initialized only if they are static. Static variables are by default initialized to 0.

   Variable declarations in Pascal have the form

   var *variable-list* : *data-type*

The *data-type* is a *type-identifier* or a type description. The *type-identifier* may be a standard type name or a user-defined type name. For example,

   type vector = **array**[1..50] **of** integer

creates a user-defined type *vector* that is a 50-element integer array.

   Pascal variables are initially undefined; if they are not assigned a value before use, an error results. A variable is local to the routine in which it is declared and is global to a routine if it is declared in a lexically surrounding routine. Declared variables have the lifetime of the routine in which they are declared. Dynamic objects generated by the storage allocator, the built-in procedure *new*, exist as long as they are accessible.

Basic types.   Data objects in C are of three basic types: *character*, *integer*, and *real*. Integers can be one of three sizes, real numbers one of two. Integers may be declared *unsigned* for bit and address manipulation.

Pascal has four standard scalar types: *Boolean*, *char* (i.e., character), *integer*, and *real*. In addition, a user can build new scalar types by enumerating identifiers that represent values for the type. An example of a user-created scalar type is

type day = (sun, mon, tue, wed, thu, fri, sat)

A variable of type *day* can have as values the identifiers *sun* through *sat*. The statement

var d1, d2 : day

declares *d1* and *d2* to be variables of the type *day*.

Pascal also includes the concept of a subrange type. A subrange of an existing scalar type is defined by specifying the low and high values for the subrange, as in the following examples:

type
    weekday = (mon..fri); {subrange of type day}
    digit = '0'..'9'; {subrange of the character set}
    index = 1..100   {subrange of the integers}

Relational operators may be used to compare values of scalar types. The ordering of the values in a user-defined scalar type is the order in which the values are enumerated. Standard functions to get the next or previous scalar value are provided.

Symbolic constants.   In C, symbolic constants are implemented via preprocessor macro definitions. The definitions

#define DAYS 29
#define WEEKS (DAYS/7)

define DAYS to be the constant 29 and WEEKS to be the expression (DAYS/7).

In Pascal the *const* statement is used to define constants. It has the form

const *name-value*

Value can be an integer, a real, a value from an enumerated scalar type, or a string constant, but not an expression.

Structured types.   C supports two basic data-structuring mechanisms: the *array* and the *structure*. The form for declaring an array is

storage-class element-type name [*size*] . . . ;

Element-type may be any type, but *size* must be a constant integer expression. The elements of the array *name* have indexes from 0 to *size*−1.

Structures in C are objects consisting of one or more fields where each field is an object of any type; the following structure *date* is an example:

```
struct date {
    int day;
    char month[4];
    int year;
};
```

If *birthdate* is an instance of the structure *date*, then

```
birthdate.year
```

refers to the field *year*.

There are also two variations on structures: *unions* and *bit fields*. In a union, each of the fields is mapped to the same area in storage. This allows the bit representation in storage to be interpreted as different types. In a bit field, each field is mapped to a portion of a word. Bit fields allow partial words to be addressed symbolically. For example, using bit fields, an instruction word might be defined as

```
struct instruction {
    unsigned opcode : 8;    /*opcode is first 8 bits*/
    unsigned operl : 4;     /*operl is next 4 bits*/
    unsigned oper2 : 4;
};
```

Pascal has four data structuring mechanisms: *arrays*, *records*, *sets*, and *files*. The form for declaring an array is

```
name:array[index-type, . . .] of element-type
```

Index-types are character, Boolean, subranges, and enumerated types. *Element-type* can be any type. For example, using the previously defined type *day*, the elements of the array *sales*, declared as

```
var sales : array[day] of real
```

are accessed by

```
sales[mon], sales[tue],
```

and so on.

The Pascal compiler may be instructed to store an array compactly by defining the array to be **packed.** This usually results in better storage utilization, but slower access time. The procedures *pack* and *unpack* are provided so that the representation of an array can be changed dynamically. Strings are packed one-dimensional character arrays of fixed length.

Pascal records have the form

record
   fixed-part;
   variant-part
end

where *fixed-part* consists of a number of components called *fields*, and *variant-part* consists of *variants*, each of which in turn consists of a number of fields. The variants may differ in the name, number, and type of the fields, and may be tagged or untagged. The value of the tag specifies which variant is active. This information is used to ensure access only to the fields of the active variant. If the variants are not tagged, it is the responsibility of the programmer to ensure correct access.

The predominant usage of records is with fixed parts only. This example illustrates the use of both fixed and variant parts:

```
type geometric_figure = record
                  area : real;
                  case shape : (rect, circle, point) of
                  rect : (a, b : real);
                  circle : (r : real);
                  point : ( )
          end
```

The fixed part consists of one field named *area*. The variant part has three variants, *rect*, *circle*, and *point*, plus a tag field named *shape*. As an example, for a variable *F* of type *geometric_figure* the assignment

F.shape := circle

specifies that the record consists of a fixed part *area* and the variant *circle* with field *r*. In this example, the only accessible fields are *F.area* and *F.r*. Attempting to access *F.a* or *F.b* would be illegal.

Fully qualified names must be used to access a record field. As this can be cumbersome, Pascal provides the *with* statement to eliminate the qualifier. For example, the statement

F.area := 3.1416 * F.r * F.r

may be written as

with F **do** area := 3.1416 * r * r

The *with* is also helpful to the compiler in optimizing access to record fields.

Sets with elements of enumerated, subrange, or character types can be defined in Pascal. Operations are provided for set union, intersection, membership, and construction. For example,

var digit : **set of** '0'..'9'

defines a set, *digit*, that may contain any combination of the characters '0' through '9'. The predicate

c **in** digit

tests whether or not the value of the variable *c* is in the set *digit*.

The file type in Pascal is based on the mathematical concept of sequence. Files are like arrays in that they have homogeneous elements. They are different from arrays in that they can only be accessed sequentially and their size can change dynamically. Associated with each file is a buffer variable. The standard input/output procedures *get* and *put* read the next element into the buffer variable and write the buffer variable to the end of the file, respectively. Procedures for initializing files and functions for detecting end-of-file and end-of-line are provided.

Pointers. A pointer in C points to an object of some particular type. The declarations

char *cp;
struct date *sp;

define *cp* to be a pointer to objects of type character and *sp* to be a pointer to objects of type date. The dereferencing operator is "*"; *cp* and *sp* yield addresses, *cp* yields a character, and (*sp).*day* (or equivalently $sp \rightarrow day$) yields an integer, assuming date has been defined as in the preceding section. The operator "&" returns the address of an object. Thus *sp* can be initialized by

sp = &instance-of-date

Operators defined on addresses are comparison, subtraction, and addition with an integer. Arithmetic on addresses is performed in units of the storage size of the base type for the pointer. Thus, using *cp* and *sp* from the previous example, *cp* + 1 points to the next character in memory and *sp* + 1 points to the next instance of date.

Pointers and arrays are closely related in C. An array name is a pointer to the first element of the array. Thus if *A* is an array, the first element may be accessed either by *A*[0] or by **A*. Similarly, if *cp* points to a character in a string, *cp*[0] yields the character pointed to by *cp*, *cp*[−1] yields the previous character, and *cp*[1] yields the next character.

Unlike those in C, pointer variables in Pascal can only access *dynamic* variables of a specific type. They cannot point to explicitly declared variables. The declarations

var p : ↑integer;
    f : ↑figure

declare *p* to be a pointer to an integer variable and *f* to be a pointer to a variable of type *figure*.

The Pascal procedure *new* is used to create the objects to which a pointer may refer. For example, execution of *new*(*p*) results in *p* being set to point to a newly allocated variable of type integer.

Discussion. The data types in the two languages reflect their different design goals. Pascal attempts to hide the underlying machine by presenting the programmer with a higher level machine whose instructions are the Pascal statements and whose objects are instances of the Pascal data types. C, on the other hand, does little to hide the underlying machine. Instead, it tries to provide a convenient way of controlling the machine. Although its instruction level is usually higher than that of the hardware, its objects are similar to those of the hardware.

Pascal has more interesting data types than C. Subranges in Pascal provide some security and potential storage economy. Sets in Pascal provide a more readable and reliable replacement for the flags and bit strings of C, although the usability of sets would be greatly increased if implementations did not restrict set size to word size and if a mechanism were provided to iterate over the elements in a set, as in SETL (Schwartz, 1975).

By confusing Boolean and integer types, C compilers cannot detect certain consistency errors that are easily caught in Pascal. For example, C has trouble with the following situations:

- $1 < 2 < 3$ and $3 < 2 < 1$ both evaluate to 1. (Relational expressions evaluate to 0 for false and 1 for true. $1 < 2$ yields 1 and $1 < 3$ is 1. $3 < 2$ yields 0 and $0 < 1$ is 1.)
- If i and j are integers, the expression $i < j$ erroneously written as $i + j$ cannot be detected by the compiler.

Through the use of the enumeration type, Pascal allows the use of symbolic identifiers instead of integers for classifying data or actions. Inconsistent usage of such identifiers can be detected by the compiler and through run-time checks. Though symbolic identifiers can be created in C, using the preprocessor *define* instruction to map identifiers to integers, consistency checking is impossible since the compiler only sees the integers.[7] The indexes in C arrays are limited to integers starting at zero; in Pascal, any scalar type except real can be used as an index type. Pascal requires variables to be initialized before being used, while in C static and external variables are given default initial values. Consequently, in C, errors resulting from lack of proper initialization cannot always be detected.

On the other hand, the data types in C allow access to the machine not possible in Pascal. Specific physical addresses can be referenced in C, as can particular bits within a word. Multiple precision arithmetic is available in C, but not in Pascal.

C places virtually no restrictions on where pointers may point, and allows arithmetic on addresses. Errors due to dangling references can occur in two ways: first, by reference to the address of a variable (determined by using "&") that is no longer active, and second, by referring to storage that has been explicitly deallocated. In Pascal only the second kind of dangling reference can occur. Its restrictions on pointers lead to safer programs, but they also reduce its usability. For example, it is not possible to write a general-purpose storage allocator in Pascal.

[7] The enumeration type has been added to newer versions of C.

Storage allocation and deallocation are not part of C, while they are part of Pascal. Consequently, in Pascal, the compiler can allocate the right amount of storage for an object. In C it is the responsibility of the programmer to specify how much storage is to be allocated—a potential source of errors.

In Pascal, arrays with different dimensions are of different types. Consequently, one cannot write routines that accept arrays of different sizes. For example, a library of general string-processing routines cannot be written. The lack of an initialization facility in Pascal is not only inconvenient, but also inefficient, since runtime assignments must be used to initialize variables. For example, initializing an array to build a table requires an assignment statement for each table entry.

The syntax for type declarations in C has been criticized as being cryptic and error prone (Anderson, 1980). This is because type declarations in C have the same syntactic form as the use of objects of the same type. Most languages, including Pascal, adopt a notation that reflects the structure of the type.

The result of the two approaches to data types is as expected. Because of its higher level data types and stricter type checking, Pascal programs are more reliable than equivalent C programs. However, because of this restrictive nature, some programs cannot be written conveniently, or at all, in Pascal.

4.3 Expressions

C includes operators for arithmetic, logic, comparison, bit manipulation, address manipulation, type coercion, and assignment. Because most of these operators behave as in other common programming languages, we present only some of the more unusual ones.

Assignment can be used in an expression like any other operator. The value of an assignment is the value of the right-hand operand cast in the type of the left-hand operand. A paradigm that has grown out of this property is the assignment in a loop condition. The statement

while ((x = nextvalue( )) != DONE) *process x*;

conveniently expresses that the function *nextvalue* is called one time more than there are elements to be processed.

C includes a form of assignment for updating a variable based on its current value. The expression

v += 1

is equivalent to

v = v + 1

This becomes increasingly convenient as v becomes increasingly complex. Any binary arithmetic or bit operator can be used in place of the "+".

The increment/decrement operators are another variation on assignment. The form for increment is

++*var* or *var*++

In the first case, *var* is incremented before its value is used, while in the second case *var* is incremented after its value is used.

Logical expressions involving AND (&&) and OR (‖) are evaluated conditionally from left to right. Consequently, the right-hand operand is evaluated only if the truth value of the expression cannot be determined by solely evaluating the left-hand expression.

The conditional operator (?:) takes three operands: a condition, a true part, and a false part. For example, the value of the expression

   (y != 0) ? 1/y : INFINITY

is 1/*y* if *y* is not zero and INFINITY otherwise.

The comma operator allows two expressions to be combined into one. The value of the resulting expression is the value of the right-hand expression. For example, the expression

   i = 0, j = 1

assigns 0 to *i* and 1 to *j*, and has the value 1.

C also has low-level operations to manipulate bits, such as bitwise Booleans and shifts. These operators are typically used to implement bit flags, to manipulate hardware devices, and to pack data within words.

Pascal provides the standard arithmetic and relational and logical operators. In addition it provides operators for strings and sets, as discussed in Section 4.2 under "Structured types."

Discussion.   As with data types, the operators in C reflect the underlying hardware, while the operators in Pascal reflect the higher level Pascal machine. Thus, while C has operators to manipulate the bits of a word, Pascal has operators to manipulate sets. C and Pascal also differ widely in their view of side effects. By allowing assignments within expressions C encourages side effects, which make programs less reliable and modifiable. The ability to perform assignment within an expression, though, tends to make C programs more compact than the corresponding Pascal programs. For example, compare the C and Pascal versions of reading characters into an array until end-of-file.

1. C:

   ```
   while ((s[i++] = getchar( )) != EOF);
   ```

2. Pascal:

   ```
   while not eof do
      begin
         s[i] := getchar( );
         i := i + 1
      end
   ```

Because it has only four levels of operator precedence, expressions that do not need parentheses in common mathematical notation do need parentheses in Pascal. Pascal requires, for instance,

(x > 0) **and** (y > 0)

instead of simply

x > 0 **and** y > 0.

C suffers somewhat from the opposite malady; it has 11 comparable levels of precedence. With so many levels, parentheses are often needed for readability.

The logical operators in Pascal are unconditional, while those in C are conditional (the bit operators "&" and "|" can sometimes be used to get the effect of unconditional logical operators in C[8]). The use of conditional operators can lead to better programs (Dijkstra, 1976), although unconditional operators may sometimes be necessary in an expression with side effects. The lack of conditional logical operators in Pascal results in the linear search program fragment

while (i <= n) **and** (x[i] ⟨⟩ key) **do** i := i + 1

to be written in the roundabout way

```
found := false;
while (i <= n) and (not found) do
  begin
    found := x[i] = key;
    i := i + 1
  end;
if found then i := i - 1
```

This must be done to avoid a subscript error in case *key* is not present in the array.

4.4 Statements

Any expression in C can be made into a statement by appending a semicolon; the expression is executed for its side effect and the value returned is ignored. A sequence of statements can be grouped into one logical statement by surrounding the sequence with braces.

The assignment statement in C is the assignment expression followed by a semicolon. Assignment is permitted between all types except arrays.[9] Because assignment is an expression, multiple assignments can take place in one statement, for example,

i = j = k = 0;

[8] Using the bitwise logical operators as wordwise logical operators can be dangerous. For instance, the bitwise AND of binary 10 and 01 yields 00, or false. The wordwise logical AND of 10 and 01 yields true.

[9] Although assignment of structures was added late to C, its addition had been anticipated in *The C Reference Manual* (Kernighan and Ritchie, 1978).

The basic selection construct in C is the *if* statement:

if(*condition*) *statement*$_1$
else *statement*$_2$

The *condition* is an expression that evaluates to false if it is zero, otherwise to true. *Statement*$_1$ is executed if the *condition* evaluates to true; otherwise, *statement*$_2$, if given, is executed.

The *switch* statement is used for multiple-way selection based on the value of an integral expression. If has the form

switch(*expression*) {
case *constant-integral-expression*$_1$: *statement-list*$_1$;
case *constant-integral-expression*$_2$: *statement-list*$_2$;
   ⋮
default: *default-statement-list*;
   ⋮
}

The *statement-list* associated with the *constant-integral-expression* equal to *expression* is executed. Execution proceeds to the following case unless an explicit transfer of control is given, usually by means of a *break* statement. If none of the *case* constants match and a default is given, the *default-statement-list* is executed; otherwise, the *switch* is exited.

C includes constructs for loops with the test either at the top or the bottom. The form for a loop with the test at the top is

while(*condition*) *statement*

Statement is executed as long as the *condition* evaluates to true.

For loops of the form

loop-initialization;
while(*condition*) {
   statement
   loop-reinitialization;
}

C provides an alternate syntax that brings the initializations and the condition to the head of the loop:

for(*loop-initialization*; *condition*; *loop-reinitialization*) *statement*

The initializations are expressions. As an example, the elements of the *n*-element array *A* can be set to zero by the statement

for(i = 0; i < n; i + +) A[i] = 0;

Any of the expressions of the *for* may be left null. The null expression as a *condition* evaluates to true. The form for a loop with the text at the bottom is

do *statement* while(*condition*);

C provides three unconditional transfer of control statements: the single-level *break* and *continue*, and the *goto*. *Break* exits from the innermost enclosing loop or *switch* statement. *Continue* forces the next iteration of the innermost enclosing loop. The effect of the *continue* statement in a *for* loop is to execute the *loop-reinitialization* expression before the next loop iteration is forced. The *goto* causes control to transfer to a label, whose form is that of an identifier. Transfer is allowed across blocks and control constructs, but not across functions.

Statements in Pascal are separated by a semicolon. A sequence of statements may be grouped into one logical statement by enclosing the sequence with the **"begin end"** pair.

The Pascal *assignment* statement has the form

variable := *expression*

Assignment is permitted between all identical types except files.

The Pascal *if* statement has the form

if *condition*
then *statement*$_1$
else *statement*$_2$

where *condition* is a Boolean expression.

The *case* statement selects one statement to be executed from a set of alternatives, depending upon the value of the *case expression*. If the *expression* does not match any of the *case-labels*, an error results. The *case* statement has the form

case *expression* **of**
case-label-list$_1$: *statement*$_1$;
case-label-list$_2$: *statement*$_2$;
   ⋮
end

Expression can be of any scalar type except real. *Case-labels* are constants or subranges from the scalar type of *expression*.

There are three kinds of loops in Pascal: the *for*, *while*, and *repeat*. The *for* loop is used where the number of iterations is known in advance. It has the form

for *control-variable* := *initial-value* **to** *final-value* **do** *statement*

The *initial-value* and *final-value* are expressions of any scalar type except real. The *control-variable* takes on successive values in the range specified. Neither the *control-variable*, the *initial-value*, nor the *final-value* can be modified within the loop. The value of the *control-variable* is undefined on loop exit. The direction of the iteration can be changed by replacing **to** with **downto.**

The *while* and *repeat* loops are used when the number of iterations is not known in advance. The *while* has the test at the top of the loop. It has the form

while *condition* **do** *statement*

The *repeat* has the test at the bottom:

repeat *statement-list* **until** *condition*

The body of the *while* statement is executed as long as the *condition* is true. The body of the *repeat* executes until the *condition* is true.

Pascal provides the *goto* statement for unconditional transfer of control. The labels for the *goto* are unsigned integers and must be declared. The target of a *goto* cannot be a statement inside a control construct or inside another routine.

Discussion.   Using the semicolon as a statement separator as in Pascal is more error prone than using it as a terminator as in C (Gannon, 1975). The control statements of C and Pascal are similar, the main differences being in the multiple-way switch and fixed-length iteration. In the C *switch* statement control flows from one alternative to the next. An explicit transfer of control must be used to exit from a branch of the *switch* statement. This is a potential trouble spot for program readability, reliability, and modifiability, particularly if overlapping code is used for various alternatives. The alternatives of the Pascal *case* statement are mutually exclusive. The *case* does not provide for a default alternative as does the *switch* statement. This is inconvenient because often an explicit test must be made prior to entering the *case* statement to check for the default cases.

C does not have an iterative form analogous to the Pascal *for* loop. The Pascal *for* has the properties that it will always terminate, that the direction of the iteration can be determined lexically, and that the number of iterations of the loop is known at loop entrance (as long as the loop does not exit via a *goto* statement). These properties improve readability and are useful for verification. Unfortunately, the control variable in the Pascal *for* is restricted to being changed by ± 1, which limits its usefulness.

Pascal does not provide controlled transfer analogous to the *break* and *continue* statements of C, forcing the use of *gotos* or additional Boolean variables to handle exception conditions. Also, the Pascal *goto* is not very attractive since statement labels are restricted to the nonmnemonic unsigned integers.

In assignments, Pascal allows type coercion in two cases: from a subrange to its basic type and from integer to real. C allows assignment between any pair of basic types with the value of the right-hand side being coerced to the type of the left-hand side. Pascal allows assignment between all identical types except files. C allows assignment between identical structures but not between arrays. However, implicit array assignment can occur in C if the array is contained within a structure, an inconsistency introduced by the addition of structure assignment into the language.

The introduction of array assignment would cause semantic and syntactic problems because array names, in contrast to names of other structured objects, are constant pointer values; an array name evaluates to the address of the array, while a structure name evaluates to the value of the structure. As mentioned earlier, both C and Pascal leave the rule for determining when two types are equivalent to the implementor.

4.5 Routines and Program Structure

A C program may consist of multiple routines spread across multiple source files. A program source file consists of external objects, data and functions, that may be declared to be local to the file or global to all files. All executable statements are contained within blocks, which may be nested to arbitrary depth. Variables may be declared at the beginning of any block. Most program source files begin with a prelude of preprocessor statements. Standard preludes are included by means of the inclusion facility of the preprocessor (see Section 4.7). By convention, every program has a function named *main* where execution begins. All routines in C are functions. Every function returns a value, which can be of any type except array. Parameters are passed by value, except for arrays. For arrays, the value passed is the address of the first element.

C functions return after executing the last statement or after executing a *return* statement. The *return* statement is also used to return the function value.

A Pascal program consists of a main procedure with the following form:

program *name*(*list of file identifiers*);
   label declarations
   constant definitions
   type definitions
   variable definitions
   procedure and function definitions
   program body.

The normal scope rules for objects in block structured languages apply in Pascal. Names are local to the routine in which they are declared. A name is global to routines contained within the routine in which the name is declared.

Pascal offers two kinds of routines: those that return a value, *functions*, and those that do not, *procedures*. The types of the formal parameters and the type of the value returned are declared in the routine heading. Variables may be passed by reference or value. A routine returns after executing its last statement. Functions may return any scalar or pointer value. A value is returned by assigning it to the function name.

Those routines that are used before they are defined must be declared to be *forward* before the first call to them is encountered.

Discussion.   PASCAL imposes a strict order of appearance on the parts of a program as an aid to one-pass compilation. The body of a routine does not appear next to the declaration of its data objects since they are separated by the intervening local functions and procedures. For example, the body of the main procedure is at the end of the program text. This detracts from program readability. C offers better program-structuring facilities than Pascal. Variables may be declared at the start of any block encouraging localized usage of variables.

Pascal does not have *static* or *own* variables. Consequently, either global variables or parameters must be used to remember information between successive calls to a routine. The use of global variables makes programs less readable and reliable (Wulf and Shaw, 1973).

Names in C can be confined to a physical file. This unusual way of defining the scope of variables allows a collection of routines to share private rather than global variables, enhancing reliability. However, one must use caution in merging such files to avoid name conflicts between shared variables.

Unlike C, Pascal makes a clear distinction between routines that return a value and those that do not, a distinction that aids readability. A Pascal function can return a value of any scalar or pointer type, but not of a structured type. C functions can return a value of any type except array. Unlike those in C, routines in Pascal can be nested, thus allowing the use of local routines with the same name in different scopes.

In C, parameters can only be passed by value, except for arrays, which are effectively passed by reference. To achieve the effect of passing by reference in C, an address is passed explicitly. Consequently, arguments passed by reference are accessed differently than those passed by value. This is a potential source of programming errors. Arguments in Pascal may be passed by value or reference, depending upon the declarations in the called routine. The arguments in the called routine are accessed uniformly, regardless of whether they were passed by value or by reference. One advantage of explicitly passing addresses in C is that the function call indicates which of its arguments might be modified.

An example of a design inconsistency in C is that array parameters behave differently from local arrays. The name of a local array is an address constant, while the name of a parameter array is a variable.

In Pascal, the number of actual parameters to a routine must match the number of formal parameters; it is not possible for a routine to accept a variable number of parameters. A routine in C may accept a variable number of arguments, but the implementation is often machine dependent, affecting portability, and occurs at the expense of error checking.

In contrast to C, a Pascal routine exits only upon reaching its end. This reflects the philosophy of the structured programming advocates that all constructs should have one entry point and one exit point (Dijkstra, 1972). From a practical viewpoint this is an inconvenience that is usually resolved by the use of *gotos*.

Pascal has neither external routines nor external variables. This is a serious handicap and prevents the use of libraries of routines. Consequently, most implementations have extended Pascal to provide for external routines, but at the cost of reduced program portability.

4.6 Input/Output

Routines for input/output are provided in the standard C library (Kernighan and McIlroy, 1979); they are not specified in the C language. The standard library includes routines to read and write data in blocks of arbitrary size, and to read and write formatted text. The format mechanism is used to build strings of arbitrary form, either on output or in memory. On input, the format mechanism provides pattern matching. Formats are themselves strings and can be generated dynamically.

Input/output in Pascal is accomplished by operating on files (see Section 4.2 under "Structured types"). On input, the buffer variable associated with a file always points to the next element to be read. The *read* routine gets the next element and advances the buffer pointer. For look-ahead, the next element can be accessed without advancing the pointer. The end-of-line character, although not explicitly readable in Pascal, may be written, read, and sensed using standard routines. Pascal provides a limited capability for formatted output by specifying the field width for printed values. It makes no provision for formatted input, nor does it provide an easy way to reference nonprinting characters.

Discussion. Input/output routines are part of Pascal but not part of C. By not including these routines in the language, the input/output routines in C cannot take advantage of information available to the compiler. For example, a change in the type or number of arguments to a formatted input/output routine must be reflected in the format string; type/count mismatches between the format items and the corresponding operands cannot be detected at compile time.

The look-ahead input strategy used in Pascal, although elegant for batch programming, causes problems in interactive programming. For example, if the standard input is a terminal, Pascal will wait for a character to be typed before beginning execution since it tries to look ahead one element. A similar problem arises in the routines that detect end-of-line and end-of-file.[10]

A more serious handicap for writing interactive programs that use a display screen is the exclusion of control characters from Pascal's character type. This forces programmers to use roundabout means to do things such as moving the cursor or changing the character font.

The lack of random accessing of files in Pascal restricts its utility. Again, extensions are used to ease this restriction. This is not a problem in C since operations to randomly access files come with its standard input/output library.

4.7 The C Preprocessor

The C preprocessor provides three primary capabilities: string substitution, text inclusion, and conditional compilation. Preprocessor instructions are executed prior to the compilation of a program.

---

[10] Several solutions to rectify these problems have been proposed; for example, see Joy et al. (1980).

String substitution is used to implement symbolic constants (as in Section 4.2 under "Symbolic constants"), but can be used more generally for arbitrary strings. For example, the preprocessor instructions

```
#define BEGIN {
#define END   }
```

allow the pair "BEGIN END" to be used in place of "{ }". The substitution string may include a parameter list, in which case the parameters are substituted before replacement occurs. An example of a macro with parameters is the preprocessor instruction

```
#define max(a, b) (a > b ? a:b)
```

which causes the string

```
max(x, y)
```

to be replaced by

```
(x > y ? x:y)
```

The *include* instruction allows the textual inclusion of files. One common usage of this is for the inclusion of a standard set of declarations.

Conditional compilation allows one source file to spawn different versions of object code based upon compile-time parameters. For example, if diagnostic instructions are included within a conditional section, a program may easily be compiled either with or without these instructions.

Discussion. The C preprocessor allows one to do things in C not possible in Pascal. For example, symbolic names may be used for constant expressions to enhance program modifiability and readability, and macros may be used instead of routines to improve run-time efficiency. Macros, however, are not as safe as routines since variables used within a macro share the same name space as the calling program.

5 DOMAINS OF APPLICATION

In this section, we assess the suitability of C and Pascal for a variety of programming domains. The assessment is based on how well the facilities in each language match those that we feel are important in each domain. We have ignored important environmental considerations such as language availability, existing software in a language, facilities to interface with other languages, friendliness of the operating system, and the expertise of local personnel.

Four programming domains are considered: business programming, scientific programming, the programming of operating systems, and the programming of system utilities. Our approach is as follows: for each domain, important language facilities are listed. C and Pascal are then assessed by noting the facilities they have, those that can be built using the language, and those that cannot be built or supported. In this same manner the languages can be compared for programming in other domains.

Some facilities are important in all domains and are available to varying degrees in both languages:

- A reasonable implementation of the three basic control constructs—sequence, selection, and iteration.
- A reasonable implementation of aggregate data structures including records with variants.
- External compilation (not part of standard Pascal but supported by most implementations).
- Parameter passing by value or by reference (in C, the latter is simulated by passing addresses).
- Recursive routines.
- Interactive input/output (Pascal's input facilities are clumsy).

There are other facilities, useful in all domains, provided by neither C nor Pascal:

- Abstract data types (Liskov and Zilles, 1974)
- Units of measure as a data attribute (Gehani, 1977; Hoare, 1973)

Finally, it should be remembered that this comparison is *only* between C and Pascal. Quite possibly some other language may be more suitable for a particular domain than either of these two.

5.1 Business Data Processing

Business data processing includes applications such as accounting, report generation, and database manipulation. Useful language features are

- Formatted input/output for generating reports and for reading data—floating formats are especially important for output (e.g., printing dollar amounts without a gap between the dollar sign and the most significant digit)
- A reasonable database interface
- Record level operations such as move and copy, and record level input/output
- Precision arithmetic, particularly decimal
- String processing
- Labeled files
- A facility for transforming coded data (e.g., translating abbreviations to their expanded form)

Pascal, although it can be used for business applications, is not very appropriate.

It supports record-level operations and record input/output, but it does not support formatted input or precision arithmetic, is weak in formatted output, provides little support for string processing, does not have a database interface, and does not support labeled files. Pascal's arrays facilitate the transformation of coded data to some degree since they can have characters and negative integers as subscripts.

Formatted input/output can be improved in Pascal using routines, but the routines cannot be fully general as they cannot be made to accept a variable number of parameters. Implementing precision arithmetic is both difficult and inefficient. General string-processing routines cannot be written because arrays of different sizes cannot be passed as parameters to a routine.

C is not much stronger in this domain as far as built-in facilities go. It has formatted input/output and allows routines to return records as values, but does not support record-level input/output or labeled files, and cannot have arrays with negative integers or characters as indexes. However, much of what C is missing can be implemented by means of functions; a string-processing library, for example, is easily implemented. Record input/output and precision arithmetic cannot be added easily.

Neither C nor Pascal are really appropriate for business programming. Pascal suffers from a lack of built-in facilities and limitations on building new ones. While C has the flexibility to add the features it is missing, its lenient view of data types makes it poor for detecting common kinds of errors. If one can live within the restrictions of Pascal for business programming, it is better because it is safer.

5.2 Scientific Programming

By scientific programming we mean applications that are dominated by numerical computation. Useful language facilities are

- Extended precision arithmetic
- Ability to detect overflow and underflow
- Array operations
- Complex arithmetic
- A large number of math functions
- Input and output of binary files
- Ability to pass routines as parameters
- Nonzero lower bounds for arrays

Pascal supports binary input/output and provides some common math functions (e.g., sin and ln). Arrays can have nonzero lower bounds, routines can be passed as parameters, and arithmetic on complex numbers, although not part of Pascal, can be implemented. Pascal's major deficiencies for scientific programming are that generic array functions cannot be built and that it does not support extended precision arithmetic.

C has about the same built-in facilities for scientific programming as Pascal does. It does not have any built-in math functions, but a standard library of common math functions is available. C supports extended precision arithmetic, but does not allow arrays to have nonzero lower bounds. Routines can be passed as parameters by passing pointers to the routines.

Again, many of the facilities missing in C can be easily built. Arithmetic on complex numbers can be implemented in a more natural way than in Pascal since functions can return structures. Generic single-dimensional array functions present no problem, but parameter arrays of higher dimensions are troublesome since C compilers do not pass the information about array bounds needed for index calculations.

Either C or Pascal is adequate for scientific programming though neither is well tuned for it. For example, neither language has an infix operator for exponentiation nor the facility for handling arithmetic exceptions detected by the hardware. As in business programming, if one can live within its restrictions, the safety of Pascal tips the balance in its favor.

5.3 Programming for Operating Systems

Useful facilities are

- Access to the machine, for example, to specific addresses or to bits within a word
- Ability to place code and data into specific memory locations
- Dynamic storage allocation and deallocation
- Compile-time initialization of variables (particularly tables)
- Concurrency

Pascal is very weak in this domain because it provides no access to the machine. It has no facility for manipulating the bits within a word, accessing a particular machine address, or forcing a particular representation of data. It also does not allow compile-time initialization of variables and does not support concurrency.

This is the domain for which C is best suited. The danger of its leniency is balanced by the advantages of its flexibility, particularly in accessing the hardware. However, it has neither the facility to force code or data to a particular physical address, nor does it have facilities for concurrency.

C is the clear choice for the programming of operating systems.

5.4 Programming for System Utilities

Facilities useful in building system utilities such as preprocessors and editors are

- String processing, often with variable-length strings
- Input/output of nonprintable characters

- Routines that accept a variable number of parameters
- Dynamic storage allocation
- Compile-time initialization of variables (particularly tables)
- Sets, particularly with cardinality on the order of the character set
- Files

Pascal is a fair language for writing system utilities, but its usefulness is limited by its treatment of arrays and its lack of compile-time initialization. It does support dynamic storage allocation, files, and sets. Unfortunately, Pascal files can only be accessed sequentially, and because they are typed, generic file routines (such as file copy) cannot be written. Pascal sets are weakened by the lack of a set iterator and by their cardinality being usually restriced to the size of the computer word. A big handicap for interactive programs is that nonprintable characters cannot be manipulated within the character type in Pascal.

While C is lacking many of the facilities for this domain, most are available in its standard libraries; for example, there are standard routines for string processing, dynamic storage allocation, and file manipulation. C routines with a variable number of arguments can be built, but only in a nonportable way. Nonprintable characters and compile-time initialization are handled easily in C, but the absence of sets is an inconvenience.

This is a broad domain; it should perhaps be treated by subdomain. C is better, suited for writing interactive programs. Both languages are suitable for noninteractive programs.

6 SUMMARY

In this paper we have presented and contrasted the important features of C and Pascal. We have stressed the different philosophies taken by the designers of the two languages: Pascal was designed to make clear and reliable programs easy to write; C was designed to be highly flexible.

As part of the comparison, we assessed the suitability of C and Pascal for programming in four different domains. We found neither C nor Pascal particularly well suited for business programming, although we favor Pascal because of its greater safety. While both languages are adequate for scientific programming, we again prefer Pascal because of its safety. C is the clear choice over Pascal for programming operating systems, particularly because of its ability to access the hardware. For programming system utilities, both C and Pascal are suitable; we prefer C for interactive programming primarily because of its more flexible treatment of input/output.

The choice of a programming language for a project hinges on many factors. Just because a language *can* be used for a particular application does not mean that it *should* be. And that a language can be used for simple programs does not mean that it can be used for more complex ones. In the end, for the best results good technical judgment must prevail in the selection of an appropriate programming language.

ACKNOWLEDGMENTS

We are grateful to our many colleagues at Bell Laboratories who have commented on various versions of this paper. We are also indebted to the editors and referees for their many helpful suggestions.

PRABHAKER MATETI

Department of Computer Science, University of Melbourne, Melbourne, Victoria, Australia

Pascal versus C: A Subjective Comparison

At first sight, the idea of any rules or principles being superimposed on the creative mind seems more likely to hinder than to help, but this is really quite untrue in practice. Disciplined thinking focuses inspiration rather than blinkers it.

G. L. Glegg,
The Design of Design.

1 INTRODUCTION

Pascal has become one of the most widely accepted languages for the teaching of programming. It is also one of the most thoroughly studied languages. Several large programs have been written in Pascal and its derivatives. The programming language C has gained much prominence in recent years. The successful UNIX operating system and most of its associated software are written in C.

This paper confines itself to a subjective comparison of the two languages, and conjectures about the effect various structures of the languages have on the way one programs. While we do occasionally refer to the various extensions and compilers of the languages, the comparison is between the languages *as they are now,* and in the context of general programming. The official documents for this purpose are Jensen and Wirth (1974) and the C-book (Kernighan and Ritchie, 1978). The reader who expects to find verdicts as to which language should be used in what kind of project will be disappointed and will instead find many statements supported only by personal experience and bias; when I felt it necessary to emphasize this, the first person singular is used.

1.1 "Methodology" of Comparison

We do not believe that objective (all-aspect) comparisons of programming languages are possible. Even a basis for such comparison is, often, not clear. (However, see Shaw et al., 1978.) We can attempt to use such factors as power, efficiency, elegance, clarity, safety, notation, and verbosity of the languages. But elevating these factors from the intuitive to the scientific level by tight definitions renders them useless for the purpose of comparison. For example, all real-life programming languages are as powerful as Turing machines, and hence equally powerful. It is difficult to discuss efficiency of a language without dragging in a compiler and a machine. Furthermore, many of the other notions listed above are based heavily on human psychology, as are the useful insights gained under the banners of structured programming, programming methodology and software engineering. Thus, universal agreement as to the level these notions are supported in a given language will be difficult to reach.

One of the most important factors in choosing a language for a project should be the estimated debugging and maintenance costs. A language can, by being very cautious and redundant, eliminate a lot of trivial errors that occur during the development phase. But because it is cautious, it may increase marginally the cost of producing the first (possibly bugged) version. It is well-known that a programming language affects programming only if the problem is non-trivial and is of substantial size. Also, it seems a language has little effect on the logical errors that remain in a software system after the so-called debugging stage. This is clearly highly correlated with the competence of the programmer(s) involved.

This suggests a method of comparison based on estimating the total cost to design, develop, test, debug and prove a given program in the languages being compared. However, controlling the experiment, and adjusting the results to take care of the well-known effect that the second time it is easier to write (a better version of) the same program (in the same or different language) than to write it from scratch, may prove to be infeasible. Also, very large-scale experiments with a large piece of software are likely to be so expensive and the results so inconclusive that it is unlikely to be worthwhile. In any case, I do not have the resources to undertake such an experiment.

This comparison is, therefore, necessarily subjective. And this, as can be expected, depends to a large extent on one's own biases, and faith in the recent programming methodology. When the growing evidence supporting this methodology is sufficiently convincing, we can replace the word "faith" by "xxxx."

In the following, we shall

1. Compare how "convenient" the languages are to code our favourite solution to a programming problem
2. Play the devil's advocate, and try to list all possible things that *can* go wrong in a program expressed in a language

Some of us, including myself, have reservations about the validity of the second technique for comparison, the most persuasive argument being that even though some of the features are potentially dangerous, people rarely use them in those contexts. There is certainly some truth in this, but until we have experimentally collected data convincingly demonstrating this, it is wiser to disbelieve it. Take note of the observed fact of increased difficulty in formally proving the properties of programs that use these potentially hazardous features in a safe way. This is one of the reasons behind the increased redundancy (and restrictions) of the newer languages like Alphard (Wulf et al., 1976), CLU (Liskov et al., 1977), Euclid (Lampson et al., 1977), Mesa (Geschke et al., 1977), and others.

1.2 Hypotheses

It should be clear that neither language is perfect, nor should there be any doubt about the truth of the following axiom (Flon, 1975):

> There does not now, nor will there ever, exist a programming language in which it is the least bit hard to write bad programs.

Since this is a subjective comparison, it is necessary to identify as many of the underlying assumptions as possible.

1. We believe:
   a. That programs should be *designed* (i.e., conceiving the abstract data structures, and the operations on them, detailing, but not overspecifying, the algorithms for these operations, and grouping all these) in a suitably abstract language, which may not be a formal language.
   b. That the *coding* (i.e., the translation into a formal programming language) of the abstract program is strongly influenced by the programming language. This paper offers several conjectures about these influences; the word "programming" is used instead of coding, in several places, to emphasize the unfortunate fact that many of us design our programs straight into the programming language.
2. We make a lot of trivial mistakes. Examples: uninitialized or wrongly initialized variables, overlooked typing errors, array indices out of range, variable parameter instead of value, or vice versa, ...
3. The effort spent in physically writing and typing during the development of a large program is negligible compared to the rest of effort.
4. Simple things that could be done mechanically, without spending much thought, should be done by a program.
5. Permissive type checking should be outlawed.
6. It is dangerous to use our knowledge of the internal representation, as chosen by a compiler, of a data type (Geschke et al., 1977).
7. The overall efficiency of a large program depends on small portions of the program (Knuth, 1971; Wichmann, 1978).

1.3 General Comments

One may wonder: Why compare two languages whose projected images are so different? For example, Sammet's "Roster of Programming Languages" (1978) lists the application area of Pascal as multi-purpose and that of C as systems implementation.

That Pascal was designed only with two objectives—viz., a language for teaching programming as a systematic discipline and as a language which can be implemented efficiently—is quoted often, ignoring four other aims that Wirth (1971) lists. The hidden implication of this attitude is that since Pascal is suitable for beginners learning to program, it is ipso facto unsuited for adult programming. In fact, an increasing number of complex programs of wide variety from an operating system for the Cray-1 to interpreters on the Intel 8080 are (being) written in Pascal and its dialects.

C is being promoted as a convenient general purpose language. In reviewing the C-book, Plauger (1979) pays his tributes to its authors and claims "C is one of the important contributions of the decade to the practice of computer programming. . . ."

Neither language includes any constructs for concurrent programming. The flexibility of C makes it possible to access nearly all aspects of the machine architecture; low-level programs such as device drivers can thus be written in C. One contention of this paper is that it achieves this flexibility at a great sacrifice of security. Such compromises can be added to Pascal by any implementor, but most have left it relatively pure and unchanged from that described in the revised report (Jensen and Wirth, 1974). Extensions of Pascal to include concurrent programming constructs have resulted in new languages in their own right (Concurrent Pascal (Brinch Hansen, 1977), Modula (Wirth, 1977a), and Pascal Plus (Welsh and Bustard, 1979)).

Thus I believe the domain of application of both languages to be nearly the same.

A great deal of criticism of Pascal has appeared in the open literature (Conradi, 1976; Habermann, 1973; Lecarme and Desjardins, 1975; Tanenbaum, 1978; Welsh et al., 1977; Wirth, 1974, 1975, 1977b) and in nearly every news letter of the Pascal User Group (Pascal News). The little published criticism of C that exists is by people associated with its design and implementation and hence is benevolent. Thus, this paper devotes a greater portion to criticism of C, and repeats some of the criticism of Pascal only when necessary in the comparison.

2 DATA TYPES

One of the greatest assets of both languages is the ability to define new data types. The languages provide a certain number of standard (i.e., predefined) simple types from which other types are constructed. The well-known arrays are composite types whose components are homogeneous. Records of Pascal, structs of C are composite types that (usually) contain heterogeneous components. Other composite types of Pascal that contain homogeneous elements are sets and files. Types are not allowed to be defined recursively, except when they involve a pointer type. Note that both languages consider a type to be a set of values (Morris, 1973).

2.1 Simple Types

Integers, reals, characters, and Booleans are standard types in Pascal. All other types are user defined.

```
type
      zeroto15    = 0..15;
      minus7to7   = −7..7;
      aritherror  = (overflow, underflow, divideby0);
      kindofchar  = (letters, digits, specials);
```

Whereas C has integers, reals, and characters, it does not have Booleans (which is sad), nor does it have a mechanism for defining enumerated types (like the above *kindofchar*), or subranges (*zeroto15*). Instead, in some implementations of C, by declaring a variable as *short*, or *char,* one obtains smaller sized variables; note the following statement from the C Reference Manual (p. 182):

> Other quantities may be stored into character variables, but the implementation is machine dependent.

In contrast, the Pascal declarations do not guarantee that smaller units of storage will be used; they simply inform the compiler that it may choose to do so. More importantly, they provide useful documentation; compiling with range checks on, one can have any violations of these caught at run time. In C, this is not possible. The conscious programmer may document the range of some integer variable in a comment, but the compiler cannot help enforce it.

The useful abstraction that Pascal offers in its enumerated types is of considerable value. That this is no more than a mapping of these identifiers into 0..? does not decrease its value. What we, the humans, have to do in other languages, is now done by the compiler, and much more reliably. (It is now rumored that C will have enumerated types in a future version.)

2.2 Arrays

In Pascal, the index type of arrays is any subrange of scalars (which include enumerated types), whereas in C, arrays always have indices ranging from 0 to the specified positive integer. For example, *int a[10]* declares an array of ten integers with indices from 0 to 9. Sometimes this leads to rather unnatural constructs. Consider the following example.

```
line[−1] = '*';       /* any char other than blank,\t, \n */
while   (( n = getline(line, MAXLINE)) > 0) {
      while (line[n] == ' ' || line[n] =='\t' || line[n] =='\n')
          n−−;
      line[n+1] = '\0';
      printf("%s\n", &line[0]);
}
```

(In C, = denotes the assignment, == the equality test, and ‖ the McCarthy's OR.) I find this program clearer, more elegant, and more efficient than the one on p. 61 of the C-book. However, since arrays cannot have negative indices (as in *line*[−*1*]), we are forced to write differently and use a *break* to exit from the inner loop.

Many people do not appreciate the use of sentinels. Often the argument against them is that you don't have the freedom to so design your data structure. I have not found this to be true in real life situations. This does happen in cooked up classroom situations. It rarely, if ever, is the case that you cannot modify the data structure slightly. The reason for this appears to be a misunderstanding of a fundamental principle of algorithm design:

> Strive to reduce the number of distinct cases whose differences are minor.

The use of sentinels is one such technique. In the above example it guarantees that a non-blank, non-tab, non-new-line character does appear in the array.

The usefulness of negative indices, in these and other situations, should be obvious even to the Pascal-illiterates.

One aspect of Pascal arrays that has come under strong attack is the fact that the array bounds must always be determinable at compile time. This rules out writing generic library routines. There are several suggested extensions to overcome this problem; the signs are that one of these will be incorporated into the language soon.

2.3 Records/Structures

The records and variant records of Pascal are similar to structs and unions of C. However, one important difference must not be forgotten. Pascal does not guarantee any relationships among the addresses of fields. C explicitly guarantees that "within a structure, the objects declared have addresses which increase as their declarations are read left-to-right" (see p. 196, C-book); otherwise some pointer arithmetic would not be meaningful. Some of the efficiency of pointer arithmetic is provided, in Pascal, by a much safer **with** statement.

2.4 Pointers

Pointers in Pascal can only point to objects in the heap (i.e., those created dynamically by the standard procedure *new*), whereas C pointers can point to static objects as well. It is well-known that the latter scheme has the problem of "dangling pointers," and several authors (notably Hoare, 1975) have argued for the abolition of pointers to static objects. The only argument supporting their existence appears to be that they provide an efficient access. It is not known how much this gain in efficiency is in real programs.

On the other hand, unless great caution is exercised, program clarity and correctness are often sacrificed in the process. "A very essential feature of high-level languages is that they permit a conceptual dissection of the store into disjoint parts by declaring distinct variables. The programmer may then rely on the assertion that every assignment affects only that variable which explicitly appears to the left of the assignment operator in his program. He may then focus his attention to the change of that single variable, whereas in machine coding he always has, in principle, to consider the entire store as the state of the computation. The necessary prerequisite for being able to think in terms of safely independent variables is of course the condition that no part of the store may assume more than a single name" (Wirth, 1974).

Pascal pointers satisfy the following:

1. Every pointer variable is allowed to point to objects of only one type, or is *nil*. That is, a pointer is bound to that type; the compiler can still do full type checking.

2. Pointers may only refer to variables that have no explicit name declared in the program, that is, they point exclusively to anonymous variables allocated by the *new* procedure when needed during execution.

C pointers, on the other hand, can point to virtually any object—local, global, dynamically acquired variables, even functions—and one can do arithmetic on these pointers. The pointers are loosely bound to the type of object they are expected to point; in the pointer arithmetic, each 1 stands for the size of this type. Most C compilers do not check to see that the pointers do indeed point to the right things. Furthermore, the C language definition is such that genuine type confusion occurs. The C-book claims that "its integration of pointers, arrays and address arithmetic is one of the major strengths of the language"; I tend to agree, as their current unsafe setting can be made very secure (Mateti, 1979a).

2.5 Type Checking

It is true that one of the basic aims behind the development of strongly typed languages such as Pascal, Euclid, Mesa, Alphard, CLU, etc. is to make it difficult to write bad programs. In realizing this goal, all programs become slightly more difficult to write. But this increase in difficulty is of a mechanical kind, as we now expect the programmer to provide a lot of redundant information.

Type checking is strongly enforced in Pascal, and this is as it should be. Errors caused by incompatible types are often difficult to pinpoint (Geschke et al., 1977). Strong type checking does increase the time to produce the first version of a syntactically correct program, but this is worthwhile. It is true that Pascal has not satisfactorily defined when two types (with different names) are equivalent (Welsh et al., 1977) but the problems are easily avoided by appropriate declarations. Any required type conversion occurs only through predefined functions for the purpose, or through user-defined variant records. (The latter are unsafe; see Section 9.)

In sharp contrast, all kinds of type conversions are either blessed in C, or ignored by its compilers. For example, our Interdata 8/32 C compiler detected only one error in the program of Figure 1. In fact, it is rare that you see a C program that does not convert the types of its variables, the most common conversion being that between characters and integers. More recently, however, C designers have provided a special program called *lint* that does type checking. A few points should be remembered in this context:

```
main( )
{
                /* See Section 2.5                          */
    int         /* integer                                  */
    i,
    xx,
    a[10],
    f( ),       /* f is a function returning integer        */
    (*pf) ( );  /* pointer to a function returning int      */

    printf(" exponent part of 123.456e7 is %d \n",
        expo(123.456e7));

    i = a;      /* i now points to a[0]                     */
    a[1] = f;   /* a[1] points to the function              */
    2[a] = f( );/* 2[a] is equivalent to a[2]               */
    a[3] = f(0);/* f called with 1 argument                 */

    pf = &xx;   /* pf now points to xx                      */
    i = (*pf) ( ); /* now call the "function" pointed to by pf */
    a = i;      /* This is the only illegal statement       */
                /* in this program caught by C compiler     */
                /* because a is not a left-value.           */

}


f(a,b)          /* f in fact has 2 formal parameters        */
char    a, b;
{
    if  (a)   return (b);
}


expo(r)                     /* see Section 9.2              */
float   r;
{
        static struct s {
                char c[4];          /* uses 4 bytes         */
                float f;
        } c4f;
        static char *p = &(c4f.c[3])+1;
                /* points to first byte of f                */

        c4f.f = r;
        return(*p);
}
```

Figure 1

39

1. Type compatibility is not described in the C Reference Manual. Presumably this is similar to that of Pascal, and ALGOL 68. It is not clear exactly what it is that *lint* is checking.

2. The need for type checking is much greater during program development than afterwards. In fact, a good argument can be made that the primary goal of a compiler is this kind of error checking and code generation its secondary goal; the function of type checking should be an integral part of a compiler. To separate it from the compiler into a special program whose use is optional is a mistake, unless it is a temporary step.

3. Type checking is not something that you can add on as an afterthought. It must be an integral part of the design of the language.

It is fair to say that type conversion is difficult in Pascal but frequent need for this is a sign of bad program design. The occasional real need is then performed by explicit conversions.

2.6 Control of Storage Allocation

It is possible to specify in Pascal that certain variables be packed thereby saving storage. The semantics of such variables is the same as if they were regular variables. There are standard procedures to unpack. It should be noted that specifying packing simply gives permission to the compiler to pack; however, the compiler may decide otherwise.

C does not have a corresponding facility. But C structures can have "fields" consisting of a specified number of bits. These fields are packed into machine words automatically. It is also possible to suggest that a variable be allocated a register.

3 STATEMENTS AND EXPRESSIONS

C is an expression language, à la ALGOL 68, in a limited way; only assignments, function calls, special conditional expressions have values. Thus, for example, a function that does return a value can be called like an ordinary procedure in C, which would be illegal in Pascal, as Pascal is strictly a statement language. Below, we take a more detailed look at these aspects.

3.1 Boolean Expressions

C does not have genuine Boolean expressions. Where one normally expects to find these (e.g., in *if* and *while* statements), an ordinary expression is used instead, and a non-zero value is considered "true," a zero being "false." Relations yield 1 if true, 0 if false. The operators & and | are bitwise AND and OR operators, && and || are similar to McCarthy's "logical" AND and OR operators : x && y is equivalent to the conditional expression **if** x $\neq$ 0 **then** y $\neq$ 0 **else** 0 **fi** and $x \parallel y$ is equivalent to **if** x $=$ 0 **then** y $\neq$ 0 **else** 1 **fi**. For example,

4 & 6	is	4	4 && 6	is	1
4 & 8	is	0	4 && 8	is	1
4 | 6	is	6	4 $\parallel$ x	is	1
4 | 8	is	12	0 $\parallel$ x	is	$(x \neq 0)$
			0 && x	is	0

where x is any expression, including the undefined one. The operators &, | are commutative, but &&, $\parallel$ are not. The left-to-right evaluation of the "logical" operators && and $\parallel$ of C does save, occasionally, a few micro-seconds. The traditional AND and OR operators have a nice property that they are commutative, in conformity with their use in mathematics. As a consequence, any reasoning we do using them is more readily understandable. One specific outcome of the use of the unorthodox operators is that the many cases where both the operands are indeed evaluated have to be discovered by involved inferences. A better solution is to have logical operators of the traditional kind, reserving the McCarthy's operators for use when really needed. To my mind, even when these McCarthy's operators are really required, to spell them out as in

> **if B1   then**
> > **if   B2 then**
> > > . . .

is much more readily understandable. I suspect this to be the main reason behind the warning "Tests which require a mixture of &&, $\parallel$, !, or parentheses should generally be avoided" of the C-book (p. 61).

3.2 Assignments

The symbol denoting the assignment operator is $=$ in C; it is rumored that this was a conscious choice as it means one less character to type. Pascal uses the conventional left arrow, written as $:=$. C allows assignments to simple (i.e., non-struct, non-array) variables only, at the moment; structure-to-structure and array-to-array assignments are among its promised extensions. The assignment statement has the same value as that assigned to the left hand side variable; thus, we can write conveniently,

> i $=$ j $=$ 0;

Pascal allows assignments to whole arrays as well as records. However, the assignment is not an expression, and the above has to be expanded as:

> i $:=$ 0;
> j $:=$ 0;

3.3 Operator Precedence

C has over thirty "operators" (including ( ), [], ., the dereferencing operator *), and fifteen precedence levels, compared to Pascal's six arithmetic operators, four relational operators and four precedence levels. Because of the many levels, and also because some of them are inappropriately assigned, one learns to survive either by constantly referring to the C manual and eventually getting them by rote, or by overparenthesizing; for example,

x & 07 == 0	is equivalent to	x & (07 == 0)
*++argv[0]	is equivalent to	*++(argv[0])

The basic problem is that the operators like &, or && take any integers as operands, and a missing pair of parentheses will result in a meaningful but unexpected expression.

It is necessary to parenthesize in Pascal also, but here the reason is different: there are too few levels, as arithmetic operators and Boolean operators got merged in their priority. For example,

flag   **and**   a < b

would result in type incompatibility, which should be written as

flag   **and**   (a < b)

or as

(a < b)   **and**   flag

using commutativity of Pascal **and**.

3.4 The Semicolon

Pascal uses the semicolon as a statement separator, whereas C uses it as a statement terminator. It is well-known that statement separators are the cause of many syntax errors in beginner's programs (Nutt, 1978). But it rarely is a problem for the experienced; most of us have learned to use it as a terminator (with a *null* statement following).

4 CONTROL STRUCTURES

> Control structure is merely one simple issue, compared to questions of abstract data structure.
>
> *Knuth (1974)*

For the last ten years or so, the literature concentrated on control structures, and we have learned enough to cope with their abstraction. Some significant rules of thumb have emerged; e.g., use procedures extensively, keep them short, avoid *goto*s, never jump out of a procedure. As a result, control structures play a rather local role; they are important, but their effect can be localized to these short procedures. Data structure abstraction is not well-understood, in sharp contrast to their design and choice. Many of the remaining errors in large software systems, after an initial period of development, can be attributed to "interface problems" which can be roughly described as inconsistent assumptions about data structures in different places. With this perspective, we move on to the control structures of the two languages.

4.1 Looping

In C, loops are constructed using *while*, *do-while*, and *for*. To exit prematurely from a loop, a *break* is used; to terminate the current iteration but continue from the next, *continue* is used. Similar loop structures in Pascal are, respectively, **while**, **repeat-until**, and **for**; premature termination can be accomplished only by **goto**s. But there is a world of difference between the *for* statements of the two languages.

The C *for* statement duplicates what can be done by other structures with equal clarity;

> *for* (expr1;   expr2;   expr3) statement

is an abbreviation of

```
expr1;
while (expr2) {
    statement
    expr3;
}
```

Note that the three general expressions can be arbitrarily complex. A missing *expr2* is equivalent to specifying the constant 1 as *expr* 2.

The Pascal **for** statement is an abstraction of an often occurring structure;

> **for** i := first **to** last **do** statement

loops exactly last − *first* + *1* times, if *first* <= *last,* or not at all. The control variable *i* starts with a value of *first*, takes successive values up to *last*. The values *last*, *first*, and variable *i* are all of a scalar type. A downward **for** is constructed by using **downto** instead of **to**. There have been suggestions in the literature (Hoare, 1972) that the variable *i* should be a read-only variable local to the body of the loop; Pascal compromisingly insists (Addyman et al., 1979) that the variable be local to the procedure/function/program block in which the **for** loop occurs.

4.2 Selection

The *if* statements of the two languages are very similar except that C uses general expressions, as in *while* statements, instead of Boolean expressions, and the word "then" is omitted.

```
case expression of
      cl₁ : S₁;
      cl₂ : S₂;
      ...
      clᵢ : Sᵢ;
      ...
end;
T
```

The above **case** statement of Pascal transfers control to one (say S_i) of several statements whose constant case label cl_i equals the value of the scalar expression. When the execution of S_i terminates, control is transferred to T. If the expression value does not match any case label, the effect of **case** statement is undefined in standard Pascal. A default label cannot be given either; several implementors have felt the need for this, and it is now allowed on most implementations. However, it should be emphasized that in most well-written programs the expression value belongs to an enumerated type which is exhaustively listed by the case labels cl_i.

The *switch* statement of C is primarily used to create a similar effect. However, control passes from S_i to the next S_{i+1}, unless this flow is explicitly broken by a *break*:

```
switch(exp) {
case   L₁    : S₁
case   L₂    : S₂
                  break;

       ...

case   Lᵢ    : Sᵢ
case   Lᵢ₊₁  : Sᵢ₊₁
       ...
default      : Sₙ
}
T
```

The "usual arithmetic conversion" is performed on *exp,* if necessary, to yield an integer value. The labels L_i must be manifest integer expressions. If *exp* matches no L_i, it matches the *default* and if the optional *default* label is absent, then none of the statements in the *switch* is executed. Whereas a default label is wanted in Pascal, it is needed in C as it cannot be hoped that the case labels L_i will exhaust the values that *exp* can take.

Note also that C needs a *break* because the only way to group cases is by falling through cases. For example, to combine more than one case, say 2 and 4, you write

```
case 2   :
case 4   :
         ----
         ----
      break;
```

and in such situations Pascal does not need a *break*, as labels can be grouped. The C-book wisely cautions (p. 56), ". . . falling through cases is a mixed blessing. . . . Falling through from one case to another is not robust, being prone to disintegration when the program is modified. With the exception of multiple labels for a single computation, fall-throughs should be used sparingly."

4.3 The Power of Control Structures

Loops with *break/continue* belong to the class $DREC_1$, in the genealogy of control structures (Ledgard and Marcotty, 1975). Theorems by Kosaraju (1974) show that a DREC1 structure cannot be simulated by D-structures (D for Dijkstra), which are formed by any number of *if*s, *while*s, and concatenation using original variables, actions and predicates. In fact, some $DREC_i$ structures (which contain BLISS-like (Wulf et al., 1971) multi-level *exit(i)*, exiting *i* enveloping loops, and *cycle(i)*, continuing the next iteration of the *i*-th enveloping loop) are more powerful than any $DREC_{i-1}$ structures.

With this background we make the following observations:

1. This does not mean that a given problem, for which we have a solution with *break/continue*s, cannot be solved using D-structures only but with a different choice of data structures. In fact, most *break*s used in the programs of C-book can be so avoided; some of them occur only because the array index cannot be negative.

2. Why stop at *break* and *continue*, which are equivalent to *exit(1)* and *cycle(1)*? Certainly, for $i > 1$, *exit(i)* and *cycle(i)* add flexibility and power. The primary function of control structures is to provide clarity by operational abstraction. Loops containing *exit*s, and *cycle*s are more difficult to understand. It is surprising how rarely one really needs *exit(1)* or higher *exit*s. The need for control structures at higher levels than D-structures is still unproven.

3. But, if one feels a *break* is needed in a certain situation, why not use a *goto*? Knuth (1974) argues that such use of *goto* is not "unstructured," while a lot of others [like Ledgard and Marcotty (1975)] would rather introduce a Boolean variable, or expand the range of values of an already existing variable, to eliminate the *break*.

Both languages have the *goto* statement. In Pascal, the labels need to be declared, and are always unsigned integers. C allows arbitrary identifiers as labels, which are not declared.

5 PROGRAM STRUCTURE

Pascal and C both have a simpler program structure than ALGOL 60. Pascal achieves simplicity by identifying blocks with routines (procedures/functions) and C does it by not allowing nested routines. In spite of this, C program structure, particularly the scope of variables, is more comprehensive than that of Pascal. Successors to Pascal, such as Concurrent Pascal, Modula, Pascal-Plus, have successfully blended into Pascal the notion of Simula-classes, which structures programs far more effectively.

5.1 Procedures and Functions

In Pascal, these are two distinct entities. A function returns a scalar, real, or pointer value, but has no side-effects when well-written. When a procedure is called, we expect the environment to change; when a function appears in an expression, we can evaluate it without at the same time worrying about side-effects. This is how it should be in a statement-oriented language.

C functions, on the other hand, may or may not return values. In the latter case, they are equivalent to Pascal procedures. But, C goes one step further, and permits a variable number of parameters and the use of value-returning functions as procedures. Certainly, it is more natural for some routines to have a variable-number of parameters (e.g., Pascal's *read* and *write*). But this should be the exception allowed only upon explicit request.

Another surprise in C is all the parameters are passed by value only. To achieve Pascal's **var** parameter, the address is passed as a value parameter, and the function changes the content of the cell pointed. Thus C depends too heavily on pointers, providing a classic case of type confusion as in

```
char *s;
```

(Is *s* a pointer to a character, or a pointer to an array of characters?)

5.2 Block Structure and Scope

C does not allow nested functions but the body of any compound statement is a block and can contain declarations (of *struct*, *typedef*, and variables). This feature, however, is rarely used in practice, except in the outermost block of a routine, or when register variables are needed. Such block structure can be simulated in Pascal by calls to nested routines, but this incurs the overhead of a call.

The names of functions in C are always global (unless declared *static*) and available to routines in other source files. Variables and new type names can be declared in between routines, or before the very first one, and are visible to routines below them in that file. To access variables declared in other files, explicit *extern* declarations are required. Variables can be declared, within a routine, to belong to the *static* storage class (similar to *own* variables in other languages); such variables retain their values between successive calls of that function and are visible only within that routine. These features and the ease of separate compilation make it possible to structure C programs with as much clarity (but not security) as can be achieved with the module concept. In contrast, such structuring cannot be done elegantly in Pascal.

6 LANGUAGE SUPPORT

It is clear to anyone involved in the production of software that often the support given to a language plays a more major role than the language itself. Supporting tools include source language debugging packages, execution profilers, cross-reference generators, macro (pre)processors, pretty printers, and a host of other library programs. To be sure, none of these is part of a language, but most users cannot distinguish them as being separate entities because of their careful integration into host languages.

C is a good example of this process. It uses a standard preprocessor for handling constant definitions and file inclusions. Many of these tools for C are written in C, and hence available just as widely as the language itself. In contrast, Pascal tools and separate compilation facilities (Kieburtz et al., 1978) are only now being developed by interested users. Some of these are written in non-standard Pascal and often integrate poorly with operating systems.

6.1 Preprocessors

Pascal programmers often get annoyed by the lack of some simple conveniences. *Examples:*

1. Expressions involving symbols defined at compile time cannot be used on the right hand side of a constant definition:

   const n = 10; n1 = 11;

   If we change *n* to, say, 20, then we should also change manually *n1* to 21. The following is simpler and more informative:

   const n = 10; n1 = n + 1;

   but this is illegal.
2. Body substitutions for calls to (very short) functions and procedures cannot be specified. The grouping of short sequences of tests and other operations into functions and procedures is thereby discouraged.

Both situations are quite common in programming, and to argue that they can be done easily by hand, and that execution profiles often prove that body substitutions do not yield space/time gains is simply unrealistic.

C handles the above situations, as well as inclusion of text from other files, excellently through its standard macro preprocessor. Such a processor is easy to write for Pascal too, but as there is no standard syntax for it, too many different preprocessors are bound to mushroom (Comer, 1979; Mateti, 1979b).

7 EFFICIENCY

> Don't diddle code to make it faster—find a better algorithm.
>
> *Kernighan and Plauger (1974)*

We can distinguish between two kinds of efficiency improvements: of the algorithm, of the coding. The efficiency that complexity theorists discuss often deals with the asymptotic behaviour of the execution time of algorithms. When input data are of sufficiently large size n, an $O(n)$ algorithm would in fact be faster than an $O(n**2)$ algorithm. This may, however, not always be the case on small amount of input data. If you have only a five element array to sort, bubble sort may run faster on your machine than $O(n \log n)$ quick sort.

Also, the following appears to be the case, unless the algorithm in question is a well-studied one:

> The lower the level of the language, the more afraid you are to use a more complex but significantly more efficient algorithm.

However, the practicing programmer often appears overly concerned with improving efficiency only at the statement-level of coding. This penny-wise saving of microseconds has an apparently incurable side-effect that the resulting programs are harder to understand and often incorrect. Not uncommonly, more significant global improvements are not realized because of the unmastered complexity introduced at this statement-level. This is the direct result of incomplete analysis of the program written.

The benefits of a theoretical complexity analysis are very often substantial. But leaving this aside, one can further distinguish two kinds of efficiency improvements at the coding level:

1. Measurable improvements
2. Demonstrable improvements

For example, let us take a millisecond as the unit of measurement. Then, these are not always the same—1 implies 2, but not vice versa; for, you may be able to demonstrate that program A is faster than B by executing them a thousand times and comparing the total execution times, even though A is not measurably faster than B.

We should not ignore another observed phenomenon that programs spend most of their time in very small portions of the code. If this is true of the program in question, try to improve the efficiency of only these small segments of the code.

Correctness-preserving efficiency improvements, of whatever kind, should certainly be followed provided the required effort is not too great and the resulting code is equally easy to understand, maintain, enhance and modify. When this proviso is not satisfied a careful analysis of the benefits of efficiency improvements is necessary. For example, is it worthwhile to (demonstrably) improve a program that runs only a few times a day? Is not a millisecond too small a unit for distinguishing the two kinds of improvements for cost benefits?

By providing such things as register variables, and decrement and increment operations, C gives the impression of being an efficient language. We have, as yet no solid evidence that this is so, or if so, by what factor, in the domain of systems programming. For example, the absence of negative indices for arrays and the lack of sets induces more computation than is actually necessary. While it is true that $i++$ can be compiled straightforwardly into demonstrably faster code than $i := i + 1$, it is not clear if such things make programs measurably faster. On the other hand, there is the real danger of a slight slip turning such a statement into a major disaster (see Sections 9 and 10.1).

> It is very easy to exaggerate the need for efficiency and require a performance competitive with optimal hand coding.
>
> *Wichmann (1978)*

8 PORTABILITY

Perhaps the too restrictive nature of Pascal and the ease with which its compilers can be modified are the two factors that prompt many of its implementors to 'extend' the language and make it unportable. (Is giving rise to a host of suggested extensions a characteristic of a superior language?) But programs in standard Pascal enjoy a considerable degree of portability (apart from problems caused in any language by the underlying character codes, ASCII or EBCDIC, or whatever).

This cannot be said of C. Even though most of the existing compilers are built by a rather close-knit group at Bell Labs and MIT, there are enough differences. One reason for this may be that the semantics of the language is often confused with what code the compilers produce in its Reference Manual.

Certainly, C programs have been and can be ported (Johnson and Ritchie, 1978). But this does not mean that they are portable as the word is generally understood. There is no clearly defined subset of it that would guarantee portability. A few example problems that the C Reference Manual cautions about are:

1. A pointer can be assigned any integer value, or a pointer value of another type. This can cause address exceptions when moved to another machine.
2. Integers can be assigned to chars and vice versa.

To these we can add the problems caused by assumptions made in C programs about the addresses of variables (that they are a fixed distance apart . . .). The unions of C and variant records of Pascal can both cause portability problems when misused.

9 INSECURITIES

"For the purpose of this discussion, an *insecurity* is a feature that cannot be implemented without either (1) a risk that violations of the language rules will go undetected, or (2) runtime checking that is comparable in cost to the operation being performed" (Welsh et al., 1977). It may sound paradoxical but few or no insecurities need not always be a good thing. For, we observe that assembly languages have no insecurities whatsoever, according to the above definition, for the simple reason that it does not attempt to provide any security. It is only when a language purports to provide security, either explicitly or implicitly, and then fails that we should be upset by it. Thus, we modify (1) to read "a risk that violations of the language rules and *intentions* will go undetected." It is unlikely that a useful language without any insecurities can ever be designed. We can attempt to reduce their number, and explicitly identify them so that we are not lulled into believing that programs written in the language are safe.

9.1 Unsafe Features

An unsafe feature is an insecurity that generally causes havoc and is frequently the cause of evasive bugs.

The list of unsafe features of C is rather long: pointers to static as well as dynamic variables, address arithmetic, passing addresses as value parameters, treating an object pointed to as an array, all belong to this list. But what is more important is that they constitute the most heavily used features. Some of these exist in the language purely for the sake of statement-level efficiency. The use of pointers in accessing array elements is not only efficient, but has a certain elegance of its own. However, its setting is extremely unsafe, and provides much fuel to the "pointers considered harmful" debate (e.g., Hoare, 1975). It is possible to control the use of pointers without any loss in efficiency (Mateti, 1979a). As they are now, they can be greatly misused, worse, an accidental slip can turn it into a very frustrating and harmful gremlin.

Not only is the list of unsafe Pascal features short—variant records without tag fields, functions and procedures as parameters, dangling pointers to dynamic variables—their relative frequency of occurrence is far lower.

9.2 Dirty Tricks

A dirty trick is an exploitation of an insecurity. The adjective "dirty" is used only to remind that such tricks often spring up as a nasty surprise to anyone but their originators. Contrary to popular belief, dirty tricks can serve clean and legitimate purposes. This happens when the language is put to use in a way its designer has not foreseen or wished to forbid but could not. More often, however, they provide short-cuts. Two such examples follow.

1. Suppose we wish to access the exponent part e of the representation of a positive real number x. On the Interdata 8/32, this happens to be in bits 1 to 7. Thus, the function expo of Figure 1 would do the job in C.

2. Suppose we wish to produce the 32-bit concatenation of four 8-bit quantities, or vice versa. On some machines, characters are represented as 8-bit bytes and integers as 32-bit words. Thus, declare the 8-bit quantities as characters, and

```
var dummy :
    record case Boolean of
        true : (bits32 : integer);
        false : (bits8   : packed array [1..4] of char);
        end;
    ...
    ...
with     dummy do begin
        bits8 [1] := first   8-bit quantity;
        bits8 [2] := second 8-bit quantity;
        bits8 [3] := third   8-bit quantity;
        bits8 [4] := fourth 8-bit quantity;
        end;
```

then *dummy.bits32* is the required concatenation. Code similar to this appears in some Pascal compilers. Pascal chose deliberately to provide this flexibility at the expense of security (Wirth, 1975).

10 PSYCHOLOGICAL EFFECTS

We are all psychologists.

From a book on psychology

It is with some trepidation that I write on these effects, for I am a computer scientist. However, to shy away from this "non-subject" would be to ignore the recognized importance (Weinberg, 1971) of the effects caused by our mental images of the languages and by our human limitations. If you are sceptical of what is said here, you are justified. But, I urge you to test these hypotheses out and see how true/false they are.

10.1 Error Proofing

That the ratio of all "meaningful" constructs to all syntactically legal constructs in any programming language is almost zero is a well-known fact. This is not because the said programming language is defined in a context-free grammar rather than in a more precise one such as vW grammar (Tanenbaum, 1978). (It is possible, by technical trickery, to define a "programming language" where this ratio is unity; such a language would, however, have extremely limited "expressive power".) Let us recall the assumptions of Section 1.2. In addition, the following appear to be true, but are not well-tested:

1. The number of errors in programs is proportional to the amount of detail that the writer had to handle in his program.
2. The cost of debugging is a rapidly increasing function of the number of errors (bugs), which includes the extremely trivial ones.

It is therefore important to decrease the possibilities for (unintentional) misuse. Thus it is desirable to inform the compiler of our intentions.

> How can we expect a language to aid in avoiding mistakes, if it is even incapable of assisting in their detection.
>
> *Wirth (1974)*

10.2 Understandability and Compactness

> Programming is the art of writing essays in crystal-clear prose and making them executable.
>
> *Brinch Hansen (1977)*

It can justifiably be argued that the code is not a complete source of information about a program and that a programmer understands a program by successively refining guesses about how the program operates (Brooks, 1978). However, we confine ourselves here to the understanding gained through reading the code only.

Programs in expression languages are (to me) more difficult to understand than those in statement languages. In the latter, only the statements are active in modifying the values of variables. It is for this reason that we often discourage functions with side-effects. In understanding expression language programs we have to handle more details at different levels all at the same time. We need to remember not only what the expression value is so far, but also what variables have which new values. It is also true that expression language programs are more compact. Thus, we remark that

> Readability is inversely proportional to compactness.

This is not to say anything verbose is readable. The word compactness, as it is used here, needs explanation. Electronic circuits can be made more compact by using integration. But this does not make them less complex than their discrete component counterparts. Compactness achieved in expression languages is of this kind. Unlike in mathematics, where compact notation hides detail irrelevant to a given level of discussion, expression language programs while being compact still contain all the gory details. The algorithm does not become simpler, nor is there any reduction in the number of abstract operations except that in the code generation some redundant load/store machine instructions may be avoided.

In C, a programmer can certainly choose not to be compact but

> The natural tendency of most programmers to write the "best possible" code in a given language works against writing readily understandable code.

Do give some thought to the qualification in the following quote.

> C is easy to write and (when well-written) easy to read.

McIlroy et al. (1978)

> However, although we are all psychologists at heart, not all of us are scientists.

From the same book on psychology

11 CONCLUSION

The images that Pascal and C evoke are vivid. The strength of C emanates from its identification of several practices used in assembly programming that lead to very well-written, modular, and efficient programs. In addition, C provides a modern syntax for them adding the conventional wisdom of high-level languages, notably automatic allocation of storage for variables and recursion. Its fundamental flaw is that it failed to curb the misuse of the very same features. While "misuse" is relative to one's programming "morals," the failure to provide enough redundancy to catch the accidental slip is unrealistic and can be expensive.

Pascal, on the other hand, gives the impression that it may have been designed by first synthesizing all that has been put forward in its time about "good and wholesome" programming, and eliminating features that cannot be implemented efficiently enough. Its promotion and exposition may have been, from a psychological point of view, offensive: restrictions are often resented, and rarely understood. It is true of nearly every human endeavour that it takes far greater courage, training, education and understanding to be disciplined, and computer programming is no exception.

Optimism has not, apparently, worked in the past programming projects. "Its [software] products have typically contained other than what was expected (usually less, rather than more), been delivered much later than scheduled, cost more than anticipated, been poorly documented, and been poorly designed" (Bersoff et al., 1979). One should learn this lesson, and be extremely careful at every step. Languages with convenient features whose erroneous use cannot be detected by its compilers should be avoided.

That excellent (as well as extremely ugly) programs can be written in either language is clear. However, I am concerned that it is all too easy to write incomprehensible programs in C. Even more offending are the "features" such as unbridled pointers, variable number of parameters in function calls, absence of type checking and lack of Boolean variables. . . ; these are a lot more troublesome than they are worth.

Finally, let me conclude by quoting Welsh et al. (1977):

> Pascal is at the present time the best language in the public domain for purposes of systems programming and software implementation.

> The discovery that the advantages of a high-level language could be combined in such a simple and elegant manner as in Pascal was a revelation that deserves the title of breakthrough. Because of the very success of Pascal, which greatly exceeded the expectations of its author, the standards by which we judge such languages have also risen. It is grossly unfair to judge an engineering project by standards which have been proved attainable only by the success of the project itself, but in the interests of progress, such criticism must be made.

ACKNOWLEDGMENTS

Many discussions with Paul Dunn, Robert Elz, Ken McDonnel, and Peter Poole prompted me to think about this topic and write this paper. However, they may not share my views as expressed here. I am grateful to the many authors who have influenced me and whose quotations I have so heavily used to make it clear that this paper is little more than a collage of their ideas.

B. A. WICHMANN
Division of Numerical Analysis and Computer Science, National Physical Laboratory, Teddington, Middlesex, U.K.

A Comparison of Pascal and Ada

1 INTRODUCTION

The new programming language Ada is based upon Pascal (*Ada Language Reference Manual*, 1980). It is natural, therefore, to compare them, in spite of the fact that they have been designed with quite different objectives in mind. Pascal was designed by Wirth as an educational tool (Wirth, 1971). The facilities it gives are just sufficient for modest undergraduate projects. The discipline of such a Spartan language is ideal in such an environment, but cannot be recommended for major commercial or industrial projects. On the other hand, Ada was designed to meet a wide range of objectives specified by the U.S. Department of Defense (1978), which would inevitably lead to a larger and more complex language. The requirements document prepared by David Fisher was certainly ambitious, even contradictory, but at least it provided the language design teams with a clear statement of the objectives. This paper does not survey the Ada language for which the reader can consult Barnes (1980).

2 OVERVIEW

The Ada language is five or six times the size of Pascal. One can see this at a superficial level by counting syntactic productions, pages in the manual or number of lexical units. All the indications are that compilers will be five or six times the size of that of Pascal (given comparable code quality). At a deeper level, one can enumerate the facilities that Ada contains that have no equivalent in Pascal. This gives the diagram (drawn to scale) shown in Figure 1.

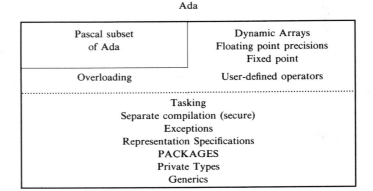

Figure 1

Above the dotted line are features which "could" be added to a Pascal-like language without radical revision. Below the line are facilities of Ada which have a major influence on the whole language design.

It is tempting to analyze a language in terms of a list of features alone, but this is not possible because of the interaction of the features themselves. The Ada design is a serious attempt to provide a coherent structure to a limited set of facilities that are essential for the intended application domain of the language.

One might suppose that Pascal would have a significant advantage over Ada in terms of having a stable and precise definition. Unfortunately, the Pascal report is defective in almost every detail, whilst giving adequate information for the ordinary programmer. Hence a formal standard was needed which would encompass the *de facto* definition (Jensen and Wirth, 1978), but would specify every detail appropriate for an international standard. The work was undertaken first by BSI (1979) and then by ISO, both groups being led by Dr. A. M. Addyman. It soon became apparent that merely giving more substance to the Jensen and Wirth report was not, in itself, adequate. Hence a language design effort was being undertaken on Pascal at the same time as that for Ada.

3 HOW SIMPLE IS PASCAL?

It has been claimed by many that Pascal is a very simple language. That it is much simpler than Ada is not in question, but a glance at the ISO standard for Pascal soon shows that it is not truly simple. This lack of simplicity can more easily be illustrated by considering a number of examples:

3.1 Type Equivalence

The Jensen and Wirth report did not say when two types were "the same." In an important paper (Welsh et al., 1977), two approaches were considered; structural equivalence, meaning that the constituents were the "same" (to be applied recursively), or name equivalence meaning that the identical identifier is used for the name of the types. Both Ada and ISO Pascal use name equivalence. However, Pascal cannot *just* use name equivalence because a string such as "ABC" has no type name associated with it. Hence it is structurally equivalent to a packed array [1 . . *n*] of char (for some *n*). Also, to make the passing of procedures and functions as parameters secure, ISO Pascal requires that the parameter specification is given for such procedures, for example:

function INTEGRATE (**function** F (*x*:real): real; lower, upper:real): real;

Any function can be passed as an actual parameter corresponding to F if it has the same parameter structure (a single real parameter by value, returning a real result).

Welsh et al. consider having a language with only name equivalence but this would require more changes to Pascal than could be accepted as part of its standardization.

3.2 Array Parameters of Different Actual Sizes

The Jensen and Wirth definition of Pascal required that formal and actual array parameters were of the same type which implied that they were of the same size. Hence standard numerical computation or even a sort procedure is not possible in original Pascal. ISO Pascal introduces an enhancement (at level 1) to overcome this. It effectively introduces structural equivalence in the parameter position for formal array parameters which are appropriately declared, for example:

procedure MATRIXMULT(
        a: **array** [allow . . alhigh, a2low . . a2high] **of** real;
        b: **array** [bllow . . b1high, b2low . . b2high] **of** real;
        c: **array** [c1low . . c1high, c2low . . c2high] **of** real);

The subscript bounds are passed over effectively as additional parameters, accessible as constants within the procedure.

This significant addition to Pascal has met with some opposition, but it provides a much wider application area for ISO level 1 Pascal, which I hope will encourage its implementation. (Procedures for string handling, similar to those of UCSD Pascal can now be written in the standard language).

3.3 Overloading

In Pascal, the function *abs* takes a real or integer parameter and returns a value of the same type. It is as if one had two functions:

```
function abs (x : real): real; . . .
function abs (x : integer): integer; . . .
```

This cannot be written in standard Pascal since an identifier cannot be declared twice in one scope. In contrast, in Ada this is permitted and mirrors the facilities with the operators such as "+" and "*", which the user can define himself.

3.4 Default Parameters

Input-output procedures and functions have a single default parameter (the file "input" or "output" as appropriate) in order to provide a more convenient interface to the user. In contrast, Ada has a standard method for default parameters which is, in consequence, available for user-defined procedures.

3.5 Input-Output Statements

Pascal has "procedures" *read*, *readln*, *write* and *writeln* for input-output, which take a variable number of parameters. Apart from the initial (possibly defaulted) file parameter, the remaining parameters are the values to be output or variables to be input. Implicit conversions to/from characters are performed for files of the special type "text." In contrast, Ada introduces no special language features for input-output, relying upon overloading, default parameters and packages to provide a comparable system to that of Pascal. To output an integer and real in Pascal to the default file one would write:

```
write (I, X);
```

whereas in Ada, with the fixed number of parameters one would have:

```
PUT (I); PUT (X);
```

where PUT is overloaded for the integer and real types involved.

4 THE EXTRA FACILITIES OF ADA

None of the additional facilities of Ada can be conveniently expressed in terms of the basic Pascal-like subset. Moreover, there is a clear need for these facilities in writing large real-time systems for which Ada was designed. For those who think that Ada is too complex, please consider how applications demanding these facilities should be programmed. The major facilities are as follows:

4.1 Arrays Whose Size Is Determined at Scope Entry

ALGOL 60 allows one to declare arrays whose size is dependent upon the data. Pascal is a backward step in this case, but an essential one if different types are to be freely composed into records and arrays. Ada provides the ALGOL 60 array mechanism, but has restrictions on how dynamic arrays can appear in records. Hence Ada provides the functionality of both ALGO 60 and Pascal at the cost of some complexity in extreme cases.

4.2 Varying Integer and Floating Point Sizes

Pascal cannot be used seriously for much numerical work because it does not permit varying precision of floating point or different integer sizes. Ada provides this by allowing compilers to implement several sizes of integer and floating point types. Dependence upon the particular hardware can be avoided by using the *derived* type mechanism. For example with

> **type** REAL **is digits** 5;
> **type** INT **is range** −1000 . . 1000;

the compiler implements REAL and INT with a hardware type which has at least the necessary precision or range. Operations on type REAL and INT are then derived from those on the hardware types. By this means, users can write truly portable Ada programs which is not possible in FORTRAN or ALGOL 68.

4.3 Fixed Point Data Types

Input and output signals from sensors are essentially fixed point rather than floating point. Although fixed point is awkward to program because of the scaling that is necessary, there are a few, but important, applications for which fixed point is essential. Floating point is not adequate in such situations, because the machine may not have the necessary hardware or perhaps because of the additional space required for floating point data. The standard functions such as SIN and COS are often programmed in fixed point (in assembler) whereas these can now be done in Ada using either fixed or floating point (Wichmann, 1981).

4.4 Exceptions

In many real-time systems it is essential for them to continue to offer a service (perhaps degraded) in spite of hardware malfunction. A telephone exchange control program or chemical plant control program would be typical. Many error situations are easily anticipated and can be handled directly at the point of detection. Others are more difficult in that the remedial action needed depends upon the circumstances which interacts with several levels of the system design. Exceptions in Ada allow one to program for these circumstances without the error handling code submerging the straightforward case. An *exception* can be raised at one level and then handled at a higher level, depending upon the calling sequence of the events which led to the exception. Ada also *defines* in a way that even ISO Pascal does not, which errors must be trapped by a compiler and those which give rise to a run-time error (i.e., an exception).

4.5 Tasking

The addition of concurrency facilities to languages like Pascal is a growth area for both academic study and serious exploitation (not incompatible!). Ada continues this tradition. The rendezvous mechanism for mutual exclusion in Ada is elegant but largely untried. Of all the extensions in Ada, this is the most ambitious and yet the one which has met with the least opposition. Only time will tell how good the particular design is.

4.6 Packages

All large Pascal programs suffer from an essential defect: they lack any clear module structure (i.e., between a procedure and a program). For instance, a compiler is naturally broken down into lexical, syntactic, semantic and code generation phases. Pascal compilers (almost always written in Pascal) only show this structure by means of comments. In practical terms, packages are probably the most important improvement of Ada over Pascal because they allow for the effective exploitation of program components. A package can consist of two parts: a specification and a body (which implements the specification). Typically, the specification and the body will be compiled separately—the first during program design and the latter during the (longer) implementation phase. Code using a package can be compiled as soon as the specification has been compiled, so that the language naturally supports top-down program development.

Apart from providing the natural unit for separate compilation, packages are also the unit for the implementation of abstract data types. Pascal, for instance, has the concept of a file built into the language. This is not necessary in Ada because files can be (and are in the standard input-output package), implemented as abstract data types. This is done as follows:

```
package I_O_PACKAGE is
    type FILE is limited private;
    procedure OPEN (F: in out FILE);
    procedure CLOSE (F: in out FILE);
    procedure READ (F: in FILE; ITEM: out INTEGER);
    procedure WRITE (F: in FILE; ITEM: in INTEGER);
private
    type FILE is
        record
        NAME: INTEGER := 0;
        end record;
end I_O_PACKAGE;
```

The part after "private" contains hidden details of the abstract type FILE so that effective compilation of users of this package is possible. (Users can declare objects of type FILE, hence the space and alignment rules for these objects must be known to the compiler). Note that the specification is quite small since it only contains the interface between the users and the implementation. In contrast, the package body is much larger, which in outline might be:

```
package body I_O_PACKAGE is
   LIMIT: constant := 200;
   type FILE DESCRIPTOR is record . . . end record;
   DIRECTORY: array (1 . . LIMIT) of FILE DESCRIPTOR:
   . . .

   procedure OPEN (F: in out FILE) is
           begin . . . end;
   procedure CLOSE (F: in out FILE) is
           begin . . . end;
   procedure READ (F: in FILE; ITEM: out INTEGER) is
           begin . . . end;
   procedure WRITE (F: in FILE; ITEM: in INTEGER) is
           begin . . . end;
   begin

   . . .
   end I_O_PACKAGE;
```

The procedure bodies for OPEN etc. are not provided, the specification of them being repeated for clarity. Objects like LIMIT are also hidden from users since it does not form part of the specification. Moreover, the package body can be changed without recompiling code using it provided it meets the same specification (which is checked by the compiler).

4.7 Compile-Time Evaluation of Expressions

In Ada the expression $(1 + 1)$ is always equivalent to 2. Any subexpression which only involves literal values is evaluated by the compiler. In contrast, in Pascal one cannot write:

```
const
   N = 10;
   M = N + 1;
```

so one is forced to write:

```
const
   N = 10;
   M = 11; {= N + 1}
```

Such subterfuges are clearly a hinderance to program maintenance. Ada also requires the evaluation of literal expressions by the compiler when the literals are reals i.e., approximate values. This places more of a burden on the compiler (which could well use a rational arithmetic package) but is in keeping with the general philosophy of allowing the programmer to write with maximum clarity at the expense of requiring the compiler to do more work.

4.8 Generics

One consequence of the strong type mechanism is that an ordinary procedure call will not suffice since the formal and actual parameters are of a different type even though the body of the procedure required is identical. As a practical example, consider two vectors **X** and **Y** and a scaler *A*. The ability to perform **Y:=Y+A∗X** is needed for a variety of scaler types: real, double length, complex, etc. Provided the scaler type has the operations "+" and "∗", the body of the procedure will be correct textually even though different machine code will be needed for the various types (Hammarling and Wichmann, 1981). Such a procedure is made generic having the type as a generic parameter:

```
generic
    type T is private;
    type T VECTOR is array (INTEGER range ⟨ ⟩) of T;
    with function '+' (X, Y: T) return T is ⟨ ⟩;
    with function '∗' (X, Y: T) return T is ⟨ ⟩;
procedure AX PLUS Y (A: in T; X: in T VECTOR; Y: in out T VECTOR) is
    begin . . . end;
```

The callable procedures are then constructed by instantiating the generic by inserting the appropriate types:

```
procedure REAL AX PLUS Y is new AX PLUS Y (REAL, VECTOR);
```

5 IS ADA TOO LARGE?

The last section illustrated that the major extensions of Ada compared with Pascal are required to meet the application area of the language. Could the language nevertheless be simplified without seriously reducing the application area? Is the size of the language a serious impediment to its use?

Firstly, it would seem possible to reduce the size of the language without materially affecting the applications. However, the size reduction is marginal—no more than 10%. Moreover, the changes are bound to make programming more difficult. My own candidates for the reduction would be as follows:*

1. Delete the pragma INCLUDE. This textual macro could be handled by a preprocessor, if needed.

---

* *Ed. note:* Two of the items in this list are not present in ANSI Ada. These are the INCLUDE pragma and the exponentiate operator (U.S. Department of Defense, 1983).

2. Delete families of entries. This facility allows for multiple queues for services, but an additional task could do this.

3. Delete the exponentiate operator. This is not present in Pascal, but is in FORTRAN. The functionality can be provided by a generic function.

4. Delete either **mod** or **rem** since having both forms of integer division is excessive.

5. Delete the **if** statement. The case statement can be used instead and is often clearer since the conditions under which the 'else part' is executed are more explicit.

Does the size of the language make it difficult to use? For the initial user, the following aspects can be ignored:

- **Tasking:** Will not be used, except in ways hidden from him.
- **Generics:** Will only use generics already written, which is quite easy compared with producing a generic.
- **Private types:** Again, will only see a simple part of this as a user.
- **Real types:** Many applications will not need this.

On the other hand, the initial user will not be able to avoid exceptions. Exceptions have to be understood because of the clear division in Ada between the static semantics (implemented by the compiler) and the dynamic semantics (implemented by the running program). This is a welcome improvement on current practice as reflected by Pascal. It is only by such understanding that the reliability of systems can be increased.

6 COULD PASCAL BE SIMPLER?

It might seem surprising that Pascal could be made simpler. The basic properties of Pascal that gives it its simplicity are that declarations do not require any executable code and that variables of one type occupy a fixed amount of storage. While retaining these properties, one could simplify as follows:

1. The functions *eof* and *eoln* need not have the default parameter (input) since this would then make them into ordinary Pascal functions.

2. The overloaded functions *sqr* and *abs* could be made true functions by using different names for the integer and real versions.

3. The language could be defined in terms of the ISO character set, substantially increasing portability and making the Pascal type char more adequately defined. RTL/2 takes this approach very successfully and Ada is similar.

4. The procedure *dispose* should be removed from the language because of its inherent insecurity. The definition of the language already permits implementations to add procedures, and since compilers (for instance) need *dispose*, it should be added as an option. The even less secure procedures of *mark* and *release* would be another alternative.

With these simplifications, perhaps one extension ought to be considered. It is particularly annoying not to be able to declare complex functions in Pascal—all functions have to return "simple" results. With this "extension," the language would actually be simpler for the user since an odd restriction in Pascal would be removed.

7 A RADICAL SUGGESTION

One reason why Ada has its current form is because of the need to make the program text as readable as possible to aid program maintenance. This assumes that program text is the sole method of communication between the programmer and the compiling system. With modern interactive computer systems, this assumption can be waived. Hence a package becomes a data-structure linked into a larger structure representing the complete library of packages. At a lower level, the user could use abbreviated keywords provided the expanded form was presented on output. Similarly, Ada is free format, but this is unnecessary for output (indeed, it is confusing). In such an environment one could design a language which has many of the attributes of Ada but is simpler as seen by the computer user.

An advantage of Pascal is that there are now a number of good textbooks on the language. The same will no doubt be true of Ada in a year or two. What would a textbook look like that was designed to teach a language based upon interactive computing? The existing books on BASIC are not encouraging in terms of teaching good discipline in programming.

It can be argued that the Ada Programming Support Environment (APSE) project (U.S. Department of Defense, 1980) could meet these requirements. Certainly syntax-oriented editors, pretty-printers and other tools can give the programmer a totally different view of a language. One reason for the success of BASIC is the simplicity of its typical environment. Similarly, the ease of using APL, even though it needs a sophisticated character set, has contributed to its success. It is not clear how significant the APSE will be in the acceptance of Ada.

8 CONCLUSIONS

Although Ada is based upon Pascal, it is quite a different type of language. Pascal is excellent as an educational tool but is inappropriate for major commercial or realtime projects. Ada is more complex than Pascal but has a capability for large systems.

The choice of a language for a project is very important. Pascal and Ada together span a potentially large part of the market. In the future, tools to convert between Pascal and Ada may be available, making an initial choice less critical (Albrecht et al., 1980). Currently, the use of Ada is restricted to long-term projects because of the absence of production quality compilers. Fortunately, with both U.S. Department of Defense and EEC funding, Ada compilers are not likely to be expensive even though they will cost more than those for Pascal. A reasonable strategy at the moment would be: (a) Use Standard Pascal where possible (especially for small projects) since this allows for an upgrade into Ada, if needed. (b) Use Ada as a design language now, since packages provide a necessary framework for project management (Wichmann, 1980).

ARTHUR EVANS, JR.
Tartan Laboratories, Inc., Pittsburgh, PA

A Comparison of Programming Languages:
Ada, Pascal, C

1 INTRODUCTION

Although the programmer dealing with systems programming now has a fairly rich choice of programming languages, there is often little guidance, other than hearsay, to help in choosing among them. In this chapter, we examine three high order languages (HOLs) and compare their features, evaluating the ability of each to meet the goals of systems programming as defined later in this section.

The three languages are now described briefly, roughly in the order of decreasing size and complexity. More details about each language, along with citations to the relevant documentation, appear in Section 2.

> **Ada:** Ada is a very large language with an extensive collection of features from which the programmer may choose. It was designed under the auspices of the United States Department of Defense for a special class of systems programming. Several compilers for the complete language have been announced and many more are under development. There are also many compilers for subsets in varying degrees of completeness.

> **Pascal:** Pascal was designed in an academic environment and was intended to be a vehicle for teaching concepts of programming languages. Given its initial goals, it has proven to be not only extremely durable but also usable in application areas far beyond its designer's intent.

> **C:** The C programming language was designed to be a simple language useful for systems programming. The intent was to provide its users with close access to the underlying hardware while permitting good efficiency and reasonable portability of programs.

Although these three language differ considerably in size and sophistication, each is a reasonable candidate for consideration for use in many system programming tasks.

The domain of application under consideration in this discussion is *systems programming*. The term is used to mean that sort of programming application characterized by most or all of the following characteristics:

Large size: The application is big, the impact of the size manifesting itself in two ways:

- The application is too big to be fully understood by a single individual, so that issues of communication among programmers are relevant.
- It is too big to be expressed in any practical way as a single compilation unit, so that issues of communication among separately compiled units are also relevant.

The implications of the large size pervade much of this discussion.

Access to hardware: In many places, the application requires close access to the underlying hardware. Such access might involve setting or examining a particular memory location or hardware register, generating a specific bit pattern, dealing with data whose layout in memory is dictated by some force (such as hardware design) outside the programmer's control, and so on.

Efficiency: In at least some parts of the application, it must be possible for the programmer to insure maximally-efficient use of the hardware resource. For example, the acceptability of the entire implementation may depend on the throughput of one key part of the program.

Portability: The application may be moved from one hardware environment to another; the pain of such moves must be minimized.[1]

Completeness: As much of the application as possible must be expressed in the HOL. Some of these applications run in a bare computer in which there is no resident operating system.

I emphasize that "big," as used in the first point, means *very* big, requiring many tens of programmers and involving many hundreds of thousands of lines of code. I also emphasize that these objectives differ in some cases from those of the language designers, as I point out in Section 2.

In this report, the three languages under consideration are evaluated with respect to their ability to meet these needs. To a large extent my comparisons are factual and should not prove to be excessively controversial. Where I express my personal opinions, I am careful to make that fact clear by use of the first person singular.

---

[1] Some have claimed that a reasonable language design goal is to reduce this pain to almost zero. I reject that goal as being unrealistic, being quite content to be able to keep the pain down to some moderate level. It seems clear to me that any program which requires access to the hardware must be changed at least a little if the underlying hardware is changed.

A word about "safety" is in order. A worthy goal espoused in many language design efforts has been to minimize the chances for certain types of errors of usage. I have no quibble with this goal, providing that attaining it does not become an obsession that unduly drives the language design. For example, early in the design of Ada there was an attempt to rule out the possibility of side effects. Later (and in my opinion, fortunately) this goal was dropped, since attaining it was impacting badly on much of the language. While I can hardly object to seeking safety, I object strongly to stripping the language of useful power in an attempt to protect from all possible consequences of a programmer's own folly.

Having made that remark, honesty requires that I acknowledge the existence of two successful large applications written in Euclid, a language which, in the interest of safety, forbids side effects, aliasing, and various other features which most systems programmers "know" that they need. One application is a Euclid compiler (Wortman, 1981), and the other is an operating system (Cardozo, 1980). Apparently, the "limitations" of Euclid were not perceived as a serious problem by the programmers who used it.

The rest of this paper is organized as follows: Section 2 contains a brief history of each language; Section 3 contains a comparison of selected features of the three languages; and Section 4 contains an examination of various metalinguistic matters, along with the goals and philosophy that lead to the language's design. Finally, Section 5 contains conclusions.

2 HISTORY AND BACKGROUND

It seems useful to say a few words about the history of each of these languages and the background that led to their creation. Although the intent of this chapter is to discuss the languages as they now exist, such discussion is more meaningful given an understanding of how they got that way.

2.1 Ada

Ada is the result of what is surely the most comprehensive language design effort ever undertaken. In 1975, the United States Department of Defense (DoD) came to the realization that its expenditures for software for embedded systems[2] were in the hundreds of millions of dollars per year, and increasing. Most such software has been written in assembly language, leading not just to high software production costs but also, much more seriously, to extremely high maintenance costs over a life-cycle that might last ten to fifteen years or more. A High Order Language Working Group, formed to oversee the design of one or more HOLs to be used to write such software,

---

[2] DoD has defined an embedded system to be a system with both a hardware and a software component whose purpose is other than computation. Examples include avionics systems, command and control, artillery fire control, digital communications networks, and so on. Such systems are in extensive use throughout DoD.

initiated a lengthy process of determining language requirements, a process which culminated in the so-called "Steelman" document (Steelman, 1978) which described the requirements to be imposed on the language design. Late in the requirements definition process, a competitive procurement for language design was initiated, ending in July of 1980 with specification of Ada. Ada's design was performed by Honeywell at its Cii-Bull affiliate in France by an international team lead by Jean D. Ichbiah. For more details about the fascinating history of Ada's development, see an interesting paper (Carlson, 1980) by members of the team within DoD responsible for overseeing Ada's design.

The first Ada Language Reference Manual (Ada, 1980a) was published in July, 1980, and the document was reprinted in November, 1980, with extensive corrections of typographic errors but with no substantive changes in content. The language was further revised and there was a new document (Ada, 1982) in July, 1982, which was adopted as Military Standard MIL-STD 1815. The final Ada Standard (Ada, 1983) was approved in February, 1983, as both a Military Standard (MIL-STD 1815A) and an ANSI Standard. During all of these revisions, the section numbers of the document have remained unchanged.

The term "Ada" standing alone in this chapter always refers to the final version, the ANSI and Military standard. When I find it necessary to distinguish among the various Ada versions, I refer to Ada-80 or Ada-82 or ANSI-Ada.

Many implementations are underway, including several extremely large ones funded by DoD that include complete environments. A current list of implementations can be found from time to time in *Ada LETTERS*, the publication of AdaTEC, the ACM SIGPLAN Technical Committee on Ada.[3] In addition, DoD has sponsored development of an Ada Compiler Validation Capability (ACVC) (Goodenough, 1980) whose purpose is to insure that any Ada compiler used for software to be delivered to DoD in fact correctly implements the entire language. At the time of this writing (October 1983), three compilers have been approved by ACVC.

2.2 Pascal

Pascal was designed in 1968 by Niklaus Wirth with the stated goal of developing "a language suitable to teach programming. . . ." It was first described in a technical paper (Wirth, 1971) in 1971 in which Wirth expounded his views about programming language design and described his new language. In 1974 Jensen and Wirth published a book (Jensen, 1974) which was for many years the closest thing to an "official" definition of Pascal that existed; this book is referred to hereafter as J&W.[4] The language described in Wirth's 1971 paper differs in significant ways from the language described in J&W.

---

[3] The July–August 1983 edition of *Ada LETTERS* lists 27 implementations in the United States and 13 in other countries.

[4] It is unfortunate that there are different printings of J&W with the same copyright date and slightly differing technical content. For example, early printings do not mention the **dispose** feature and later printings do.

In 1982 a standard for Pascal (Pascal, 1983) was adopted by ISO. The language defined by the standard is largely the same as the one defined in J&W, but the standard specifies precisely many points left vague by J&W. It is the standard language that is discussed herein.

Since Wirth designed the language to be taught, it was deliberately kept small with a minimum number of concepts. Given this limitation, it is truly impressive to see how implementations of the language have proliferated, finding acceptance in areas far beyond the designer's intent. For example, Pascal seems to be offered on most home computers. It suffers from being the oldest of the three languages—the fact that it was originally offered as an alternative to Algol-60 surely dates it. It has had an immense influence on most subsequent programming language design; in particular, Ada's design owes much to Pascal's influence.

2.3 C

The C language, designed in about 1972 by Dennis Ritchie of Bell Telephone Laboratories, is a modification of the language B (described only by Bell Laboratories internal memoranda), which is in turn a modification of BCPL (Richards, 1969). C was designed for systems programming on the PDP-11 for a community with a long tradition of programming only in assembly language.

The closest thing to a language reference manual is the book *The C Programming Language* (Kernighan, 1978) by Brian Kernighan and Dennis Ritchie; this book is referred to hereafter as K&R. I believe that K&R is inadequate as a "language reference manual." I define that term in Section 4.2 and return to my claim of inadequacy and justify it at that place.

Much of the rationale for the creation of the language is presented in a later paper (Ritchie, 1978) by Dennis Ritchie. Bell Laboratories has implemented C on the Honeywell 6000, IBM System/370, and the Interdata 8/32; many other implementations exist for many computers and operating systems.

There is an additional product which is so closely related to C that I feel it must be mentioned as part of any discussion of C: a program called *lint* (Johnson, 1979), so named "apparently because it picks bits of fluff from one's programs."[5] The C community has recognized that type checking in almost all C implementations is quite weak (as discussed in Section 3.1.4), the error detection performed by most compilers leaving much to be desired. As *lint* detects and reports many real and apparent bugs which most compilers make no attempt to find, it can be thought of as a somewhat more rigorous enforcer of language standards than the C compilers.

2.4 Further Comments

A strong case could be made for restricting this chapter to a discussion of languages that already exist in the sense that there be usable implementations. In that sense, Ada just barely exists. However, many useful implementations of Ada will surely

---

[5] (Kernighan, 1978), page 3.

exist within the next few years, and the nature and influence of its sponsor (the Department of Defense) is such that it will come into extensive use. Thus it is a strong candidate for the kinds of applications I discuss herein.

There is an additional consideration which is more important: Ada probably represents the most labor-intensive programming language design effort ever undertaken, an effort that has had the benefit of advice from most of the international programming language community. It is not surprising that there is much of excellence in it. It is therefore completely appropriate to include it in any comparison with existing languages—both to evaluate Ada as well as to provide a standard against which to measure other languages.

3 FEATURE COMPARISON

In this section, I compare the three languages with respect to the way each treats certain specific language features. I address in turn data types, placement of data in the computer's memory, expressions and side effects, statements and structured programming, program structure, parallel processing, input/output, and other topics.

3.1 Data Types

3.1.1 Basic types.   All three languages support a collection of basic types, used both to declare scalars and to build aggregates. Each such type is discussed in turn.

Boolean.   Both Ada and Pascal support a distinct class of booleans with values *true* and *false*; in C these values are represented as non-zero and zero, respectively. C's punning eliminates the possibility of the compiler's being able to detect certain kinds of programming errors. For example, each of the expressions

$$1 < 2 < 3$$
$$3 < 2 < 1$$

is a correct C expression, each of which is true (i.e., has the value 1).

Enumerations.   The enumeration, an important concept in modern programming language design that was introduced by Pascal, provides programmer-selected names for a small class of objects with type checking of those names. Although small integers can be used to encode such data, use of enumerations permits the compiler's type checking feature to detect many programming errors. Both Ada and Pascal include enumerations with essentially the same syntax.[6] Further, Ada and Pascal permit subranges of enumerations. The C programmer is clearly at a loss here. The C programmer can use the preprocessor to assign symbolic names for

---

[6] Ada's design was strongly influenced by Pascal.

such constants and recent releases of the C compiler from the Bell Laboratories support enumerations. However, as these are just names of integers, there is no type checking.

Integers.   Although all three languages support integers, Ada and C provide extra features to accommodate the programmer's need for more than one size of integer, while Pascal has only integers and subranges of integers, with no control over the space required for each.

In Ada, every integer type is in fact a subrange of the (mathematical) integers. A standard prelude may well predefine types such as *short_ integer* or *long_ integer* to match the hardware's capabilities. Ada also supports nonnegative integers, which it calls *natural*, and positive integers, which it calls *positive*.

C has *int*, *short*, and *long*, where the number of bits of each is implementation-dependent and out of the programmer's control. In general, two or perhaps even all three of these may be the same size. Since C has no concept of subrange, an important kind of error detection is missing.

Ada and C give the programmer at least some control over how much space is to be allocated for an item of each type. Although Ada has considerable fineness of control and C's control is rather coarse, even that of C is probably adequate for most real applications. Ada permits the programmer to put enough information into the text of a program to guarantee safety when a program is ported; C permits enough for safety to be highly probable most of the time.

As this is the first of several situations in which I find C to be "probably adequate most of the time," I include an example. One problem in carrying a program from one computer to another is differing word sizes. Consider the following fragment:

```
unsigned int FUNNY;     /* Declare unsigned integer var. */
int X, Y;               /* Declare two integer variables. */
. . .
FUNNY = 0177777;        /* An octal constant—see footnote⁷. */
X = 0177777/3;
Y = FUNNY/3;
```

One might well expect *X* and *Y* to be left with the same values by this fragment. In fact, that expectation would be met if the code were running on a VAX. However, on a PDP-11, *X* would be left at zero since on that computer the constant would be interpreted as signed and therefore have the value −1. The difficulty is not just that there is a machine dependency or that there is no way to obtain a warning message from the compiler, but that the C community does not perceive this sort of problem as important. After all, "C gets it right most of the time." This is an excellent example of my major concern with C.

Real Numbers.   All three languages support some sort of approximation to real arithmetic. Ada distinguishes between floating point, characterized by a relative precision (the number of digits in the mantissa), and fixed point, characterized by an absolute precision. (Neither of the other languages includes fixed point.) Alone

---

⁷ It is the leading zero that indicates to the C compiler that the constant is octal.

among the three languages, Ada's definition is sufficiently precise to permit the calcula-
tion of error bounds of numeric computations.[8] A prelude may well define types
such as *long_float* or *short_float* that match the hardware's capabilities.

C supports two sizes of floating point numbers (*float* and *double*) to match
the hardware. Pascal merely supports a single type *real*.

Although Ada's definitional power in this area is impressive, I doubt that systems
programming requires such power. On the other hand, as many embedded applications
that include an interface to analog-to-digital hardware are expressed most readily
using fixed point computations, there is a weakness here in Pascal and C.

Character Data.   All three languages support character data and permit literals
of this type, and all three languages accept string literals as syntactic sugar for an
array of characters. Pascal has the unfortunate inability to distinguish between a
character constant and a string of length one, in that

'abc'

denotes a string whose length is three characters while

'x'

denotes a character.[9]

Ada is committed to the ASCII character set with its attendant advantages.
C implementations support either ASCII or EBCDIC. Pascal, in the interests of
accommodating the whims of other character sets, says less about the characteristics
of characters and thereby achieves less portability. A Pascal implementation is not
required to include lower-case letters.

Logical Data.   None of the languages supports logical data (as opposed to
Boolean), which are in effect bit strings, with operations such as **and** and **or** and
shifts. C defines these operators but they operate on integers. Ada provides arrays
of Booleans and the operators **and** and **or** on them; the facility is at best barely
adequate for convenient expression of specific bit manipulation operations.

Conclusions.   Ada provides the user with a rich collection of basic types in
a safe manner. Pascal's lack of logical data is a serious limitation in systems programming. C provides all the requisite power, but, by doing much of it with integers,
gives away a lot of safety. Pascal provides a simple set of types in a fairly safe way.
It would be quite awkward or impossible to express certain bit-manipulating calculations in Pascal.

3.1.2 Structured data.   All three languages provide two kinds of structured
data: *arrays* and *records*.[10] Pascal also supports *sets*. In addition, all three languages
have some sort of pointer mechanism.

---

[8] The required assumption is that the implementation is "correct." Again, Ada's definition is sufficiently complete that it permits appropriate testing for correctness as part of validation.

[9] The distinction is the same as that between an integer and an array of length one of integers.

[10] The term *structure* is used by C for what Ada and Pascal call a *record*. (C follows the lead of
BCPL in this matter.) I use hereafter the more conventional term, record.

Arrays. All three languages provide arrays of objects of any type supported by the language, including arrays of arrays and arrays of records. Ada permits multidimensional arrays as part of the language; Pascal and C achieve the same effect with arrays of arrays. The major difference I choose to focus on is how the languages treat a *flexible array*, an array in which one or both subscript limits is not known until run-time. Such an array might be used in any of three contexts:

- As a formal parameter to a routine with bounds set on entry to the routine to the limits of the actual parameter
- As local data with bounds set on entry to the scope in which the data are declared
- As heap data with bounds set when the object is allocated

Ada permits flexible arrays in all three of these contexts. The Pascal standard permits no flexible arrays at all, a serious deficiency, but the standard also defines "level 1 Pascal" which permits flexible arrays as formal parameters.

C's approach to arrays is rather quaint. If X is an array, then the bit pattern which is X's value is the address of the array's zeroth component.[11] (All arrays in C start at subscript zero.) Thus, the following expressions, in which X is an array and N is an integer, are all equivalent:

$$X[N] \qquad *(X + N) \qquad *(N + X) \qquad N[X]$$

Here the prefix operator "*" stands for "contents of." The semantics of "+" used to add a pointer (i.e., an array) and an integer is that, before the addition the integer is multiplied by the number of address units occupied by each element of the array.

Although C requires that local arrays have limits known at compile-time, it relaxes that restriction for a formal parameter which is a one-dimensional array. Since there is no language-defined heap, the subroutine package to implement one could easily allocate variable-sized objects. Of course, the size desired would have to be passed as an explicit parameter since the compiler would have no way to calculate it.

Records. Pascal and Ada provide variant records in which parts of the record can vary in different situations. There may be only one variant and the variant must be the last item of the record, but that variant may itself have variants. An important advantage of Ada over Pascal is that the compiler will insure (unless the check is suppressed) that the tag is correct for the field being accessed. Some Pascal implementations may perform the check but doing so is not required by the standard.

C's union provides the same functionality provided by variant records. The union is more flexible since there is no restriction for only one union at the top level of a record. The union is also slightly less convenient to use since there is an extra level of naming.

Sets. Although a set is little more than a (packed) array of booleans, the presence of sets in the language can be an important advantage for the programmer, particularly in writing an expression whose value is to be such a set. Pascal supports

---

[11] C's designers copied this feature from BCPL.

sets; Ada and C do not. As the Pascal standard does not establish a minimum set size that each implementation must support, an implementation is free to have a fixed maximum size (perhaps dictated by the word length) that is too small for many uses.

Pointers.   Although all three languages provide pointers, Ada's designers opted instead for the phrase "variable of an access type." The intent, presumably, was to avoid the bad connotations ascribed to pointers in much of the literature of the time.

Ada and Pascal provide a heap (a storage area maintained by the support system from which space may be obtained) and restrict pointers so that they can point only into the heap. In C a pointer can point anywhere at all. There are probably safety advantages to keeping pointers from pointing to anything, although programmers often complain that they "need" this feature. Heap storage and its use are discussed in Section 3.2.3.

In architectures in which hardware registers or I/O control registers are addressable, C programmers achieve access to them by using absolute pointers. An Ada programmer can accomplish the same effect by using a representation specification to direct the compiler to place a given item at a given address.

3.1.3 Routines and labels.   Language designers differ on whether or not to include objects of type routine or label in the language.[12] Constants of these types exist, a label constant being the identifier used to label a statement and a routine constant being one declared by a function or procedure declaration. The question of interest is whether or not values of type label or routine can be passed as parameters, or whether there can be variables which take them as value.

Following Strachey (Barron, 1963), let us define the concept of "classes of citizenship" for types as follows:

First class: A type is a *first class citizen* if there can be objects of that type which can be passed as parameters. Most types are in this class.

Second class: A type is a *second class citizen* if objects of the type can be used as parameters but there cannot be variables of the type. Labels and routines are second class citizens in many languages.

Third class: A type is a *third class citizen* if no objects of the type can be used at all.

The language designer planning to admit routines into a language as first or second class citizens faces two major problems: efficiency and safety. Consider a routine INNER declared within the body of another routine OUTER. In the usual block-structured language, the code within the body of INNER can access variables declared at the beginning of OUTER. The efficiency problem concerns the ability to

[12] The term *routine* refers to either a procedure or a function. The term *label* refers to the possible target of a *goto*, not a block label in Ada.

be able to find OUTER's variables while INNER is running. A display mechanism solves this problem but always at some cost in run-time. The safety issue arises if routines are first class citizens and INNER is assigned to a variable whose lifetime exceeds that of the block containing OUTER. It is then possible for INNER to be invoked at a time when OUTER's stack no longer exists. This disaster can, in general, be detected only at run-time and then awkwardly, at best.

An interesting solution to both of these problems is the so-called "BCPL scope rule" which provides that it is not possible to access any non-local data which are resident on the stack within a routine body. This curious restriction, a very clever idea of Martin Richards' that was incorporated into the design of BCPL (Richards, 1969), means that no run-time mechanism, such as a display or static chain, is required. Further, routines can be first class citizens without incurring run-time overhead and without violating safety. On the other hand, nested routines are distinctly less convenient to write.

Type checking is a third issue of interest if routines can be passed as parameters (i.e., they are first or second class citizens). Then the question is whether or not strong type checking of parameters is still in effect when the routine which is a formal parameter is invoked.

Ada.   In Ada, routines and labels are third class citizens and cannot be passed as parameters. However, a generic routine can be parameterized at compile-time by a function or procedure; since the effect is at compile-time, there is no compromise of strong typing. (Ada's generic facility is discussed briefly in Section 3.8.1.) Thus, routines have a partial promotion to second class citizenship, but only at compile-time.

Pascal.   In Pascal, routines are second class citizens and there is type checking of parameters[13] when a formal routine is invoked. Labels are third class.

C.   In C, routines are first class citizens.[14] Because routines cannot be nested, the problem solved by the BCPL scope rule does not arise and there is no efficiency loss.

Labels are third class citizens, although many C compilers will apparently permit a pointer to a label.

Conclusions.   Some applications are naturally expressed by a vector of routines, an effect that can be achieved only in C.[15] Although it is possible to achieve the effect in other ways, doing so is not so convenient.

My personal view is that it is desirable to promote routines to first-class citizenship but that there must not be serious loss in efficiency or safety as a result. Unfortunately, these requirements are incompatible.

---

[13] This checking is required by the standard; it was not required by J&W.

[14] More precisely, a pointer to a routine can be passed or assigned although a routine cannot. This distinction is important to the programmer but does not affect the conclusions reached by this discussion.

[15] The distinction pointed out in the previous footnote is relevant.

3.1.4 Type checking.   Given the fact that modern programming language design theorists now seem to be in general agreement that typed languages are to be preferred, it is not surprising that all three languages claim to be typed. However, their approaches to data types differ considerably. Let me first define my terminology:

> A language is said to be *typed* if every object has a type which is known to the compiler.

> A language is said to be *strongly typed* if the compiler is able to and, in fact, does enforce the type of every object, insuring that no value of an incorrect type is assigned to it.

All three languages are typed, but only Ada is strongly typed; Pascal comes close but has gaps, discussed later. I claim that C is not strongly typed.

Some have claimed that strong typing is neither needed nor desired in systems programming. I believe the following things:

- Strong type checking at compile-time is a requirement of modern programming languages. Furthermore, it is necessary that strong typing be enforced over separate compilation, both for shared data and for parameters.
- Programmers sometimes require the ability to circumvent the type checking rules.
- A properly designed language should provide an explicit mechanism for such circumventing.
- Every use of the mechanism should be immediately obvious to the most casual reader of the code.

These definitions and beliefs are important to the ensuing discussion.

Ada.   The type facility in Ada is extremely rich, extremely powerful, and extremely complicated. The programmer is provided a rich collection of mechanisms dealing with types. (The chapter on types in the Ada Standard is 44 pages long.) The richness of the overloading feature, which permits multiple instances of a routine with a given name (selection of the proper one depending on the types of the actual parameters), makes it difficult for both programmers and compilers to determine which one is invoked at a given place. Further, overloading (at least to some extent) removes some of the important advantages of strong typing since certain expressions that would be reported as a type-matching error without overloading might turn out to have a legal (though perhaps unintended) meaning. I think Ada has provided too much richness here, at least for systems programming.

Ada provides an explicit mechanism to circumvent type checking: the predefined generic library procedure UNCHECKED_CONVERSION that can force the compiler to view any given value as having any specified type. This mechanism is an excellent solution to the problem. The requisite functionality is provided, it is a bit awkward to use (with the long name), and every use is immediately obvious to the casual reader.

Pascal.   Wirth, in his description of Pascal, claims that the language is strongly typed. However, the design provides no intentional mechanism for circumventing type checking although such a mechanism exists: overlaying variant fields of a structure. Since Pascal provides no mechanism for tag checking, variant fields are always potentially unsafe. Wirth discusses this matter in a reflective paper (Wirth, 1975) written in 1975. Although he admits that Pascal's failure to check the tag (and, worse, its option to omit a tag entirely) leads to unfortunate programming practice, he nonetheless concludes that the design is justified on efficiency grounds. I suspect that now, eight years later, Wirth might take the opposite position. I do.

Pascal avoids the problem of type checking across separate compilation by the simple expedient of not providing separate compilation. Although many implementations do provide it, they do so in different ways with differing degrees of type checking; further discussion is beyond the scope of this chapter.

C.   Although C has types (unlike its grandparent BCPL) and most compilers seem to do some type checking, it is difficult to support the claim that the language is strongly typed. All C compilers are quite concerned about the *size* of an object (i.e., the number of bytes of storage it requires), but they rarely care very much about any other aspect of type. In fact, a major function of *lint* (see Section 2.3) is to detect violations of type checking that are not caught by compilers. C admits many ways to circumvent type checking; just a few are mentioned here. The first two are properties of (apparently most) implementations but not inherent in the language; the last two are language properties.

- Pointer assignment is not checked so that, for example, a pointer-to-integer may be assigned to a pointer-to-float.
- In an expression such as

    $P \rightarrow \ldots$

    in which P is to be a pointer to a field of a structure, there is no check on the type of P.
- Arguments to functions are not checked.
- The *union* mechanism is advertised as being a way to circumvent type checking.

There is no reason to discuss "beating the compiler" in this area. Most C compilers just do not care.

Conclusions.   Ada provides all the type checking needed to assist the programmer in finding many bugs at compile-time. In particular, it attacks and solves the important problem of type checking between separate compilation units. (Pascal avoids this problem by omitting separate compilation entirely.) Further, it provides a mechanism to circumvent type checking when needed, meeting the requirement that doing so be immediately apparent to the casual reader of the program.

It is my belief that the provision of overloading in Ada defeats, at least to some extent, some of the advantages to be had from strong type checking. Further, it makes the whole problem of type matching much more difficult. On the other hand, of course, it provides the programmer an often useful feature.

C can barely, if at all, claim to be a strongly-typed language, although C with *lint* can make the claim. K&R contains, on page 3, the following statement:

> Programs which pass unscathed through *lint* enjoy, with few exceptions, freedom from type errors about as complete as do, for example, Algol 68 programs.

If that claim is true, and if *lint* is assumed to be part of the definition of C, then the situation is not so bad as I have claimed. Unfortunately, the details of the checking *lint* performs are not documented.

3.1.5 Declarations and scope rules.

I define the *scope* of a declaration of an identifier to be that part of the program text in which that declaration controls the properties of that identifier.[16] For the most part, all three languages are block-structured, as the term was first defined in the Algol-60 Report [Naur 63]. Ada and C provide ways to import names into a scope from elsewhere, a feature that is required for separate compilation.

Ada.   Although Ada is largely a block-structured language, the ability to import names into a scope for separate compilation is a departure from strict block nesting. Also, because of the presence of overloading, some declarations of routines which in Algol-60 would result in a hole in a scope have in Ada a different effect. Indeed, Ada's visibility rules are extremely complex. I believe that Ada has gone too far in this area and would be a better language for systems programming had overloading been omitted.

Pascal.   Pascal does not admit nested blocks, an extremely serious restriction in writing programs of any size at all. The major effect of this omission is that a declaration must often be much too far from the place of use of the item declared— the modern idea of locality is violated. A related problem is that the controlled variable in an iteration statement must be declared in the surrounding block, thereby letting the programmer use its value after completion of the iteration. A better design is to make it declared by the iteration statement and local to its body, as in Ada.

C.   C does not permit nested routines, thereby avoiding the whole issue of the BCPL scope rule (see Section 3.1.3) and still not paying any efficiency cost. C uses the *file* for scope control. Static data declared in a file outside of any routine have scope consisting of the rest of the file. Such items may also be exported so that they have global scope.

The kindest way I can describe C's declaration syntax is to call it a disaster. An item's type is specified by giving a sort of template of its use. Further, there are three slightly different syntaxes for types: for declaring variables, for declaring

---

[16] Ada introduces the additional term *visibility*; although understanding visibility is a requisite to learning the language, the concept can be ignored in this discussion.

types (with *typedef*), and for explicit conversions. Rather than go into details, I refer the reader to an informative and amusing diatribe on the subject by Bruce Anderson [Anderson 80] who points out that the documentation is incomplete and inconsistent and that compilers differ from each other, from themselves, and from the documentation.

Conclusions.   Pascal and C present a curious pairing, the former rejecting nested blocks and the latter rejecting nested routines. Ada, as it does so often, opts to provide both kinds of nesting; I like Ada's decision.

3.2 Storage Allocation and Placement of Data

One of the requirements of system programming is the ability to control precisely where the application's data are to be placed into the computer's storage. Four aspects of such control are storage allocation, placement, heap storage, and shared data.

3.2.1 Storage allocation.   The term *storage allocation* has to do with layout of specific fields in records. All three languages provide a default layout for records that is moderately efficient in both time to access fields and space to store them. Each language then gives the programmer some abilities to override that default. There are two reasons for wanting such control. First, the programmer may want to specify a packing discipline that optimizes efficiency as appropriate for the needs of the application, minimizing either access time or space occupied, as desired. Second, the layout of the fields in the record may be outside the programmer's control, dictated by hardware (e.g., the fields in an interrupt status word) or external protocol (e.g., a message header in a communications system).

Ada.   The pragma PACK may be applied to a record type to request[17] the compiler to optimize so as to minimize the space occupied at the cost of time required to access its fields. The programmer requiring finer control must specify where each field is to go, using a representation specification. Complete control is available.

Pascal.   The programmer either accepts the implementor's default or specifies *packed*; there is no other control. A *packed* type occupies less space than the corresponding unpacked type but is usable only in restricted contexts.

C.   The programmer may control exactly how fields are to be laid out in records.

Conclusions.   Ada and C provide adequate control; Pascal is completely inadequate in this area.

3.2.2 Placement.   The term *placement*, which was coined for this purpose by Douglas T. Ross,[18] refers to placement of compiled program or of data (scalars, records, arrays, or whatever) in specific places in the computer's memory. If the

---

[17] We use "request" rather than "direct" because an Ada compiler is free to ignore pragmas.

[18] Personal communication.

application runs in multiple processors with shared memory, there is the problem of placement of data in that memory. The problem is particularly severe if the processors are not all of the same type. An additional complication is that different processors may perceive the shared memory to be at different addresses. The shared memory may contain a heap with records that contain pointers to other parts of the heap. This problem is exacerbated by the preceding problem.

None of the languages under discussion addresses adequately the problem of placement, although Ada attacks some aspects of it. To my knowledge, it is solved only in Praxis (Walker, 1981), in which the programmer may specify the location of the code for a procedure, the static storage for a procedure, the constants for a procedure, or any static data item. Here "specifying the location" means specifying which segment is to be used and then specifying with a compiler directive how each segment is to be treated by the loader. The language design addresses and solves the problem of shared memory accessed by several processors, even if the processors view the memory as having different addresses. I am surprised that no other systems language has addressed these problems.

3.2.3 Heap storage.

The term *heap* refers to an area of memory from which the user may, by explicit action, obtain space during run-time. For real systems applications (as opposed to classroom exercises), there must also be a way to recover such space when it is no longer needed. Ada and Pascal support a heap. C does not, although routines that supply a similar service are part of C's usual library.

In Ada and Pascal, space is obtained from the heap using a special syntactic construct to invoke the appropriate library routine, a routine that cannot be invoked directly by the user because there is no way type checking can succeed.[19] In Ada, the space so obtained can be initialized as part of the act of obtaining it, a distinct advantage.

Although both Ada and Pascal use the reserved word *new* to obtain heap space, Ada uses it as a function whose value is a pointer to the space. Pascal uses it as a procedure which sets its argument to be the pointer. I find Pascal's design distinctly less felicitous.

A much more important difference between Ada and Pascal has to do with *garbage collection* (GC), which is reclaiming space that is no longer needed. Ada apparently assumes a full marking garbage collector and promises to retain any heap data as long as they can still be accessed, as implied by the following quotation (from Section 4.8(7) of the Ada Standard):

An implementation must guarantee that any object created by the evaluation of an allocator remains allocated for as long as this object or one of its subcomponents is

---

[19] The problem is that the function returns a pointer to what is being allocated and there is no way to declare "pointer to whatever." One could write a generic function in Ada; it would have to be instantiated for each type to be allocated.

accessible. . . . An implementation may (but need not) reclaim the storage occupied by an object created by an allocator once this object has become inaccessible.

Although reclaiming inaccessible space is evidently optional, the fact that no real-time application can continue to allocate space, unless that space is somehow reclaimed, means that any useful implementation of Ada must either provide GC or permit writing programs that do not use it.

Ada provides the generic procedure UNCHECKED_DEALLOCATION for freeing space no longer needed, although the language definition fails to promise that the space deallocated will in fact be available for other use.

Pascal's *dispose* feature is identical in effect to Ada's UNCHECKED_DEALLOCA-TION, even to failing to promise that the space freed may be reallocated.

In this matter, Ada has erred, since I believe that GC is inconsistent with the requirements of systems programming.[20] The problem is not that Ada includes GC but rather that much essential power of the language is eliminated if the programmer must eschew those language features whose implementation requires it. I believe that it is a requirement of these kinds of languages that it be possible to program in such a style that the program incur no overhead costs, either in space or in time, arising from the fact that automatic GC is provided in the language. Ada provides a mechanism to give the programmer control of allocation and deallocation (see Sections 4.8(8) through (12), 13.2(b), and 13.10.1 of the Ada Standard), but I cannot be absolutely sure from the description that my requirement can be met. On the other hand, I acknowledge that I cannot find a flaw.

3.2.4 Shared data. If the application requires parallel processing, whether the language supports it or is implemented by the programmer, there must be a way to deal safely with data shared between processes.[21] An important problem is to be able to insure that two processes do not simultaneously attempt to alter such shared data. Although some claim (I do not) that the language design should enforce solution to this problem, none of our languages attempts to do so. At least, the language designer must provide the programmer the tools needed to accomplish this task.

Two kinds of tools are needed. First, a synchronization mechanism is needed so that two processes may, for example, insure that they are not both accessing the same shared object; this topic is discussed in Section 3.6. Second, control is needed of the compiler. A modern optimizing compiler may choose to keep a given item in a live register to improve code efficiency, thereby defeating the programmer's attempt to deal safely with shared data. This same issue arises when it is necessary to write a given bit pattern into some location, as in hardware (such as the PDP-11) in which

---

[20] Ada, of course, was designed for embedded applications rather than for systems programming. However, my claim that Ada has erred is based on my belief that GC is equally inappropriate for embedded applications.

[21] Ada's design clearly is predicated around a different mechanism—rendezvous between processes—to deal with shared data. See Section 3.6.

I/O is controlled that way. A good optimizing compiler will eliminate all except the last of several successive writes into the same location; it must be possible to suppress this optimization.

Only Ada addresses these problems at all, providing the pragma SHARED which directs that, for the variables named in the pragma, every mention of the variable in the program text corresponds to an access of or store into memory. (See Section 9.11 of the Ada Standard.) The Pascal or C programmer has no way to control the compiler in this important regard. Of course, as Pascal provides no parallelism, the Pascal programmer has no need for the feature.

3.3 Expressions

Expressions are those constructs of a language that are evaluated to return a value; there may perhaps also be a side-effect as a result of the evaluation. Since there are few significant differences between the languages in what can be in expressions, I confine my discussion to side effects.

Briefly, Ada and Pascal take the attitude that side effects are not only undesirable but probably somewhat immoral and that their use should be avoided. C's design actively encourages their use.

Starting in the early 1960s with the publication of the Algol-60 report (Naur, 1963), there has been a vocal group of language specialists who have cried out against side effects. Almost all concerned agree that unconstrained use of side effects is bad. What is controversial is the extent to which a language should be designed so as to render it difficult or even impossible to write them. Wirth originally intended to design Pascal so that side effects could not occur, stating the following dictum:

> In order to eliminate side-effects, assignments to non-local variables are not allowed to occur within a function.[22]

This intention was weakened in Wirth's final design, the following quotation appearing on page 79 of J&W:

> [Side effects] often disguise the intent of the program and greatly complicate the task of verification. . . . Hence, the use of functions producing side effects is strongly discouraged.

As mentioned in Section 1 of this chapter, the early attempt in Ada to make side effects impossible or at least difficult to write was abandoned. Ada retains some of this flavor, though, still requiring that parameters to functions have mode **in** and not **in out** or **out**.

It is accurate to say that the design of C encourages side effects. Although C distinguishes between expressions and statements, the construction that in most languages is called an *assignment statement* is in C called an *assignment expression*. It

---

[22] Page 39 of (Wirth, 1971).

is treated as an expression with a value (that of the right side) which can, therefore, be used in any context where a value is required. C includes operators such as "++" which increments its argument and then returns it, encouraging the programmer to write statements such as

A[J++] = B[K++]

inside a loop to copy vector B into A. Here the assignment statement both copies an element of the array and increments the indices J and K.

A real difference in design philosophy is revealed here. My view is that while side effects are needed from time to time in the real world of systems programming, their use should be the rare exception rather than the common occurrence. Most modern language designers would agree.[23] The C design is clearly at strong variance with this viewpoint. In designing C's predecessor B in the late sixties, the desire was to get maximal efficiency from the PDP-11, and the efficient implementation of the "++" operator by the autoincrement addressing mode surely seemed quite clever. While this decision may have been right fifteen years ago, it cannot be defended in today's world.

3.4 Statements and Structured Programming

A statement is elaborated for its effect rather than to calculate a value. As statements have been around for a long time and seem to be well understood, I have very little to say about their details.

3.4.1 Structured programming.
The modern trend in programming languages is suggested by the phrase *structured programming* which describes a particular philosophy of program construction. All three languages make an attempt to be consistent with this philosophy, with varying degrees of success.

Ada.   Ada's collection of structured statement forms is completely adequate.

Pascal.   Although one of Wirth's stated design goals in developing Pascal was structured programming, this goal was not attained in the sense that there remained many contexts in which there was no reasonable alternative to the *goto*. For example, Pascal omits any convenient structured way to break out of an iteration or return from a procedure.

C.   In its usual way, C has a minimal but adequate collection of features to deal with the issue. C programmers rarely need to use a *goto*, but there are a few situations in which one is required. One is escaping from a nested loop since the *break* statement breaks out of only one level; the other is dealing with an error discovered while deeply nested in routine calls. Ada solves the former problem with block labels and the latter problem with exceptions.

---

[23] Honesty, once again, requires that I mention the Euclid experience discussed in Section 1 of this chapter. Two large applications were successfully written in a language whose design precludes side effects, and the implementors apparently experienced no pain.

3.4.2 Exceptions.   Ada provides exception processing; Pascal and C do not. This feature provides the programmer with a way to detect and process hardware errors (such as overflow), system errors (such as end-of-file or heap-exhausted), and programmer-defined exceptions. The lack of this feature can be a particularly serious inconvenience in Pascal since the programmer has no alternative. Although the C programmer can get much of the effect with appropriate library routines, the result is less convenient than having the feature built into the language.

3.4.3 Miscellaneous topics.   A few topics relevant to statements have found no home elsewhere.

Statement Labels.   The use of integers as statement labels in Pascal is clearly bad design and reflects the age of that design.

Full Bracketing.   Ada requires of every statement-level bracketing construct in the language that it have a unique matching end bracket. For example, **if** is terminated by **end if** and **while** by **end while.** In Pascal, bodies must be bracketed by **begin . . . end,** and in C by {. . .}. I think full bracketing represents the wave of the future, with important advantages in readability and programmer convenience.

3.5 Program Structure

The requirements for systems programming listed in Section 1 mention the need to build extremely large systems, systems which are too large by several orders of magnitude to be comprehended by any one person or to be compiled as a single piece. To deal with such large systems, it is necessary to break up the program into manageable pieces each of which is small enough to be dealt with both by human programmers and by the compiler. To a large extent, the ability of the programming team to deal with these systems depends on extralinguistic tools such as loaders, dependency checkers, configuration managers, cross reference generators, and others. Such tools are, of course, beyond the scope of this chapter. I, therefore, confine my attention here to the languages themselves and the extent to which their features help or hinder the programmer in dealing with this problem.

The major issue is controlled communication between pieces of an application which are compiled separately. "Communication" means referring in one unit to items which are defined in other units. The control has to do with extending strong type checking (as the term defined in Section 3.1.4) to inter-unit references.

Ada.   Ada was designed with the problem of separate compilation very much in mind. A routine or package body may be compiled as a separate unit. An important aspect of Ada's scheme is that resolving names between separately compiled units is done entirely by the compiler, with no assumption that a "linker" or "loader" or "task builder" exists which maintains a global name space for an entire program. Thus, there is little chance of accidental conflict of external names between unrelated parts of the program.

Pascal.   Pascal has no provision for separate compilation and so is quite unsuited for large applications, including the very large ones of concern here. Separate compilation facilities have been proposed and many implementations have this feature.

C. The unit of separate compilation in C is the "file," a collection of data and routine declarations stored as a unit in a "file system." A name declared at the top level of a file may be accessed from other files by declaring the name in the other files to be "external" and specifying its type; there is no check that the types match. (*lint* may be directed to make this check.) The loader (usually) performs the required resolution of names. The features are adequate for large problems but might be inadequate for very large ones. The problem I anticipate is that the loader is used to maintain the names of routines and static data that are shared. There is, thus, a single name space for the entire application with the possibility of name conflicts between unrelated parts of the program.

3.6 Parallel Processing

Some computations are described most naturally by a model which envisages more than one task at a time proceeding in parallel. Ada provides a powerful tasking feature. Pascal and C have no features at all in this area.

Three features are needed for parallelism: a concept of *process*, a method for *synchronization* (or *mutual exclusion*) between processes, and control of *shared data*. The usual model of computation involves a single process doing all the work. With parallelism, multiple processes exist (at least conceptually), each proceeding in parallel to accomplish the task in some cooperative manner. Given multiple processes, there is then the need for a way to achieve synchronization or mutual exclusion to permit the programmer to insure that, for example, a critical data base is not being altered simultaneously by more than one process. The closely related matter of data shared between processes is discussed in Section 3.2.4.

Ada. Ada's model for parallelism is quite powerful. A process is realized in Ada as a *task*, and synchronization and mutual exclusion are achieved by a rendezvous; there is no other method. The reader interested in this topic is advised to study Chapter 9 of the Ada Standard.

I regard Ada's tasking model as elegant in the extreme. Ada proponents have demonstrated conclusively that the various classical problems in parallelism can be programmed in Ada both effectively and naturally. They have also shown how to deal with a wide spectrum of real applications. My sole misgiving has to do with efficiency. Because the only way to achieve mutual exclusion is with a rendezvous, that feature must be used in situations in which a more primitive mechanism (such as a semaphore or even a spin lock[24]) is more natural.[25] If it turns out that tasks and rendezvous can be implemented with adequate efficiency, my misgivings will vanish. There is a lengthy discussion of these and related issues in a paper (Roberts, 1981) of which I am a co-author; unfortunately, the language discussed is Preliminary Ada, which differs in important ways from ANSI-Ada.

[24] A *spin lock* is an interlock which has the property that a process wishing to lock it and finding it already locked waits in a tight loop till the lock is released.

[25] Clearly, what is "natural" is largely a matter of taste. The Ada design team apparently finds this use of rendezvous as being quite natural; I am not quite so sure.

Pascal.   Standard Pascal has no provision for parallelism. However, the dialect Concurrent Pascal (Brinch Hansen, 1975) provides the requisite features. There is no practical way to achieve parallelism in Standard Pascal.

C.   Although C provides no features for parallelism, its general low-level approach to things is such that suitable primitives could readily be written in C. The only feature missing is some sort of interlock which would have to be implemented by code written in assembler.[26]

Conclusions.   Ada is the only language in which high-level parallel processing is built in; the Ada design team has worked very hard on this matter. I am concerned that Ada provides only a very high-level solution (the rendezvous) to the problem, the language providing no access to the low-level primitives in terms of which the rendezvous is implemented. If in fact the rendezvous is the "right" solution, all is well; if not, low-level primitives will have to be implemented, at least partially in assembler. Although there is no problem in doing so, Ada is then no better than C in this respect. Further, the user is paying for a lot of language complexity which is not being used, as well as extra costs in compiler and (probably) run-time complexity.

The key question, then, is this: "Is the rendezvous the right solution?" I do not know, and I see no way to find out until we have experience with it in extensive use in the field. However, there is an analogy that suggests that some of my concern may be misplaced. When Algol-60 was first announced, programmers and compiler writers wailed about the horrible inefficiencies inherent in such features as stack storage, flexible arrays, and recursion. After a few years of research, fairly efficient solutions to most of these problems were found and we discovered that the residual inefficiencies were acceptably small in cost given their payoff in programming power. I will not be surprised if the rendezvous turns out to have the same fate, but I do not yet know. The jury is still out.

3.7 Input/Output

The term "input/output" refers to two kinds of activity. *High-level I/O* is communication of data, usually formatted for human consumption, between a program and the external world; it is usually device independent. *Low-level I/O* concerns transmission of bits as part of the application; it is usually dependent on the details of the device being communicated with. Consider, for example, a communications network in which high-level I/O is used for formatting messages to an operator and low-level I/O is used for the actual communication function of transmitting bits over the communication links. Note that the routines that implement high-level I/O must in general invoke routines which perform low-level I/O.

In my opinion, features for high-level I/O need not be built into a systems programming language, although it is desirable for the language definition to include the specification of a library of routines for the purpose. Only Pascal provides high-level I/O in the language itself, the other two providing a standard I/O library. As

---

[26] Required is an indivisible test-and-set operation. Usually a compiler does not compile this instruction unless there is a special linguistic feature for it.

none of the languages provides explicitly for low-level I/O, I confine my discussion to ways available for the programmer to achieve it. Note that in hardware such as that of the PDP-11 in which I/O is controlled by accessing a specific address, the ability to address specific memory locations suffices; otherwise, it must be possible to execute the special hardware I/O opcodes.

Ada.   The Ada Standard in Chapter 14 defines a comprehensive high-level I/O library for communicating with files, where the term *file* is defined to be an external ordered collection of data all of the same type. It is this view of file (the "all of the same type" phrase) that keeps this part of Ada from being useful for low-level I/O. The features defined are clearly adequate for high-level I/O.

There is also package LOW_LEVEL_IO (Section 14.6) which is intended to provide the requisite functionality. I have my doubts. However, since Ada provides for addressing specific memory locations, for inhibiting optimization with pragma SHARED, and for code inserts, any low-level I/O can be programmed in Ada.

Pascal.   The Pascal Standard defines a limited amount of high-level I/O, similar in spirit to that in Ada but much less ambitious. Low-level I/O cannot be performed at all and it is awkward to program high-level I/O beyond what is provided by the design.

C.   C provides no I/O in the language but there is a standard library of high-level I/O routines which is described in Chapter 7 of K&R. Low-level I/O might well require routines coded in assembly language if hardware I/O operations require special opcodes.

Conclusions.   Although systems programming (as defined in Section 1) does not require very much high-level I/O, at least rudimentary functions are required. Ada surely provides much more than is needed. The inability to do low-level I/O in Pascal is a serious limitation. C, in its usual way, is adequate.

3.8 Other Features

3.8.1 Generics and macros.
Ada has generic subprograms and packages, templates which can be parameterized by generic invocation at compile time. The actual parameters supplied at such invocation may be types or routines, even though neither a type nor a routine may be a parameter to a regular routine. In principle, generic instantiation could be done by macro substitution in a prelexical phase, providing that nonlocal names were bound properly. In practice, efficiency considerations require of an acceptable compiler that in many cases bodies be shared between instantiations. Although generics provide the Ada programmer considerable convenience in writing code, their presence in the language surely provide major problems in writing a high-quality compiler.

C includes a preprocessor which expands text macros, performing string substitution. The feature is often used to give symbolic names to constants to improve the readability of the code. When used with care, the effect can be quite good. However, there is no type checking, as usual in C. Further, although macros can surely be helpful in writing programs, only the most judicious avoids playing havoc with readability. The modern approach to language design emphasizes readability over writability.

3.8.2 Initialization.

It is often convenient for both program writing and program understanding to be able to initialize a variable as part of declaring it.

Ada permits an initial value to be associated with a variable declaration or with any field of a record or with any acquisition of space from the heap. Pascal has no facilities for initialization, although some implementations permit data declared in the outer block to be initialized. C permits initialization of some variables as part of their declaration.

Initialization as part of variable declaration is clearly a useful property of modern programming languages, desirable on methodological grounds. I believe that a modern programming language should provide at least Ada's capabilities. C, as usual, has a barely adequate facility, and Pascal, lacking any initialization of variables, is inadequate in this area.

3.8.3 Assertions.

An assertion is an expression inserted in the code which the programmer claims is true whenever control reaches that point. Use of assertions can ease the debugging task, make code easier to understand, and sometimes improve the quality of code generated. Earlier versions of Ada included assertions but the final version does not. Experience with Euclid (Wortman, 1981) suggests that assertions are immensely helpful in debugging.

Although the C language does not have assertions, the "standard" package of macros includes such a facility. C programmers report it to be easy to use and helpful in debugging.

3.8.4 Case sensitivity.

C, alone among the languages, is case sensitive.[27] Although I happen to prefer case sensitivity, I am aware that it is a controversial topic. I, therefore, confine myself to pointing out that C has the feature and refrain from drawing conclusions.

4 METALINGUISTIC MATTERS

The preceding section contains language comparison on a feature basis. This section turns to metallinguistic matters which I feel deserve discussion. In successive subsections, language size and then the related issues of documentation and standardization are investigated.

4.1 The "Size" of the Language

It is useful to briefly examine the size and "power" of each of these languages. In an important theoretical sense, all have equal power since any computation that can be expressed in one can be expressed in each. However, that statement, like a

---

[27] The term "case sensitive" refers to distinguishing between upper- and lower-case letters.

mathematical existence theorem, often has little impact on the real world of programming. For example, a common requirement in systems programming is to access a specified machine address or register. This requirement implies a functionality in a direction which is orthogonal to that of the "power" of the language. (Both Ada and C have this particular functionality.)

The three languages differ immensely in size, C being quite small and Ada being quite large. Perhaps the most interesting comment to be made about the size of each of these languages is this: Each design team undoubtedly feels that it has selected the "right" size, given the intended audience and area of application contemplated by the designers. We will discuss the evaluation criteria (my definition of "systems programming" in Section 1) that differ from the application area intended by some of the designers.

Ada.   I believe that Ada is too big, both for the embedded applications for which it is intended and for the systems programming applications considered here. It is not the Ada design team that I fault in this matter but rather the requirements process that preceded (and accompanied) the design. A committee, as is well known, is an organism which produces something resembling a camel when it sets out to design a horse. Although the language itself did not fall victim to this syndrome, largely due to the strong leadership of Jean Ichbiah, the requirements list (i.e., Steelman) was influenced by too many inputs of the form "Well, while we are designing a language, we surely must include the . . . feature."

Although it is my opinion that any language whose design was required to meet the requirements of Steelman would, of necessity, be too large, there is an item of possibly conflicting evidence that deserves consideration. After Phase 1 of Ada's design, a group at Carnegie-Mellon University became concerned with the large size of the four candidate languages and set out to show that a language of modest size could meet the Ironman[28] requirements. The resulting language, called Tartan (Shaw, 1978a), largely met the requirements and was described in a 23-page document. (The possibility of such a small description was one of the design goals of the Tartan effort.) There was also an accompanying rationale (Shaw, 1978b).

Is the existence of Tartan a counter example to my stated belief that Ada's size is an inevitable consequence of Steelman? The answer depends on how one interprets "largely" in the phrase "Tartan *largely* meets Ironman requirements." With one or two notable exceptions (such as the total absence of the fixed-point data type from Tartan), Tartan's designers perceive Tartan as meeting the *spirit* of Ironman's requirements; they did not regard it as necessary to meet the *letter* of the requirements. At the time, the community surrounding Ada's design was much more concerned with the letter of the law than with speculating on what Ironman's authors might have intended. I continue to believe that large size is an inescapable consequence of meeting the letter of Ironman, that Ada's designers perceived that doing so was necessary (i.e., required by the people who were funding the design), and that a

---

[28] Steelman was developed in stages. The latest version at the time was called Ironman.

but langs are not committee based?

markedly smaller language would largely satisfy the intent of Ironman. Further speculations may be of historical interest; I do not pursue this topic further.

Ignoring now *why* Ada is too big, let us consider the effects of its large size. There are three important objections:

- The learner has a high threshold to overcome in order to start using the language. At the very least, the learner must know enough about all the features to avoid accidental use of a key word as an identifier.
- Each of the many features impacts with each of the rest of them. This combinatorial complexity affects both the user of the language and its compilers.
- Any compiler to be at all acceptable must be quite big and, therefore, both expensive and hard to debug.

The last point deserves more attention.

Because the requirements for embedded systems and for system programming include extremely good object code, high-quality optimizing compilers are required. Compilers for large languages are hard to write and debug as are high-quality optimizing compilers for languages of moderate size. An excellent compiler for a language as large as Ada is a truly formidable task.

Pascal.   Although Pascal's size presents no problems, its failure to provide such features as separate compilation and low-level access to the hardware rules it out for the kinds of applications under consideration.

C.   I have no problems with C's size.

4.2 Documentation and Standardization

A poorly documented language (or any other software) is not really useful. There are three requirements that good documentation must meet:

Accuracy: The documentation must be correct. If there are dialects of the language, the user must have correct documentation for the one in use.

Readability: Accurate documentation is not useful if it is not possible to find what is wanted or if, once found, the text is unclear.

Completeness: Basically, there is a single goal to documentation: The reader must be able to use it to find a clear answer, with only a reasonable level of effort, to questions of the form "What happens if I write . . . ?"

Although readable introductions and primers are surely desirable, I am most interested here in the extent to which a language reference manual or standard definition meets the above criteria.

A closely-related issue is the extent to which the language has been standardized, either officially or unofficially. An accepted standard provides important advantages, including the existence of precise documentation, a pool of programmers who know the language well, existence of software tools (an extremely important advantage), higher likelihood of ease in porting, higher likelihood that the implementations match the documentation, and so on. The three languages under consideration vary widely in this area.

Ada. Ada is described in the Ada Standard (Ada, 1983). It is, in my opinion, a good example of what a reference manual for a programming language should be. Although it is *not* a primer, a plethora of introductory texts on Ada are now becoming available.

There is also a draft formal definition (Ada, 1980b) for those inclined to such things. Unfortunately, the formal definition is for the obsolete Ada-80 and it appears quite unlikely that the formal definition will ever be completed or upgraded to ANSI-Ada. There is also a Rationale (Ichbiah, 1979) for Preliminary Ada. Unfortunately, the differences between that Ada and ANSI-Ada are nowhere listed.

Ada achieves all the advantages of standardization listed above. In particular, the Department of Defense has undertaken development of an Ada environment which will include various software tools built around Ada. Once this environment exists, this metalinguistic issue should be given serious attention by anyone choosing a language.

Further, the Department of Defense has announced its intention to exercise two forms of control to insure that Ada compilers conform to the standard. First, DoD has established an Ada Compiler Validation Capability (Goodenough, 1980) which will test any candidate compiler to determine whether or not it conforms to the standard. DoD has stated that it will require in its software procurement that vendors use only compilers approved by ACVC, thereby providing an extremely strong financial incentive to insure adherence to the standard. Second, DoD has registered the term "Ada" as a trademark when used as any form of reference to a programming language and has further announced its intention to restrict the usage of this term, in ways yet to be determined. This strong commitment to control of the language definition and implementation will be a major plus in its acceptance.

Pascal. For years, J&W was the only source of Pascal specification and it was a most unsatisfactory specification. It consists of two parts, the first ("User Manual," about 130 pages) being a moderately friendly overview of the language and its implementation on the CDC 6000 series computers, and the second ("Report," about 34 pages) being a short definition of the language. Both documents are sufficiently imprecise that many important questions about Pascal cannot be answered by studying them.

After much labor, the international Pascal community has finally accepted a standard Pascal (Pascal, 1983), one which was produced by IEEE and accepted by ANSI. Like most such documents, it is precise but not easy to read. In writing this chapter, I have found the readable book by Doug Cooper (Cooper, 1983) to be of considerable help in interpreting the standard.

C. The "official" definition of C is K&R (Kernighan, 1978) which contains a one-chapter primer, five chapters of greater detail, and a 42-page appendix titled "The C Reference Manual." (Additional chapters describe the I/O library, which is not part of the language, and the UNIX system interface.) A later paper (Ritchie, 1978) by Dennis Ritchie contains much of the history of C and its design motivation. Many introductory texts on C have been written.

K&R is not a suitable Language Reference Manual, given the definition of good documentation stated at the beginning of this section. K&R is neither accurate nor complete, either in the main part of the text or in the appendix titled "C Reference Manual." In writing this chapter, I often was totally unable to determine answers to questions about C by studying K&R. When I asked experienced C programmers, I was often told, "Oh, well, that's not in the book, but everyone knows that . . . ."

Recently, an effort to standardize C has been started under the sponsorship of ANSI. The intent is to standardize the language, the environment (including some aspects of the operating system interface), and the library. It is currently anticipated that "Standard C" will be largely unchanged from the language of K&R but will be specified more precisely. Much of the fuzziness of C should be eliminated by the existence of a standard and I believe the C community will benefit greatly from this effort.

5 CONCLUSIONS

The philosophy of programming language design espoused by the designer has a significant impact on the final result. In some cases, the designers have left us to study explicit statements of philosophy, and in others it is necessary to deduce the philosophy from clues left in the design. A group from Carnegie-Mellon University has performed (Shaw, 1981) an important contribution to language comparison by emphasizing philosophy rather than features in comparing FORTRAN, COBOL, Jovial, and (very old, unfortunately) Ada.

5.1 Ada

A major factor influencing the philosophy of Ada is the set of design requirements embodied in Steelman. As I have already indicated (in Section 4.1), I believe that Ada is too big and that the large size is a consequence of the Steelman requirements. Because the requirements as delineated in Steelman were largely outside the control of the design team, and because I have already discussed their effect, I ignore their impact in the remainder of this discussion.

With few exceptions, the Ada design reveals a commendable attempt to retain the simplicity and elegance of Pascal, from which it was derived, while correcting the deficiencies which have been found in that language. Ada uses similar syntax for similar constructions, as **case** and **when** in both variant records and the **case** statement, and the similar **when** in exception handlers. The long design and redesign and review process has removed most of the rough edges and awkwardness that usually plague new languages. Most importantly, though, the design team had a strong leader in Jean Ichbiah who maintained a commendable evenness and consistency of approach.

5.2 Pascal

Pascal suffers very much from its age, as mentioned in Section 2.2. It suffers additionally in this discussion from the fact that the designer's original goal (that it be a vehicle for teaching about programming languages) is largely inconsistent with the systems programming criteria which I have selected for this analysis. Although advances during the last thirteen years in the science (or is it an art?) of programming language design have dimmed the luster of the original elegance of the language, it, nonetheless, remains well-suited for the applications for which it was originally intended. Unfortunately, it is not at all well-suited for large systems programming tasks—tasks which are far from what Wirth had in mind during his original design.

5.3 C

I find C to be a rather curious mixture of things. I get the impression that C's designers were personally charged $1000 for every reserved word in the language and $2000 for each concept, that C programmers are charged $5 for every character in each program they write, and that minimizing these costs was a major design goal. It is, in my opinion, very much the wrong metric. Although C is apparently not bad to program in, C programs are often not easy to read—a serious fault. I can point to no instances in which functionality is lacking since anything the programmer might want to do can be done somehow. However, I find some mechanisms distinctly less than felicitous.

What role does *lint* play? If *lint* is taken to be part of C's definition, then much (but not all) of the looseness of the design goes away. *lint* was written in the same environment that produced C, but by a different author. It is not documented in K&R but it is mentioned there. I find this fuzziness about the status of *lint* to be compatible with much of the fuzziness about C.

6 ACKNOWLEDGMENTS

This chapter is an extensive revision of an earlier paper which I wrote in May 1981 at Bolt Beranek and Newman Inc.; it was published there as BBN Report No. 4634. The writing of that report was supported by Lawrence Livermore National Laboratories under contract 1493601 to BBN. The original version included discussion of a fourth language, Praxis, which had been developed at BBN for LLNL. As I was the leader of the team which designed Praxis, an important purpose of the original paper was to compare the design with existing languages.

In the present revision I have made major changes to the discussion of Pascal to reflect the ISO standard which did not exist when the paper was originally written. Also, I discuss ANSI Standard Ada rather than the older Ada-82.

I am grateful to C. Robert Morgan for illuminating discussions on many of the issues reported in this document and to Alan G. Nemeth and Daniel L. Franklin for their patience in answering my frequent questions about C.

I am grateful to Tartan Laboratories for providing me the opportunity to complete this final version.

ASSESSING PROGRAMMING LANGUAGES

The most important test for any programming language is that of actual usage. C and Pascal have been used sufficiently that an assessment can be written based on experience. For these two languages we have included assessments by the designers of the languages. At this time, Ada is too young for a similar discussion; instead, we have included an assessment of Ada based on academic experience and language analysis.

Wirth, in his paper "An Assessment of the Programming Language Pascal," explains and motivates some of the decisions he made in the original design of Pascal. Since that original design in 1969, Pascal has been widely discussed and modified. Wirth agrees with some of the criticism of Pascal and suggests ways of overcoming some of its well-known inadequacies. He also reflects on the lessons he has learned about designing and choosing a programming language, and finally laments

> It is probably the most disheartening experience for a language designer to discover how features provided with honest intentions are ingeniously misused to betray the language's very principles.

The assessment of C is extracted from a paper titled "UNIX Time-Sharing System: The C Programming Language" by Ritchie, Johnson, Lesk, and Kernighan. Ritchie is credited with the design of C and the others have been influential in its development. Like Pascal, C has evolved since its original design, particularly with respect to the treatment of data types. In this paper the authors describe their experiences with the language and discuss some of the changes. On the whole they have found C a hospitable language both for system and application programming.

The final paper in this section, Gehani's "An Early Assessment of the Ada Programming Language," is based on extensive study of and experimentation with the Ada language. In the paper Gehani expresses his opinion that despite its problems, Ada represents a considerable advance over existing languages, since it incorporates many of the results of programming language research from the 1970s. He claims that Ada is weakest in its facilities that implement the most recent research results, especially the derived type mechanism and the facilities for concurrent programming.

NIKLAUS WIRTH

Federal Institute of Technology (ETH), Zürich, Switzerland

An Assessment of the Programming
Language Pascal

1 WHAT IS RELIABLE SOFTWARE?

Reliable is the attribute for a person, an organization, or a mechanism that you can trust, that you can depend on, that is worthy of your confidence. For example, a reliable clock is one that indicates accurate time even during an earthquake, a reliable railway system is one where trains run punctually even during a snowstorm, a reliable bridge is a bridge that doesn't crack even under heavy load, and a reliable transistor is one that operates for years, possibly under extreme temperature and radiation. The common enemy of reliability in these examples are adverse circumstances and influences that may cause a deterioration of the physical properties of material. The accumulation of these influences is called aging. Reliability is achieved by dimensioning the mechanisms properly, taking such adverse conditions into consideration. In a railway system the schedule is arranged such that it leaves room for catching up on lost time, and an ample supply of spare engines is kept on the alert for emergencies. A bridge is built stronger than actually needed most of the time— and a transistor is equipped with cooling devices and radiation shields.

What does this all have to do with software? Well, we all have experienced failures of computer systems; and we all would like them to be reliable too. When a computer fails, the first question among its intimates is usually: is the hardware or the software the culprit? Most customers of a computation center show signs of relief when the latter is announced, for the disruption of service is then quickly ended by a so-called deadstart, and life goes on as if (almost) nothing had occurred.

Indeed there had been neither an earthquake, nor a snowstorm, nor a weighty load, nor heat or radiation. Instead, merely unpredictable circumstances had led to a state of computation for which the logical structure of the program had not been designed, which the system's designers didn't anticipate. And when pressing the deadstart button, the computer operator is reasonably confident that these circumstances won't reoccur too soon.

What must we conclude? We understand by the term software the collection of programs that deterministically prescribe a system's detailed behaviour and transitions of state. These programs are constants and are independent of any "adverse conditions" of an environment. Hence, software cannot fail because of unpredictable happenings and age, but only due to defects in its logical design. This leads us to a replacement of the attribute "reliable" by "correct."

We may be accused of nitpicking with words. To this I can only reply that the choice of words often reveals a speaker's *attitude* more profoundly than is clear to him. The attitude through which we content ourselves at producing "reliable" software instead of correct software, bears the danger that we may also consider various *degrees* of reliability. Software may then be termed reliable and "more reliable"; we may also call it correct, but certainly not "more correct."

The difference in these words is also manifested in the techniques to be employed in producing reliability in software versus in clocks, bridges, and transistors. In most technical phenomena, reliability is achieved by overdimensioning the components, by using high quality material, or by supplying standby equipment that automatically goes into action when a failure occurs. In programs, merely repeating a logical test ten times instead of performing it once does not help, if the logical structure is correct and the underlying hardware is reliable. In fact, the degree to which a program is unreliable is exactly the probability with which its incorrect parts are executed. But this measure is *not* a property of the program itself.

Reconciling ourselves with the word correct in place of reliable has the advantage that we more readily identify the causes of failures of our products to meet their goal. They are not to be sought in external, unforeseeable, adverse circumstances, but solely in our own inadequate minds, and in our failure to communicate, if several people participate in a program's design. The advantage of this recognition is that we know where to concentrate our efforts; its unpleasant part is the fact that it will be a neverending crusade, because committing mistakes is a truly human characteristic.

The most sensible targets in our drive at producing correct software are evidently *the programmers themselves.* Nothing whatsoever can replace a sound, systematic training in precise reasoning. Other sensible targets are the tools that we employ to assist our reasoning. These include primarily the *formal languages* in which we express our thoughts and abstractions, and by which we transmit them to other people. We have directed our efforts to improve our programming tools since more than a decade, and I will therefore devote the main part of this paper to a report and an evaluation of the latest product, the language Pascal, in the light of the topic "reliable software" (Wirth, 1971b).

The justification to discuss Pascal in the context of the issue of reliable software is derived from the fact that several large programs have been written in this language. They include several compilers which have been widely distributed and thus can be considered as genuine software engineering products. The value of using a high-level language for such systems has been demonstrated most convincingly in the first effort to transport the compiler onto another computer (Welsh and Quinn, 1972), which I consider a landmark in the technology of software engineering.

The following brief assessment of Pascal begins with an enumeration of features that proved to be valuable in constructing correct programs and at the same time do not impair the conceptual simplicity and efficient implementability of the language. It is followed by a short selection of features that give rise to some issues and even controversies (Habermann, 1973). Intentionally we refrain, however, from suggesting extensions to the language, although we fully recognize the legitimacy of many wishes in view of certain areas of application. The aim is to evaluate a language that was designed in 1969 and is in practical use since five years, as we feel that it is more important to report about factual experiences than to postulate additional, unproven, and sophisticated facilities at a time when the large majority of programmers and engineers still operates with languages and techniques conceived 20 years ago. For a general overview and details of the language we refer to the published literature (Jensen and Wirth, 1974).

2 IMPORTANT FEATURES OF PASCAL WHICH CONTRIBUTE TO TRANSPARENT PROGRAMMING

Experience with Pascal has shown the following features to be essential in making programs transparent and in avoiding and detecting mistakes. Their common and distinguishing characteristic is that they provide a compiler with redundant information that is used in checking for consistency of the program, without causing appreciable overhead in program execution. The most essential facility in this respect is the type definition, and in particular the distinction between *types* and *variables*. In fact, declarative features contribute not only to transparence and reliability, but also to the efficiency of the compiled code.

2.1 Symbolic Scalar Types

Example:

> **type** color = (red, yellow, green, blue)

This declaration lets the compiler check against inconsistent use of variables of this type, and it prohibits the application of incompatible operations (such as arithmetic to colors). The use of suggestive names for constants is particularly helpful. The above declaration is easily processed by a compiler into a mapping of colors onto a suitable subset of the integers.

2.2 Record Types

Example:

type person = **record** name: alfa;
                      age: integer;
                      sex: (male, female);
                      . . .

                end

A sensible generalization of the array which allows compound data with components of different types (heterogeneous structures).

2.3 Set Types

Example:

type tint = **set of** color

The set provides for an appealing formulation of what so far had been expressed in terms of *bitstrings*. The representation of sets by their characteristic function assures utmost simplicity and efficiency of implementation (Hoare, 1967; Wirth, 1971a). Together with the feature discussed in Section 2.1, this feature has proved to be an invaluable asset in the description of compilers and operating systems.

2.4 Subrange Types

Example:

type index = 0. .99

A variable of this type possesses the properties of variables of the base type (integer in the example) under the restriction that its value remains within the specified range. The declaration provides a compiler with information that may be used to choose a most economical use of storage (e.g., a variable of type index can be represented by 7 bits only) and to accompany each assignment with the necessary checks against violation of the specified invariant property. In practice, this facility has turned out to be equally helpful in detecting logical flaws as built-in bound checks upon array indexing.

2.5 Simple Forms of Iterative and Selective Statements

In the realm of control structures, the simple and flexible **while**, **repeat**, and **case** statements are a great asset. Together with the **if** statement and a drastically trimmed version of the **for** statement of Algol 60 they suffice to formulate the vast majority of programs as a nested, hierarchical structure of these fundamental composition schemes. This contributes in a most essential way to the ease of understanding and verifying programs, and greatly facilitates the task of code optimization for compilers.

3 FACILITIES AND CONVENTIONS THAT HAMPER THE CLARITY OF PROGRAMS

3.1 Operator Precedence

In the interest of simplicity and efficient translatability Pascal aimed at a reasonably small number of operator precedence levels. ALGOL 60's hierarchy of 9 levels seemed clearly too baroque. An additional incentive for change was the replacement of the equivalence operator for Boolean expressions by the equality operator. Since these two operators reside on different priority levels in ALGOL 60, some departure from the old rules was mandatory. In retrospect, however, the decision to break with a widely used tradition seemes ill-advised, particularly with the growing significance of complicated Boolean expressions in connection with program verification.

ALGOL 60	Pascal	
$\uparrow$		$\neg$
$*/\div$	$*/$ **div mod**	$\wedge$
$+-$	$+-$	$\vee$
$=\neq<\leq\geq>$	$=\neq<\leq\geq>$	
$\neg$		
$\wedge$		
$\vee$		
$\supset$		
$\equiv$		

Examples of expressions in ALGOL 60 and Pascal:

$$\neg\, x < y \qquad\qquad \neg\,(x < y)$$
$$x < y \wedge y < z \qquad\qquad (x < y) \wedge (y < z)$$
$$x < y \equiv y < z \qquad\qquad (x < y) = (y < z)$$

3.2 The goto Statement

There is hardly any doubt that the use of **goto** statements which disassociate the control structure of a process with the textual structure of its program is a frequent source of mistakes and impairs the verifyability of programs. This was perfectly clear even when the decision to include the **goto** statement in Pascal was taken (Dijkstra, 1968). Yet even now there is no general agreement on an adequate replacement. Placing further restrictions upon the **goto** statement—for instance, allowing only forward jumps—may be one solution. But clearly, allowing integers only instead of identifiers as labels is no sufficient deterrent to programmers who have previously worked with FORTRAN! In teaching programming, the use of a subset Pascal system *without* the **goto** statement is strongly recommended.

4 THE EXPLICIT DISTINCTION BETWEEN "TYPES" AND "VARIABLES"

The most widely used technique of program verification is based on the explicit statement of assertions about the state of the computation at different points in the program. Recently, it has been recognized that it would be even more useful to attach assertions to specific variables rather than program points.

Declarations are essentially a statement of invariant properties of the respective variables. In Pascal, every variable is said to be of a certain *type*, and a data type can be defined explicitly by the programmer. It implies essential invariants needed for the verification of programs, and it moreover supplies a compiler with sufficient information to decide on a suitable storage representation. In essence, a compiler translates a type definition into a storage template to be used upon allocation of each variable of this type.

Moreover, the type definition determines the set of operators that is applicable to variables (sometimes called "instances") of that type.

It follows that a type definition should combine all attributes of a variable that are constant and known at the time of compilation (static). In fact, Pascal goes so far as to exclude *all* information from a type definition that cannot be determined from a simple textual scan. This rule has its important merits, but also bears some inconveniences, as shall be explained below. Our experience shows that the advantages of explicit type definitions are enormous and indispensible, if program transparence and efficiency of compiled code are both an issue.

Unfortunately, the Pascal concept of type has also stirred some controversy (Habermann, 1973). It seems to be largely originating from a too strict interpretation of the word *type* based on its use in the world of mathematics. There, the concept of types distinguishes between numbers and truth values, between numbers and sets of numbers, or between sets and sets of sets, but not between integers and natural numbers (a subrange of the former) or between small sets and larger sets. In the world of programming it is both natural and necessary to extend this concept of type, because objects can become different (types) because of far more (detailed) reasons than in abstract mathematics, where problems of representation are immaterial.

Which were, then, the negative consequences of adhering to the rule of strictly static type definitions? They became manifest in the form of two restrictions in the use of arrays, as compared to ALGOL 60. The first is the exclusion of so-called *dynamic arrays*, because the array type definition includes the specification of its size. There are good reasons for wanting dynamic arrays, but also convincing arguments against them (Lecarme and Desjardins, 1974). The fact remains that dynamic arrays in the sense of ALGOL 60 are sort of a hermaphroditic (hybrid) species:

their size can neither be determined at compile time, nor can it be changed during program execution. Instead, it is fixed upon block entry.

The second drawback is in practice much more severe. It originates from the essential requirement that formal procedure parameters specify their types. But in the case of *array parameters*, this once again includes their size. As a consequence, a given procedure can only be applied to arrays of one fixed size. This rule hardly contributes to program security and transparence, but seriously impairs the highly desirable flexibility of procedures.

Both problems can be overcome by allowing type definitions—in particular array types—to be parametrised. The following example shows the use of such a *parametrised type*.

```
type table(m,n) = array[m. .n] of integer;
var  t1: table(1,100);
     t2: table(0,999);
function sum(t:table;u,v:integer):integer;
     var i,s: integer;
begin s : = 0;
     for i : = u to v do s : = t[i]+s;
     sum : = s
     . . .
end;
begin.=
     s1 : = sum(t1,1,100);
     s2 : = sum(t2,0,999);
     . . .
end.
```

From this example we can see both the utility and the dangers of such a generalization, and possibly also the consequences upon a compiler. A most sensible decision is to restrict parametrization to the index bounds of array types, and to allow for constants only as actual parameters (in variable declarations). This already solves the dilemma of array parameters. If dynamic arrays are to be allowed, the latter rule may be relaxed. I would caution, however, against any further generalization: Allowing the component type of an array to be a parameter too, for example, would destroy many advantages of the Pascal type concept at once.

5 AN IMPORTANT CONCEPT AND A PERSISTENT SOURCE OF PROBLEMS: FILES

In Pascal, files are understood to be strictly sequential files, and are defined in terms of the mathematical notion of a *sequence*. Like the array, they are homogeneous structures, but in contrast to the array, their size changes (truly) dynamically. Naturally, we not only aimed at a simple and consistent mathematical definition of files and their operators, but also kept in mind their efficient realization, particularly with a view towards the involvement of secondary storage media. As it turned out, the original file concept was right in terms of implementation, but not in terms of mathematical axiomatization which seemed highly desirable for a tool to construct reliable software. Therefore, the whole scheme was slightly modified in a revision of the language made in 1973 that was summarized in (Hoare and Wirth (1973)). (It is noteworthy that apart from the replacement of constant-parameters by value-parameters it constitutes the only change of the language that had appreciable and non-trivial consequences upon existing programs.) Although the revised file facility proved to be a definite improvement, some inherent difficulties became evident only after extended usage. This may be the reason that the file concept had never been mentioned in any critical commentary about Pascal.

What are these deficiencies, and where do they have their roots? I presume that the main culprit is the attempt to hide from the programmer and the verifier the fact that files must be allocatable on secondary storage media. In this case, an efficient buffering mechanism is involved. Indeed, such technicalities may well be withheld from the programmer who is concerned with correctness only, if the scheme presented to him is rigorously defined and faultless, and if the consequences on efficiency are fully understood and accepted.

Originally, a file f was viewed as a sequence in which at any time only a single element was accessible, if there existed one. Conceptually, one could think of a window, through which that element, denoted by $f\uparrow$, could be seen (the arrow denotes the "window position"). But that description isn't honest, of course, if $f\uparrow$ actually represents a buffer variable in primary store, via which data are transferred to and from secondary stores (tapes, disks). Therefore the appealing fiction of a sliding window was dropped in favour of a distinct *buffer variable*. But of course, also this isn't quite honest, if the true buffer comprises several logical file elements, such that the operation $put(f)$ will actually be effectuated by a mere pointer updating until the buffer is full. For then it is difficult to explain why $f\uparrow$ suddenly changes its value during the operation $put(f)$. In reality we now have a buffer of which a single component is visible through a sliding window; and this situation is slightly too complicated to be neatly expressed by a simple scheme of axioms.

I wish to suggest two possible solutions to this dilemma. Characteristically, the choice depends on the intended application of the language. If Pascal is to serve for system construction purposes, then the file facility might be dropped entirely, because the very purpose would be the description of possible file mechanisms in terms of more primitive concepts. If, however, Pascal is viewed as a general purpose language in which files are an indispensible concept, then the basic operators *get* and *put* might be replaced by *read* and *write* statements defined in terms of the former as follows:

$$read(f,x) \equiv x := f\uparrow;\ get(f)$$
$$write(f,x) \equiv f\uparrow := x;\ put(f)$$

This makes it possible to hide the chosen buffering mechanism entirely, and to ignore the existence of a window or of a buffer variable. (Incidentally, Pascal states exactly these abbreviations, but allows them only for textfiles. The relaxation of this restriction is an obvious step.)

A premise of the axiomatic scheme was that the predicate $eof(f)$ be always defined (true, if the part of the file to the right of the reading position is empty, false otherwise). This implies that a file access must be made before the program actually specifies any reading. The solution lies in combining the rewinding of the file with the initial loading of the buffer. Emptyness can be recognized during this operation. The unpleasant consequence is that a program can never leave a file in a properly rewound state. This may itself not be of any concern, as long as we remain strictly in the world of the Pascal program; but if this program is considered as one action upon a more permanent environment, it must be considered as a deficiency. Indeed, the appropriateness of the primitive $rewrite(f)$ appears at least questionable. It is, from a theoretical point of view, indispensible, because it is the only operation by which a file variable can be given an initial value, namely the empty sequence (see Hoare and Wirth, 1973). In practice, however, rewinding (a tape) is considered as the basic operation, and rewinding does *not* cause the tape to be erased. An obvious "solution" consists in splitting $reset(f)$ and $rewrite(f)$ into the "more primitive" operations as follows:

```
reset(f)   ≡ rewind(f); openread(f)
rewrite(f) ≡ rewind(f); openwrite(f)
```

The drawbacks are that the state of the predicate $eof(f)$ and the buffer $f\uparrow$ are undetermined in between, and that a programmer is liable to forget to specify the *openread* or *openwrite* operation.

The most unsatisfactory consequences of the Pascal file concept lie in the area of substructures, and in particular textfiles. Originally, the idea of substructures could well be ignored. Texts were considered as sequences of characters, separated into lines by control characters. This concept is also embodied by the ISO (and ASCII) conventions, and proved to be most conveniently implementable. On a CDC 6000 computer with 6-bit characters and a set of 63 printing characters, the obvious choice was to introduce a 64th control character *eol* to signal the end of a line.

A program reading a textfile f, performing an operation L at the beginning of each line and an operation P after reading each character, is easily expressed by the following schema:

$$
\begin{aligned}
&\textbf{while } \neg eof(f) \textbf{ do}\\
&\quad \textbf{begin } L;\ read(f,ch);\\
&\quad\quad \textbf{while } ch \neq eol \textbf{ do}\\
&\quad\quad\quad \textbf{begin } P(ch);\ read(f,ch)\\
&\quad\quad\quad \textbf{end}\\
&\quad \textbf{end}
\end{aligned} \tag{1}
$$

But then, alas, a new operating system came along with a set of 64 characters. It supposedly incorporates a true miracle: the coding of 64 characters *and* a line separation within 6 bits only! How can reliable software be constructed at all on the basis of such premises?

The new situation left no escape from providing textfiles with an explicit substructure: a textfile was to be considered as a sequence of lines, each line being itself a sequence of characters. In analogy to the predicate *eof*(*f*), a predicate *eoln*(*f*) was introduced to indicate the end of a line. Evidently, also a pair of new operators became necessary, *writeln*(*f*) to terminate the generation of a line, and *readln*(*f*) to initiate the reading of a next line.

Another problem arose simultaneously. At the end of a line, the predicate *eoln*(*f*) becomes true. Should at the end of the last line the predicate *eof*(*f*) also become true simultaneously? Probably so, because evidently the end of the last line is also the end of the text. Once again, we are faced with a dilemma: when reading the end of a line, we either find out whether there exists a next line, and we therefore read on (which may not be the intent of the programmer), or we refrain from looking ahead, and must leave the definition of *eof*(*f*) up to a further explicit *readln* instruction. Neither solution is fully satisfactory.

In the latter case (as in rev. Pascal), the program corresponding to schema (1) is

```
while ¬eof(f) do
begin L;
   while ¬eoln(f) do
     begin read(f,ch); P(ch)
     end;
   readln(f)
end
```
(2)

In the former case, the resulting program is slightly but significantly different:

```
while ¬eof(f) do
   begin readln(f); L;
      while ¬eoln(f) do
         begin read(f,ch); P(ch)
         end
   end
```
(3)

The difference may appear to be minimal, even negligible. It lies not so much in the form of the program but in the underlying concepts. And frequently such details decide ultimately about the acceptibility—the healthiness—of a language. The issue of files is a typical case of the devil persistently and successfully hiding in the details.

6 SECURITY VERSUS FLEXIBILITY: TYPE UNIONS

It is sometimes desirable that a variable may assume values of different types. Its type is then said to be the *union* of these types. There appear to be three different motivations behind the desire for union types.

1. The need for *heterogeneous structures*. For example, in an interpreter a stack may have to consist of integer, real, and Boolean components. If the stack is represented by an array, its homogeneity is a hindrance. Although each "stack" element assumes only one fixed type during its lifetime, the underlying (static) array element appears to have a varying type.

2. *Storage sharing* (overlays). This implies the use of the same storage area—expressed in the language as "the same actual variable"—for different purposes, i.e., for representing different abstract variables whose lifetimes are disjoint.

3. Realization of implicit *type transfer functions*. For instance, a variable of type real is interpreted as being of type integer for the purpose of printing the internal representation in, say, octal form.

The dangers of the type union facility lie in the possibility to err about the current type of a variable and in the difficulty to identify the mistake. If it occurs in an assignment, the consequences may be disastrous. Efforts must be made to provide automatic checking facilities. We therefore distinguish between *discriminated* and *free unions* (Hoare, 1972). In the former case, the variable carries along a tag which indicates the currently valid type (which is one among the types specified in the definition of the union type). In the latter case, no such direct information is stored. Clearly, the latter provides greater freedom in programming, the former increased security through automatic consistency checks.

In Pascal, the concept of type union is embodied in the form of *variants of record structures*. The discriminated union inherently dictates a record structure, because every value consists of (at least) two components: the actual value and the tag value identifying its current type. *Example*:

```
type stackelement =
  record
      case tag: (A,B,C) of
              A: (i: integer);
              B: (r: real);
              C: (b: Boolean)
  end;
var s: array[1..100] of stackelement
```

In a program with these declarations, the occurrence of a variable designator $s[i].r$ is only valid, if at this point that variable is of type real. It is so, if and only if $s[i].tag = B$. A compiler may generate this test automatically, provided that it also ensures an appropriate setting of the tag upon assignment. This, however, implies an appreciable, although worthwhile overhead. Suggestions have been made to provide syntactic structures which let the compiler determine the current tag value from context. One such feature is the *"inspect when"* statement of Simula (Birtwistle et al., 1974). But these constructs sometimes turn out to leave insufficient freedom to express a given situation in a natural way.

No such facility was included in Pascal; to the contrary, in its revised version

(1973) the tagfield of a variant record definition was declared to be optional. If it is omitted, we obtain the equivalent of a free type union, and a compiler has *no* chance of checking consistency in its application. One may rightly criticize this development which clearly opens the door for a very dangerous sort of programming error, but there seem to exist applications where the discriminated union is insufficiently flexible. (Even so, my advice is to refrain from using variants without tagfields.)

The issue of type unions is a clear example of a case where a language may offer added security only at the expense of flexibility, or vice versa. The programmer must make his own choice. Yet, we have the impression that a more satisfactory solution must be found. It will not necessarily be found in new language facilities, but may lie in a different approach to data organization.

The truly disconcerting fact is that facilities such as the record variant, provided for a genuine need for flexibility (motivation 1 above), can be (and are!) easily misused. The example for the third motivation (see above) is characteristic for programmers who (habitually) think in terms of machine facilities and assembly code, and (love to) show that their techniques can also be expressed in a higher level language. It is probably the most disheartening experience for a language designer to discover how features provided with honest intentions are "ingeniously" misused to betray the language's very principles.

7 SUMMARY AND CONCLUSIONS

We have argued that the concept of a *degree of problem reliability* is ill conceived and helps to foster a mistaken attitude in software engineering. Instead, a program can be called *correct*, if and only if its operations are fully consistent with static specifications of the expected results of the dynamic process. As programs used in practice are enormously complex and have a tendency to become even more complex in future applications, programming errors will always be with us. Instead of relying too much on either antiquated "debugging tools" or on futuristic automatic program verifiers, we should give more emphasis to the systematic construction of programs with languages that facilitate transparent formulation and automatic consistency checks.

The language Pascal was designed with exactly these aims. Five years of experience in its use have proved its significant merits with respect to ease of programming, suitability for formal program verification (Igarashi et al., 1973; Marmier, 1974), efficient implementability, and practical portability. They have also revealed some weaknesses and some remaining difficulties. After analysing the roots of these problems, we are tempted to list a few conclusions about the design and the choice of languages for "reliable programming."

- The language must rest on a foundation of simple, flexible, and neatly axiomatised features, comprising the basic structuring techniques of data and program.
- Language rules must not deviate from widely accepted traditions of formal

notations, even if these traditions are sometimes inconsistent or inconvenient. More importantly, *new* features must be designed with utmost care to notational regularity and consistency.

- The urge to gain flexibility and "power" through generalizations must be restrained. A generalization may easily be carried too far and have revolutionary consequences on implementation (e.g., full parametrization of types).

- Every basic feature is to be governed by a consistent set of "obvious" rules (axioms). The rules must be such that efficient implementability does not depend on particular (or even peculiar) properties of a specific computer system (e.g., on the existence of a line-end-character).

- In many cases, security and flexibility are antagonistic properties. Security is obtained through redundancy which is used by the system to perform consistency checks. Often, redundancy is cumbersome to provide, and the programmer must decide whether to choose a straight-jacket providing relative security, or a free language where the responsibility is entirely his own (e.g., discriminated vs. free type unions).

- Every rule of the language must be enforceable by the system. It follows that rules should preferably be checkable by a mere textual scan, but also run-time checks should become widely used. (In our Pascal system, run-time checks can be turned off; but we have learned the merits of leaving them on, even after having "proved" the program to be correct.)

- A rich language may be welcome to the professional program *writer* who's principal delight is his familiarization with all its intricate facets. But the interests of the program *reader* dictate a reasonably frugal language. People who want to understand a program (including their own), compilers, and automatic verification aids all belong to the class of readers.

- In the interest of increased quality of software products, we may be well advised to get rid of many facilities of modern, baroque programming languages that are widely advertised in the name of "user-orientation," "scientific sophistication," and "progress."

ACKNOWLEDGMENT

I wish to acknowledge the criticism and suggestions of members of the IFIP Working Group 2.3 which helped to clarify this presentation.

D. M. RITCHIE, S. C. JOHNSON, M. E. LESK, AND B. W. KERNIGHAN
Bell Laboratories, Murray Hill, New Jersey

UNIX* Time-Sharing System:

The C Programming Language

C is a general-purpose programming language featuring economy of expression, modern control flow and data structure capabilities, and a rich set of operators and data types.

C is not a "very high-level" language nor a big one and is not specialized to any particular area of application. Its generality and an absence of restrictions make it more convenient and effective for many tasks than supposedly more powerful languages. C has been used for a wide variety of programs, including the UNIX operating system, the C compiler itself, and essentially all UNIX applications software. The language is sufficiently expressive and efficient to have completely displaced assembly language programming on UNIX.

C was originally written for the PDP-11 under UNIX, but the language is not tied to any particular hardware or operating system. C compilers run on a wide variety of machines, including the Honeywell 6000, the IBM System/370, and the Interdata 8/32.

[*Material Deleted*]

1 EXPERIENCE WITH C

C compilers exist for the most widely used machines at Bell Laboratories (the IBM S/370, Honeywell 6000, PDP-11) and perhaps 10 others. Several hundred programmers within Bell Laboratories and many outside use C as their primary programming language.

* UNIX is a trademark of Bell Laboratories.

1.1 Favorable Experiences

C has completely displaced assembly language in UNIX programs. All applications code, the C compiler itself, and the operating system (except for about 1000 lines of initial bootstrap, etc.) are written in C. Although compilers or interpreters are available under UNIX for FORTRAN, Pascal, ALGOL 68, SNOBOL, APL, and other languages, most programmers make little use of them. Since C is a relatively low-level language, it is adequately efficient to prevent people from resorting to assembler, and yet sufficienctly terse and expressive that its users prefer it to PL/I or other very large languages.

A language that doesn't have everything is actually easier to program in than some that do. The limitations of C often imply shorter manuals and easier training and adaptation. Language design, especially when done by a committee, often tends toward including all doubtful features, since there is no quick answer to the advocate who insists that the new feature will be useful to some and can be ignored by others. But this results in long manuals and hierarchies of "experts" who know progressively larger subsets of the language. In practice, if a feature is not used often enough to be familiar and does not complete some structure of syntax or semantics, it should probably be left out. Otherwise, the manual and compiler get bulky, the users get surprises, and it becomes harder and harder to maintain and use the language. It is also desirable to avoid language features that cannot be compiled efficiently; programmers like to feel that the cost of a statement is comparable to the difficulty in writing it. C has thus avoided implementing operations in the language that would have to be performed by subroutine call. As compiler technology improves, some extensions (e.g., structure assignment) are being made to C, but always with the same principles in mind.

One direction for possible expansion of the language has been explicitly avoided. Although C is much used for writing operating systems and associated software, there are no facilities for multiprogramming, parallel operations, synchronization, or process control. We believe that making these operations primitives of the language is inappropriate, mostly because language design is hard enough in itself without incorporating into it the design of operating systems. Language facilities of this sort tend to make strong assumptions about the underlying operating system that may match very poorly what it actually does.

1.2 Unfavorable Experiences

The design and implementation of C can (or could) be criticized on a number of points. Here we discuss some of the more vulnerable aspects of the language.

Language level.   Some users complain that C is an insufficiently high-level language; for example, they want string data types and operations, or variable-size multi-dimensional arrays, or generic functions. Sometimes a suggested extension merely involves lifting some restriction. For example, allowing variable-size arrays would actually simplify the language specification, since it would only involve allowing general expressions in place of constants in certain contexts.

Many other extensions are plausible; since the low level of C was praised in the previous section as an advantage of the language, most will not be further discussed. One is worthy of mention, however. The C language provides no facility for I/O, leaving this job to library routines. The following fragment illustrates one difficulty with this approach:

printf ("%d\n", x);

The problem arises because on machines on which *int* is not the same as *long*, x may not be *long*; if it were, the program must be written

printf("%D\n", x);

so as to tell *printf* the length of x. Thus, changing the type of x involves changing not only its declaration, but also other parts of the program. If I/O were built into the language, the association between the type of an expression and the format in which it is printed could be reconciled by the compiler.

Type safety. C has traditionally been permissive in checking whether an expression is used in a context appropriate to its type. A complete list of examples would be long, but two of the most important should illustrate sufficiently. The types of formal arguments of functions are in general not known, and in any case are not checked by the compiler against the actual arguments at each call. Thus in the statement

s = sin(1);

the fact that the *sin* routine takes a floating-point argument is not noticed until the erroneous result is detected by the programmer.

In the structure reference

p − >memb

p is simply assumed to point to a structure of which *memb* is a member; *p* might even be an integer and not a pointer at all.

Much of the explanation, if not justification, for such laxity is the typeless nature of C's predecessor languages. Fortunately, a justification need no longer be attempted, since a program is now available that detects all common type mismatches. This utility, called **lint** because it picks bits of fluff from programs, examines a set of files and complains about a great many dubious constructions, ranging from unused or uninitialized variables through the type errors mentioned. Programs that pass unscathed through **lint** enjoy about as complete freedom from type errors as do ALGOL 68 programs, with a few exceptions: unions are not checked dynamically, and explicit escapes are available that in effect turn off checking.

Some languages, such as Pascal and Euclid, allow the writer to specify that the value of a given variable may assume only a given subrange of the integers.

This facility is often connected with the usage of arrays, in that any array index must be a variable or expression whose type specifies a subset of the set given by the bounds of the array. This approach is not without theoretical difficulties, as suggested by Habermann (1973). In itself it does not solve the problems of variables assuming unexpected values or of accessing outside array bounds; such things must (in general) be detected dynamically. Still, the extra information provided by specifying the permissible range for each variable provides valuable information for the compiler and any verifier program. C has no corresponding facility.

One of the characteristic features of C is its rather complete integration of the notion of pointer and of address arithmetic. Some writers, notably Hoare (1975), have argued against the very notion of pointer. We feel, however, that the facilities offered by pointers are too valuable to give up lightly.

Syntax peculiarities. Some people are annoyed by the terseness of expression that is one of the characteristics of the language. We view C's short operators and general lack of noise as a benefit. For example, the use of braces {} for grouping instead of **begin** and **end** seems appropriate in view of the frequency of the operation. The use of braces even fits well into ordinary mathematical notation.

Terseness can lead to code that is hard to read, however. For example,

*++*argv

where *argv* has been declared *char **argv* (pointer into an array of character pointers) means: select the character pointer pointed at by *argv* (*argv*), increment it by one (++*argv*), then fetch the character that *that* pointer points at (*++*argv*). This is concise and efficient but reminiscent of APL.

An example of a minor problem is the comment convention, which is PL/I's /* . . . */. Comments do not nest, so an effort to "comment out" a section of code will fail if that section contains a comment. And a number of us can testify that it is surprisingly hard to recognize when an "end comment" delimiter has been botched, so that the comment silently continues until the next comment is reached, deleting a line or two of code. It would be more convenient if a single unique character were reserved to introduce a comment, and if comments always terminated at an end of line.

Semantic peculiarities. There are some occasionally surprising operator precedences. For example,

a >> 4 + 5

shifts right by 9. Perhaps worse,

(x & MASK) == 0

must be parenthesized to associate the proper way. Users learn quickly to parenthesize such doubtful cases; and when feasible **lint** warns of suspicious expressions (including both of these).

We have already mentioned the fact that the *case* actions in a switch flow through unless explicitly broken. In practice, users write so many *switch* statements that they become familiar with this behavior and some even prefer it.

Some problems arise from machine differences that are reflected, perhaps unnecessarily, into the semantics of C. For example, the PDP-11 does sign extension on byte fetches, so that a character (viewed arithmetically) can have a value ranging from −128 to +127, rather than 0 to +255. Although the reference manual makes it quite clear that the precise range of a *char* variable is machine dependent, programmers occasionally succumb to the temptation of using the full range that their local machine can represent, forgetting that their programs may not work on another machine. The fundamental problem, of course, is that C permits small numbers, as well as genuine characters, to be stored in *char* variables. This might not be necessary if, for example, the notion of subranges (mentioned above) were introduced into the language.

Miscellaneous.   C was developed and is generally used in a highly responsive interactive environment, and accordingly the compiler provides few of the services usually associated with batch compilers. For example, it prepares no listing of the source program, no cross reference table, and no indication of the nature of the generated code. Such facilities are available, but they are separate programs, not parts of the compiler. Programmers used to batch environments may find it hard to live without giant listings; we would find it hard to use them.

2 CONCLUSIONS AND FUTURE DIRECTIONS

C has continued to develop in recent years, mostly by upwardly compatible extensions, occasionally by restrictions against manifestly nonportable or illegal programs that happened to be compiled into something useful. The most recent major changes were motivated by the extension of C to other machines, and the resulting emphasis on portability. The advent of *union* and of casts reflects a desire to be more precise about types when moving to other machines is in prospect. These changes have had relatively little effect on programmers who remained entirely on the UNIX system. Of more importance was a new library, which changed the use of a "portable" library from an option into an effective standard, while simultaneously increasing the efficiency of the library so that users would not object.

It is more difficult, of course, to speculate about the future. C is now encountering more and more foreign environments, and this is producing many demands for C to adapt itself to the hardware, and particularly to the operating systems, of other machines. Bit fields, for example, are a response to a request to describe externally imposed data layouts. Similarly, the procedures for external storage allocation and referencing have been made tighter to conform to requirements on other systems. Portability of the basic language seems well handled, but interactions with operating systems grow ever more complex. These lead to requests for more sophisticated data descriptions and initializations, and even for assembler windows. Further changes of this sort are likely.

What is not likely is a fundamental change in the level of the langauge. Realistically, the very acceptance of C has compelled changes to be made only most cautiously and compatibly. Should the pressure for improvements become too strong for the language to accommodate, C would probably have to be left as is, and a totally new language developed. We leave it to the reader to speculate on whether it should be called D or P.

[The following works were consulted in the preparation of this article: Habermann (1973), Hoare (1975), Johnson and Kernighan (1973), Kernighan and Ritchie (1978), and Richards (1969).]

NARAIN H. GEHANI

Bell Laboratories, Murray Hill, New Jersey

An Early Assessment of the Ada*
Programming Language

I have always worked with programming languages because it seemed to me that until you could understand those, you really couldn't understand computers. Understanding them doesn't really mean only being able to use them. A lot of people can use them without understanding them.

Christopher Strachey (Horowitz, 1983)

1 INTRODUCTION

The design of the Ada programming language (U.S. Department of Defense, 1983), in response to a set of requirements, was an engineering effort that incorporated many of the advances made in programming language design in the 1970s (Barnes, 1982; Gehani, 1983; U.S. Department of Defense, 1978). The Ada language[1] is not in widespread use today, primarily because of the lack of high quality compilers that would allow the Ada language to be used in production programs and because

---

* Ada is a registered trademark of the U.S. Government—Ada Joint Program Office.

[1] The Ada language discussed in this paper is the ANSI standard version (U.S. Department of Defense, 1983). The language design that was eventually named Ada was initially named GREEN. GREEN was modified and renamed Ada—this version is designated as Preliminary Ada (U.S. Department of Defense, 1979a). An evaluation of Preliminary Ada discovered inadequacies in the language which resulted in its modification and lead to the release of a new reference manual—this version is called the July 80 Ada (U.S. Department of Defense, 1980). Subsequently, the Ada language was modified once again—Ada 82 (U.S. Department of Defense, 1982)—in the process of adoption as an ANSI standard—ANSI Ada (U.S. Department of Defense, 1983). The Ada langauge was adopted as an ANSI standard in February 1983.

of changes that had been anticipated in the design of the Ada programming language as a response to the ANSI standardization effort. Production quality compilers, implementing the full Ada language, are expected by 1984; some good compilers implementing Ada language subsets are now available. Because of enormous backing, both economic and political, the use of the Ada language is likely to spread rapidly with the availability of good and reliable compilers.

Despite the lack of widespread use of the Ada programming language, there has been much analysis and academic use of the Ada language, including the design of some large programs. Ada implementations are in progress at scores of universities and companies, journals dedicated to the Ada language have appeared and several books have been written on the Ada language. The primary reason for all this activity is the support of the Ada language by the United States Department of Defense.

Ada is an elegant, albeit somewhat large and complex,[2] language. Its complexity is a direct consequence of the large number of requirements its design had to satisfy (U.S. Department of Defense, 1978). Most of the facilities in the Ada language are convenient and easy to use. As you read you will see that I generally, but not always, agree with Peter Wegner when he states (Wegner, 1982)

> The designers of Ada have done their homework well, having learned from earlier languages and correcting [sic] their inadequacies. Ada provides greater type security and better facilities for modular programming than other languages. It represents the end product of a remarkably open and fair design competition, and contains a number of features that can increase program reliability and programmer productivity if they are properly used.

The Ada programming language is not the *be all and end all* of programming languages. There are places where it can be simplified and improved. Some facilities are awkward to use or just inappropriate. In fact, the many dissections of the Ada language have themselves been a major factor in advancing the understanding of issues in the design of programming languages, especially those destined for widespread use in a variety of applications. Moreover, the design of the Ada language has stimulated much interest and new research in programming language design.

1.1 Basis of the Evaluation

There has been much debate over the appropriateness of the facilities in the Ada language and of its complexity. My assessment of the Ada programming language is based on writing many Ada programs that span a wide spectrum of application domains. These programs were written so that I could understand the Ada language better and as examples for a book about the Ada programming language (Gehani, 1983a). The programs were tested using the New York University (NYU) Ada Compiler.

---

[2] The *Reference Manual for the Ada Programming Language* (U.S. Department of Defense, 1983) is about 320 pages—including the appendices, and the index.

1.2 Some Words of Caution

I have qualified my assessment of the Ada programming language as "early" to emphasize the fact that this assessment is based on running Ada programs on a prototype Ada compiler. No production quality Ada compilers are available at present. With the recent exception of the NYU Ada Compiler, which is excruciatingly slow, currently none of the other Ada compilers implements the full Ada language.

I must warn the reader that my assessment is based on writing relatively small Ada programs. Although the programs were realistic insofar as possible, they were not "real" in the sense that they were not intended for extended use by me nor were they designed for use by others. Exhaustive testing of the programs was not possible because of the enormous amounts of resources—both memory and execution time—required by the prototype NYU Ada Compiler. Moreover, programs to control devices were tested only in a simulated environment.

Consequently, any extrapolation of my evaluation of the facilities in the Ada language to "real" and large programs[3] should be done with some caution.

1.3 Comments on the Contents/Organization of the Paper

In this paper, I shall point out some strengths of the Ada language and discuss some of its weaknesses. I will evaluate facilities in the Ada language but I will not compare them in any detail with the facilities in other languages such as FORTRAN, C or Pascal. When evaluating the Ada language, I shall try to distinguish between factual information, the goals of the Ada designers and my opinions about the Ada language.

Although the bulk of the discussion in this paper focuses on weak points of the Ada programming language, I have enjoyed using the Ada language; I have found it to be a good programming language. My experience with programming languages suggests that the facilities in the Ada language will help in the construction of reliable, modular and potentially portable[4] programs.

This summary and assessment of the Ada programming language is partitioned into functional areas such as types and objects, sequential programming, concurrent programming, error handling and program structuring facilities. But first, here is an example illustrating the Ada language.

---

[3] Large programs are systems consisting of many program components, usually written by many people (DeRemer and Kron, 1976).

[4] I have qualified *portable* with the adverb *potentially* because I did not actually port the programs to another system. There are two reasons for my not porting the programs. I did not have access to another Ada compiler. Moreover, at the time I was running Ada programs, the NYU Ada Compiler was the one that implemented the largest subset of Ada. Therefore, it is likely that the programs I wrote would probably have not run on the other compilers. Many facilities in the Ada language have been designed with the goal of easy program portability. Whether or not Ada compilers achieve this very desirable goal remains to be seen.

2 EXAMPLE ILLUSTRATING THE ADA LANGUAGE (GEHANI, 1983a)

The flavor of Ada programs is illustrated by a small program, CALCULATOR which simulates a simple calculator that can add, subtract, multiply and divide. The data appears as a list of operations in the format

A operator B

where *operator* is one of the symbols +, −, * or /, and the operands A and B are real numbers.

The reader familiar with high level languages ought to be able to understand most of the program CALCULATOR and much of the conventional part of the Ada language without undue difficulty:

```
--comments begin with two dashes and continue until the end of the line
with TEXT_IO; use TEXT_IO; --makes input/output available
procedure CALCULATOR is
    type REAL is digits 10;
        --precision of real values is specified to be at least 10 digits
    package IO_REAL is new FLOAT_IO(REAL); use IO_REAL;
            --input/output for REAL values is now available

    A, B: REAL;   --A and B are declared to be real variables
    OPR: CHARACTER;
    RESULT: REAL;
begin
    while not END_OF_FILE(STANDARD_INPUT) loop
            --function STANDARD_INPUT returns the default
            --input file
        GET(A); GET(OPR); GET(B);   --read the input
        case OPR is--case statement
            when '+' => RESULT := A+B;
            when '−' => RESULT := A−B;
            when '*' => RESULT := A*B;
            when '/' => RESULT := A/B;
            when others => PUT("ERROR***BAD OPERATOR");
                    exit; --exit from the loop on bad input
        end case;
        PUT(RESULT); NEW_LINE;
    end loop;
end CALCULATOR;
```

Procedure CALCULATOR is an Ada main program. Any Ada subprogram can be executed as a main program provided all the *contextual information* needed by the subprogram has been specified. The contextual information

with TEXT_IO; use TEXT_IO;

makes CALCULATOR complete, i.e., CALCULATOR can be compiled and executed. The *with* clause specifies that CALCULATOR needs to use the predefined package TEXT_IO containing the text input and output facilities. The *use* clause allows subprograms in TEXT_IO to be referenced in CALCULATOR without explicitly stating that they belong to TEXT_IO. Package TEXT_IO provides subprograms to do input and output for some predefined types (e.g., CHARACTER), while for other types it provides templates of subprograms. Using the template FLOAT_IO for floating point input and output given in TEXT_IO, the declaration

package IO_REAL **is new** FLOAT_IO(REAL);

creates a package containing input and output subprograms for values of floating point type REAL.

3 TYPES AND OBJECTS

The Ada language provides the standard set of basic types and type structuring mechanisms. Basic types such as integers, reals, boolean and character are provided. Users can define enumeration types.

The type structuring mechanisms provided are the *array*, the *record* and *pointer*. The *unconstrained* array type, in which the array bounds are left undefined, allows the parameterization of array types and allows a procedure to be called with arrays of different sizes. Portions of arrays, called slices, can be referenced. Record types can be parameterized and can have a *variant* part—a portion of the record that depends upon values of the parameter.

Users can define their own types—the underlying representation can be hidden by declaring a type to be *private* (private types may occur only in packages) in conjunction with the *package* facility.

The range of integer and real types can be specified along with the accuracy of representation for the real types. The real type is based on a model of real computation that ensures accurate representation of real values. All Ada compilers are required to provide an accurate implementation of the model values. This requirement serves as the basis for the consistency of real arithmetic across different machines, even if they have different word sizes, and guarantees the portability of programs with real arithmetic—giving Ada compilers an opportunity to eliminate a notorious irritant. Only time will tell whether or not Ada compilers will be able to accurately implement the model of real computation on machines with different word sizes and with different representations of real values.

Strings are arrays of characters. This implementation of strings leads to several problems primarily because now the size of a string object is considered to be part of its type (Kernighan, 1981). String variables cannot grow or shrink in length. A string variable must always be assigned strings of the same length even though this may require padding with blanks. This inconvenience can even be wasteful of storage, e.g., in an array of error messages the array element size must be equal to that of the longest error message.

String usage differs significantly from general array usage. Consequently, a programming language should provide a predefined string type in which the length of a string is not considered to be part of the string type. All strings will be of the same predefined string type, regardless of their length.[5]

The only operations allowed on pointers are assignment and comparison—in the interest of error detection and safety. Restrictions on pointers are specifically included to prevent the uncontrolled use of pointers which lead to problems such as stray and dangling references.

All variables can be explicitly initialized. Surprisingly, the only type definition that can be explicitly initialized (so that all variables of this type have the same initial value) is that of a record type—an example of non-uniformity. (If a pointer variable is not explicitly initialized, then for reasons of safety, it is implicitly initialized to the value **null**).

Another example of non-uniformity is that only array type definitions can be used directly in the declaration of objects, e.g.,

A: **array**(1 . . 10) **of REAL**;

In case of record and access types, the type must be first given a name and that name is used in declaring objects, e.g.,

```
type COMPLEX is
  record
    X, Y: FLOAT;
  end record;
    ⋮

  P: COMPLEX;
```

Parentheses are used to subscript arrays rather than square brackets—unlike C and Pascal. The use of square brackets enhances program readability by making it easy to distinguish function calls from references to array elements.[6] One argument made

---

[5] This implementation of a string type will require that strings be implemented as a *covert* access type (Wetherell, 1983). Providing a string type would not add to the complexity of an Ada implementation. The storage management required for access types could also be used for strings.

[6] An esoteric example for the Ada expert! Charles Wetherell, a colleague at Bell Labs, disagrees with the use of parentheses for subscripting arrays; he illustrates the resulting lack of program clarity by means of the following Ada example:

```
type ELEM is (R, G);
type VECTOR is array(ELEM) of ELEM;
X: ELEM;
function F(A: ELEM := R) return VECTOR is
  Y: VECTOR;
begin . . . return Y; end F;
    ⋮

begin
    ⋮
  X := F(R);
    ⋮
```

Is there a type error in the assignment statement $X := F(R)$;? There is no type error and it is left to the reader to figure out why. *Hint*: Actual parameters corresponding to formal parameters that have default initial values may be left out.

in favor of using parentheses for array subscripting is that this allows an array to be substituted for a function, and vice versa, without having to make many changes to the rest of the program—the *uniform reference* principle. While this argument might be appropriate in languages like Lisp, it does not hold much water in the Ada language because changing a function to an array or vice versa will require many changes in Ada programs. For example, since functions are not full fledged objects like arrays, they cannot be passed as parameters. Moreover, the uniform reference principle has been violated elsewhere in the Ada language, e.g., in the notation for selecting record components.

Another weak argument in favor of using parentheses is the fact that implementations with limited character sets may not have square brackets. Transliteration of square brackets to parentheses could be allowed just as transliteration has been allowed for some special characters.

3.1 Strong Typing

Ada is a *strongly typed* language—each object has one type, the type can be determined syntactically and the typing mechanism can be bypassed only by using a mechanism provided explicitly for this purpose (Gehani, 1983a). It is even more strongly typed than Pascal from which it derives its type philosophy.

Strongly typed languages lead to increased program clarity and reliability (Gannon, 1977) and increased program portability (Feuer and Gehani, 1982). For example, violation of strong typing, by viewing the representation of an integer value as a real value (as is possible by using the EQUIVALENCE statement in FORTRAN) will hamper program portability because different machines may have different word sizes and different representations of integers and reals. My experience with the strong typing in the Ada language has been extremely positive. Almost all my semantic errors, such as type mismatches and illegal direct references to objects, the majority of them occurring when I was still learning the Ada language, were detected at compile time.

Opponents of strong typing argue that the typing mechanism is a barrier to programming ease and programmer flexibility—a problem that I did not encounter except with the derived type mechanism (discussed later). Another problem with strongly typed languages, often cited by strong typing opponents, is that programs such as a *storage allocator* that violate strong typing cannot be written. The Ada language provides a mechanism *UNCHECKED_CONVERSION*, for use in isolated places, by which strong typing can be breached and by which programs such as a storage allocator can be written easily. Programs breaching strong typing can be easily identified by their use of UNCHECKED_CONVERSION—an asset in maintaining programming standards.

3.2 Type Equivalence

Name equivalence is used to define equivalence between two types. Each type definition introduces a new type, i.e., each type name denotes a distinct type. Consequently, two objects have *equivalent* types only if they are declared with the same type identifier.

This rule is strictly enforced in the Ada language, making it easy for both the reader and compiler to determine whether or not two objects have the same type. Type equivalence was left undefined in Pascal, the language that popularized strong typing. This omission caused portability problems since different Pascal compilers used different rules for determining when two types were equivalent.

3.3 Subtypes

Suppose the variable CUR_FLOOR is to be used to indicate the current floor number in a program to control the elevator in an eight-floor building. CUR_FLOOR can be declared to be of type INTEGER, but in this case erroneous assignments to CUR_FLOOR outside the range 1 to 8 will not be automatically detected. It would be desirable to restrict the values of CUR_FLOOR to lie between 1 and 8 so that attempts to assign values outside this range to CUR_FLOOR are automatically flagged as errors.

The *subtype* mechanism is used to specify such a restriction. For example, CUR_FLOOR is declared to be of the subtype STORIES which is declared as

subtype STORIES is INTEGER range 1..8;

to restrict the legal values of all objects of the subtype STORIES to be the integers between 1 and 8.

By declaring a subtype, a user provides additional information that enhances program readability, allows a compiler to ensure that all values assigned to variables of the subtype satisfy the constraints associated with it and also allows the compiler to optimize storage by allocating just the necessary amount of storage required for the restricted set of values.

3.4 Derived Types

Consider, as an example, two real variables PRICE and WEIGHT, of type FLOAT, that represent the price of a computer disk and the weight of the disk. Since both PRICE and WEIGHT are of the same type, errors such as the inadvertent or mistaken addition of PRICE and WEIGHT, or the assignment of WEIGHT to PRICE cannot be automatically detected.

PRICE and WEIGHT can be specified more precisely in the Ada language by declaring them to be of the user-defined types DOLLARS and POUNDS, respectively. DOLLARS and POUNDS have the same set of values and the same operations as FLOAT, but are different from each other and from FLOAT. Mistaken use of variables of type DOLLARS for those of type POUNDS or FLOAT, and so on, can then be detected automatically. The ability to define similar but distinct types such as DOLLARS and POUNDS is provided by the *derived types* mechanism in the Ada language.

The use of derived types is illustrated by simple operations related to a *rectangular parallelepiped*. Consider the following derived type declarations

```
type LENGTH is new FLOAT;
        --keyword new indicates that a type is being derived
type AREA is new FLOAT;
type VOLUME is new FLOAT;
type FORCE is new FLOAT;
type PRESSURE is new FLOAT;
```

and the variable declarations

```
L, W, H: LENGTH;  --the three dimensions of the parallelepiped
A: AREA;
V: VOLUME;
F: FORCE;         --force on one of the sides
P: PRESSURE;  --pressure = force/area
```

Each of the types LENGTH, AREA, VOLUME, FORCE and PRESSURE has the same set of values and operations as FLOAT, but these values and operations are distinct from those associated with FLOAT and from each of the other derived types. Essentially, the derived type mechanism just allows the user to paint distinct colors on otherwise identical types.

From a logical viewpoint, the derived type mechanism will correctly flag as errors the semantically meaningless operations

```
L+A
A+V
A:=V;
```

but incorrectly flag as errors the semantically meaningful operations

```
L*A
A:=L*W;
V:=L*A;
P:=F/A;
```

and allow semantically meaningless operations such as

```
L:=W*H;
```

The incorrect flagging of these operations as errors could be avoided by appropriately defining additional operators to allow mixing of the different derived types. For example, the operation V := L*A could be made legal by defining * for arguments of type LENGTH and AREA and to return a result of type VOLUME—a process that will require two conversions.

Not only is the overloading process cumbersome and inelegant, since many operators will have to be defined, but it is also dangerous since the definition of these operators requires overriding the derived type mechanism by means of explicit type conversions. Moreover, the rules for determining the operations inherited from the parent type and associated with the derived type are complicated (U.S. Department of Defense, 1983).

A simpler and better approach than the derived types approach is *units of measure* (Gehani, 1983b) in which the units of quantities represented by the objects are specified. The validity of the operations depends upon whether they conform to the rules of *units analysis* (also called *dimensional analysis*). For example, the above variables would be declared as (in Ada-like notation)

```
L, W, H: FLOAT {feet};
A: FLOAT {feet²};
V: FLOAT {feet³};
F: FLOAT {pounds};
P: FLOAT {pounds feet⁻²};
```

Unlike derived types, units of measure flags only the semantically meaningless operations as errors and does not flag meaningful operations as errors. The semantically meaningless operation

```
L+A
```

is flagged as an invalid operation while the semantically meaningful operation

```
L*A
```

is not flagged. Moreover, no overloading, no explicit conversions and no subversion of the units of measure rules is necessary.

Derived types have been perceived as the source of much unneeded complexity in the Ada language by many of the distinguished reviewers of the Ada language design effort. However, a proposal to remove derived types from the Ada language was unsuccessful (Fisher, 1983). The verbosity, inconvenience and inelegance of the derived types approach may discourage a programmer from using derived types— perhaps to the point of complete avoidance (Gehani, 1983b).

4 SEQUENTIAL PROGRAMMING

Facilities for sequential programming in the Ada language are similar to, although more elaborate than, those found in languages such as Pascal. Operators and some statements[7] of the Ada language are discussed in this section since sequential program execution consists mainly of expression evaluation and statement execution.

---

[7] In addition, there are statements for use in conjunction with other facilities, such as those for concurrent programming and exception handling.

4.1 Operators

The Ada language provides the normal kinds of operators found in a programming language. Listed in order of increasing precedence, they are

logical	**and** | **or** | **xor** | **and then** | **or else**
relational/membership	= | /= | < | <= | > | >= | **in** | **not in**
adding (binary)	+ | − | &
adding (unary)	+ | −
multiplying	* | / | **mod** | **rem**
highest precedence	** | **abs** | **not**

The operators have their usual meanings. The six operator precedence levels in the Ada language are probably appropriate since Pascal's four precedence levels require parentheses in many expressions that require no parentheses in common mathematical notation. On the other hand, C has eleven comparable levels of precedence, and parentheses are often needed for readability (Feuer and Gehani, 1982).

The conditional logical operators **and then** and **or else** facilitate the convenient writing of program segments such as those used for searching an array (Gehani, 1983a). Unlike conditional operators, both operands of unconditional operators **and** and **or** are evaluated. For example, suppose an array A has an upper bound equal to N. Execution of the following program segment will then result in a subscript error when I is equal to N+1 because the second operand of **and** is always evaluated:[8]

while I <= N **and** A(I) /= X **loop** ⋯ I := I + 1; **end loop**;

This error can be avoided by suppressing the evaluation of the second operand $A(I)$ /= X of **and** if the first one is FALSE—exactly the facility provided by the conditional operator **and then**.

Operators (along with subprograms) can be *overloaded* by the programmer, i.e., the definition of an operator can be extended to include values of other types. Operator overloading is convenient because it is natural, in some cases, to extend definitions of the operators provided for built-in types such as INTEGER and FLOAT to new types. For example, overloading operators such as +, −, * and / for the user-defined type COMPLEX allows COMPLEX expressions to be written in conformance with common mathematical notations and eliminates the necessity of having to use functions with names such as ADD_COMPLEX and MULTIPLY_COMPLEX.

Unfortunately, the assignment operator := cannot be overloaded—a handicap in some situations. Consider, for example, the definition of a new string type for

---

[8] Most languages (Ada included) do not define an order for the evaluation of operands of ordinary operators. Hence it is even possible that the second operand of an operator may be evaluated before the first.

which the programmer does explicit storage allocation and deallocation. When assigning a string variable a new value, the storage used for its old value is reclaimed. Since it is not possible to overload assignment, the programmer cannot extend := to include this deallocation. Instead the programmer will have to declare a procedure ASSIGN_STRING, which will include this storage deallocation (Wetherell, 1983) to be used for string assignment.

4.2 Statements

The Ada language provides the usual control statements for sequential programming such as the *null, assignment, if, case, loop, block, exit, return*, and *goto* statements. There are three kinds of loops corresponding to the *for* and *while* loops and a loop that executes for ever.

The *null* statement must be used whenever a null action is to be performed, e.g., an empty alternative in a *case* statement. The use of the *null* statement for a null action, instead of an empty space, as in Pascal, enhances program readability and prevents unintentional omission of statements.

As in Pascal, assignment is allowed between all identical types, e.g., assignment is allowed between two array variables provided they are of identical array types, i.e., same array type name. Not only is this facility elegant, since structured types are treated in a manner similar to simple types, such as integers, but it is also very convenient.

All *compound* statements must be explicitly delimited, e.g.,

if ⋯ **end if;**
case ⋯ **end case;**
loop ⋯ **end loop;**

This requirement eliminates the syntactic ambiguity problem that arises when nesting *if* statements in ALGOL 60 and Pascal—such an ambiguity is usually resolved by some extra syntactic means.

The *case* statement allows the specification of an *others* clause that covers all the cases not explicitly specified—correcting a need often felt in Pascal's *case* statement. I never felt it necessary or desirable to use the *goto* statement—the *exit* statement was sufficient in the rare cases where I needed to exit from the middle of a loop.

5 PROGRAM STRUCTURING

The Ada programming language provides standard facilities for the construction of small programs, e.g., subprograms, packages and tasks. According to Wegner (1983), the Ada language also provides an adequate basis for the development of large and evolutionary programs with facilities such as separate compilation, context specification and strong typing.

5.1 Subprograms

Two kinds of subprograms are provided—functions and procedures. Subprograms can be compiled *separately* and are called *compilation units* (packages and generic units are the other compilation units). Functions are used to return values while procedures are executed for their effect, e.g., changing values of their arguments. Parameters may be specified in the positional or named notation in subprogram calls:

SQRT(A, 0.001)
SQRT(EPS=>0.00001, X=>A)

where X and EPS are the formal parameters of SQRT.

Formal parameters can be given default initial values. Actual parameters corresponding to these formal parameters can be left out—a convenience especially in the cases when the default values suffice most of the time. For example, if SQRT is declared as

procedure SQRT(X: FLOAT; EPS: FLOAT := 0.001) **return** FLOAT **is**
⋮
end SQRT;

it may be called as

SQRT(A)

or

SQRT(X=>A)

Subprograms can be overloaded, allowing the use of the same subprogram name for different subprograms—a convenience for the programmer. For example, the name SORT can be used for subprograms to sort arrays of characters, strings, reals, integers and employee records. Of course, the same name should be used for subprograms that are conceptually similar—a discipline that cannot be enforced by a compiler.

Subprograms cannot be passed as parameters. Such a facility is necessary in writing some kinds of programs, e.g., a procedure INTEGRATE that integrates the function supplied as a parameter between two limits. However, this restriction is not really a handicap in the Ada programming language since the generic facilities allow generic formal parameters to be subprograms. Consequently, instead of a normal procedure INTEGRATE, a programmer can declare a generic procedure INTEGRATE and use instantiations of it with the desired function as the generic formal parameter.

5.2 Packages

Packages can be used to group together logically related entities such as constants, procedures and types. As an example, consider the package PLOTTING_DATA, which consists only of a group of common variables and which has no corresponding package body (U.S. Department of Defense, 1982).

```
package PLOTTING_DATA is
  PEN_UP: BOOLEAN;
  CONVERSION_FACTOR,
  X_OFFSET, Y_OFFSET,
  X_MIN, X_MAX,
  Y_MIN, Y_MAX: FLOAT;
  X_VALUE: array(1..500) of FLOAT;
  Y_VALUE: array(1..500) of FLOAT;
end PLOTTING_DATA;
```

All variables related to plotting data can be easily found since they are encapsulated in one place, i.e., the package PLOTTING_DATA. Not only does this localization of related variables by using the data encapsulation facility enhance program readability but it also enhances program modifiability.

5.3 Tasks

Tasks are similar to packages in that they can be used to group logically related procedures (called *entries*). Unlike packages, tasks are active objects—the task body executes in parallel with the program component activating the task. Entities in a package specification may be concurrently accessed by many tasks while the entries in a task can be accessed only one at a time—concurrent accesses are serialized, i.e., tasks provide *mutual exclusion*.

Consequently, tasks may be used in preference to packages to group logically related procedures when it is desirable to have the maximum amount of parallelism and/or provide mutual exclusion.

5.4 Programming-in-the-Large

Any program can be partitioned into smaller program components—subprograms, packages and tasks. Each program component has two parts—a specification and a body. The user of a program component need know only the specification of that component, thus allowing many people to work on a large project once the specifications of the program components have been decided.

Subprograms and packages (and bodies of tasks) may be *separately* compiled, i.e., independently compiled along with type checking. This facility allows independent development and testing of program components. Systems can thus be incrementally compiled with new modules being added when completed. Moreover, modification of a program component does not in general require recompilation of the whole program—an important economic and time consideration for large software projects.

Strong typing ensures that program components, separately compiled or not, are used consistently with respect to their specifications. It also protects the user of a program component from arbitrary changes to the specification of program components. Moreover, the body of a program component must conform to its specification—the specifications that the users of the program component rely upon.

Contextual information specifying the environment (e.g, the program libraries) with which a subprogram or package is to be compiled can be simply specified. The contextual information can be easily changed allowing for easy program modification.

I must warn the reader that I myself did not write any large programs. However, since these facilities substantially meet DeRemer and Kron's (1976) criteria for programming language support in the writing of large programs, I am of the opinion that the facilities in the Ada programming language for programming-in-the-large represent a substantial improvement over the facilities in any other major programming language.[9] Just by themselves, these facilities make Ada an attractive language to use.

6 DATA ABSTRACTION—PACKAGES AND TASKS

Data abstraction in the Ada language is provided by means of packages and (surprisingly) tasks. Packages are primarily an information hiding and data encapsulation facility. Packages consist of two parts—specification and body.

Only the entities specified in the public part of a package specification[10] are visible to the user. Moreover, all the information specified in the body of the package is hidden from the user. As an example consider the package SET_PACKAGE that provides facilities for declaring and manipulating sets of integers:

```
package SET_PACKAGE is
    type SET is private;
    procedure ADD(S: in out SET; X: in INTEGER);
    procedure DELETE(· · ·);
      ⋮
private
    type SET is · · ·;    ––representation details of type SET
      ⋮
    end SET_PACKAGE;
```

Set variables are declared using the *private* type SET. Because SET has been designated as a private type, the only operations allowed automatically for SET variables are assignment, equality comparison and parameter passing. The only additional operations allowed for set variables are the ones defined in SET_PACKAGE, e.g., ADD and DELETE.

The body of SET_PACKAGE is

[9] I am by no means implying that Ada has facilities that support the management of large software projects. Support of software project management is to be provided by the Ada Programming Support Environment (Buxton, 1980).

[10] Representation details of private types are given in the private part of the package specification, instead of the package body, to help the compiler to allocate storage for variables of private types. Remember, a program component, using a package, can be compiled successfully with just the specification of the package.

```
package body SET_PACKAGE is
  --local variables, bodies of ADD, DELETE, etc.
  :
end SET_PACKAGE;
```

All implementation details of type SET are hidden from the user. Hiding the details prevents a user from making programs dependent on the implementation, and accidentally or maliciously violating the integrity of an abstract data type object by manipulating its representation in undesirable ways.

6.1 Abstract Data Types

Abstract data types are user-defined types that are declared and manipulated in exactly the same way as the predefined data types in the language. Although packages can be used to implement abstract data types by using the private type, packages are conceptually not a true abstract data type facility, e.g., the operations on the private type are associated with the package and not the type (Gehani, 1983a; Schwartz and Melliar-Smith, 1980; Wegner, 1983).

6.2 Tasks

As mentioned earlier, tasks can be used to provide a collection of logically related operations and therefore they can be used to implement data abstraction. Task types can be declared and used in a manner similar to the declaration of other user-defined types. Consequently, it is possible to declare an array of tasks, to pass them as parameters and so on. However, it is not possible to declare package types. As a result, tasks come closer to being an abstract data type facility than packages. Unfortunately using tasks as abstract data types may impose a heavy implementation overhead since, as mentioned before, tasks are active objects with their own flow of control that also requires scheduling.

7 ERROR HANDLING

Error handling in the Ada language is supported by means of an elaborate exception facility. Exceptions in PL/I are used as a normal programming technique. In contrast, exceptions in the Ada language are intended specifically for handling errors and limiting conditions. Exception handlers are therefore specified separately from the normal statements in program units. Execution of the normal part of a program unit is suspended when an exception occurs; execution of an exception handler (if any) is initiated after which the program unit terminates. Exceptions are necessary to handle some kinds of errors, e.g., numeric errors that occur in the middle of an expression.

The exception facilities in the Ada language enhance program clarity by separating the normal program statements from those used for error handling. These exception facilities have been reasonably well defined and have uniform semantics. In contrast, the exceptions in PL/I[11] were not very precisely defined nor was their treatment uniform.

The utility of exceptions may be limited by the fact that no contextual information related to an exception, such as the location where the exception occurred and the reason for its occurrence, is passed to the exception handler. Moreover, exceptions cannot be parameterized to pass explicit contextual information. For example, in one of the programs I wrote, the exception TEMP_OUTSIDE_LIMITS was raised whenever the temperature of the nuclear vessel went outside some predefined limits. It was not possible to pass information, indicating whether the exception was raised because the temperature exceeded the upper limit or fell below the lower limit, directly to the corresponding exception handler. However, since an exception handler has access to the entities declared in its associated program unit, it was possible to deduce the above information in the exception handler.

Although I was not hampered by the limitations of the exception facility in my examples, I feel that their impact may be felt in case of large programs.

8 CONCURRENT AND REAL-TIME PROGRAMMING

The concurrent programming facilities of the Ada language are orthogonal to the rest of its facilities. Based on Hoare's "Communicating Sequential Processes" (1978), they are elegant and easy to use. The ability to express concurrency in a programming language is desirable for two reasons. First, many algorithms are described naturally using concurrency. Second, programs with concurrency explicitly specified may be implemented more efficiently on multicomputers and multiprocessors than can sequential programs.

Parallel processes are called *tasks* in the Ada language. A concurrent program may be viewed as consisting of several cooperating tasks. Tasks interact by first synchronizing, then exchanging information and finally continuing their individual activities. This synchronization or meeting to exchange information is called the *rendezvous*.

A task may have *entries* which are called by other tasks. Two tasks A and B *rendezvous* at entry E of B when A calls E and the entry call is accepted by B. If A calls E before B is ready to accept the entry call, then A waits until B is ready. Similarly, if B is ready to accept an entry call, then it must wait until some task issues that entry call. Calling an entry corresponds to sending a message while accepting an entry call corresponds to receiving a message.

My understanding of concurrent programming has benefited a great deal from using facilities in the Ada language. Within a short time I was able to write concurrent programs with ease—even device drivers such as those for controlling a keyboard, a display and a traffic light, were easy to write because interrupts are treated like entry calls.

---

[11] PL/I was the first language to provide elaborate exception handling facilities.

Ada is the first major general purpose programming language to provide **high level** concurrent programming facilities. Moreover, it is the first language to base its concurrent programming facilities on the rendezvous concept. Consequently, it is natural to expect problems and limitations of these facilities, such as those enumerated below, to be discovered with use and experience:

- *Level of concurrency:* The *task level* concurrent programming facility in the Ada language is not very appropriate for writing some kinds of concurrent programs e.g., concurrent versions of *divide and conquer* algorithms. Such programs have several recursive calls that have to be executed in parallel and there is no easy way to express that in the Ada language. For example, there is no easy way of saying that the two recursive calls in a quicksort program (Cohen, 1982; Gehani and Wetherell, 1983c), e.g.,

  procedure QUICKSORT(···) **is**
  ⋮
  ⋮
  begin
  ⋮
  ⋮
  QUICKSORT(···); QUICKSORT(···);
  ⋮
  end QUICKSORT;

  are to be executed in parallel.

- *Parallel numerical computations:* The design of concurrent programming facilities in the Ada language has been motivated by the kind of concurrency that appears in operating systems problems, e.g., the producer-consumer problem, rather than that found in numerical applications. Consequently, it is hard and circuitous to write parallel numerical computations, e.g., parallel vector operations (Blum, 1982).

- *Polling bias:* The facilities supporting the rendezvous lead to and encourage the design of programs that poll—the *polling bias* (Gehani and Cargill, 1983). As an example consider entry families[12] which can be used to implement programmer controlled scheduling (Gehani, 1983a; U.S. Department of Defense, 1979b). The only general way to handle calls to an entry family is by polling to determine whether or not an entry member has been called. Polling is generally, but not always, undesirable because it wastes system resources. Ada programmers, especially novice programmers, must be aware of this bias to avoid writing polling programs inadvertently.

- *Determination of self identity by a task:* Tasks cannot determine their identity—an inconvenience in many applications. Suppose, for example, that an array of tasks has been declared. An element task cannot determine its index in the array. The lack of a facility to allow tasks to determine their identity means that some sort of identification, e.g., the index in the array, must be supplied

---

[12] An entry family is really an array of entries.

explicitly to the tasks. As a specific example, consider the dining philosopher's problem (Dijkstra, 1971; Gehani, 1983a), in which 5 philosophers eat spaghetti using 2 forks each. There are 5 forks and the ith philosopher can use only forks i and i **mod** $5 + 1$. If an array of tasks is used to implement the philosophers, each task must first be supplied with its identity i so that it knows that it should only use forks i and i **mod** $5 + 1$. Preliminary Ada (U.S. Department of Defense, 1979a,b) had a facility that allowed tasks to determine their identity. Instead of the task types, Preliminary Ada had task families. The attribute INDEX when used in the body of a member of the task family yielded its index in the family.[13]

- *Array of device drivers:* Task types cannot be parameterized; this limits their usability. For example, an array of device drivers, say for a set of identical terminals, cannot be declared because their buffer, register and interrupt addresses cannot be supplied as parameters.

- *Interrupts and entry families:* It is not possible to associate entry families with a set of interrupts. Consequently, an entry family cannot be used to handle a number of functionally similar interrupts such as those corresponding to the elevator buttons in a computer-controlled elevator mechanism.

- *Tasks and global data:* The only way to write tasks that can simultaneously access the same data is by using global variables. It may be desirable to allow several tasks to simultaneously read shared data, but allow only one task at a time to update the shared data. The user of global variables has been considered harmful (Wulf and Shaw, 1973) and the presence of the additional dimension of concurrency makes the situation worse.

8.1 Real-Time Programs

A real-time programming language should provide facilities for (Stotts, 1982; Young, 1980)

1. Explicit control of task scheduling to meet critical timing constraints
2. Timeout in task communication
3. Direct communication with hardware devices (it should also be possible to confine interrupt handling to well defined language constructs)
4. Error handling

Ada is reasonably suitable as a real-time programming language since it provides facilities that substantially meet the above requirements:

---

[13] Task families in Preliminary Ada were replaced by task types in ANSI Ada to solve some problems with the tasking facilities, e.g., tasks could not be passed as parameters and tasks could not be created dynamically. With task types, tasks can be created dynamically using access types with objects of a task type in conjunction with the storage allocator *new*.

1. Scheduling of a task can be done explicitly by requiring the task to register its request by calling an entry of the server task which gives it an index of some member of an entry family. The requesting task then calls this member of the entry family—the call being accepted according to the desired scheduling policy (Gehani, 1983a). Implicit scheduling is possible by specifying the priority of a task by using the PRIORITY *pragma* (i.e., an instruction to the compiler). Task priorities cannot be changed dynamically.

2. The timeout facilities in the Ada language are the *timed entry* calls for the task calling an entry and the *delay* alternative in the *selective wait* statement for the acceptor of an entry call.

3. Direct communication with hardware and high level handling of hardware interrupts devices is provided by the *representation clauses*.

4. Elaborate error handling facilities are provided by the exception mechanism. Errant tasks in Ada programs may be unconditionally terminated by means of the *abort* statement.

Again, as in case of large programs, I do not have realistic experience with real-time programs since I was not able to actually execute any real-time programs—as mentioned earlier, the NYU Ada compiler is very slow and my version of it did not allow a program to directly communicate with hardware devices.

My analysis of the facilities provided in the Ada language leads me to think that the Ada language seems to be appropriate for most real-time programming applications. However, the Ada language does not provide the programmer with sufficient control over the scheduling discipline (Roberts, 1981). There is no way to specify a run-time limit for a task or to deschedule a task explicitly. For example, when implementing a time-sharing system in the Ada language it would be natural to implement user processes as tasks. For fairness, time-sharing systems usually allow each process to run for some prespecified time limit. If this limit is exceeded, the executing process is suspended, rescheduled for later execution and another process is allowed to execute.

9 RELATIONSHIP OF PROGRAMS WITH THE OUTSIDE WORLD

The relationship of a program with the outside world is determined by how a program gets its data, outputs its results, builds and accesses program libraries and interfaces with the underlying hardware.

9.1 Input/Output

Input and output facilities are not part of the Ada language but are provided by means of standard library packages—TEXT_IO, DIRECT_IO and SEQUENTIAL_IO. (A package LOW_LEVEL_IO is also provided for controlling physical devices directly.)

These input/output facilities are straightforward and easy to use. Use of these facilities does require that the programmer understand the concepts of *packages*, *generic* facilities, and *exceptions*. For example, many of the facilities in the above packages are templates (i.e., generics) which must be instantiated before use. Exceptions may have to be used in handling interactive input. However, input/output can be made easy, especially for the novice user, by providing appropriate instantiations of the TEXT_IO package.

One problem area is interactive input in which the Ada language suffers from a problem similar to that in Pascal (Feuer and Gehani, 1982). For example, use of the paradigm

```
while not END_OF_FILE(STANDARD_INPUT) loop
    Prompt for data from user
    Read data
    :
end loop;
```

to read input interactively from a terminal causes trouble. Function END_OF_FILE cannot be evaluated when there is no data, since it cannot be determined whether the data has been exhausted or that the data has not been supplied as yet. Consequently, evaluation of END_OF_FILE will be delayed until the user supplies the data—but the user has no way of knowing that the program is waiting for the data because the prompt will not be printed.

However, the Ada language provides alternate facilities that can be used to avoid the above problem. For example, the following paradigm (Gehani, 1983a), that uses the exception END_ERROR which is raised when an attempt is made to read past the end of file, can be used to read input from an interactive terminal:

```
begin
    loop
        Prompt for data from user
        Read data
        :
    end loop;
exception
    when END_ERROR => null;
            --Control is transferred here when an attempt is made
            --to read past the end of the file; the null
            --statement is executed and the block exited.
end;
```

This solution is inelegant since it requires the use of an exception and enclosure of the program segment reading the data in a *begin* block (so that the exception can be handled locally) and the use of a null exception handler.

A better solution (Wetherell, 1983) that avoids the above problems is

```
loop
    Prompt for data from user
    exit when END_OF_FILE(STANDARD_INPUT);
    Read data
       ⋮
end loop;
```

9.2 Program Libraries

Program libraries consisting of subprograms and packages can be easily built in the Ada language since they can be compiled individually. Strong typing ensures that the library subprograms and packages, like other subprograms and packages, are used in a manner that is consistent with their specifications. Accessing program libraries is straightforward.

The Ada language also provides a mechanism for accessing programs written in other languages, e.g., FORTRAN. Such a mechanism is extremely valuable, both from an economic viewpoint and in making the changeover to programming in the Ada language, since it allows utilization of the tremendous amount of existing software written in other languages. It remains to be seen how well Ada compilers will be able to implement such a mechanism.

9.3 Representation Specifications

The Ada language provides facilities for interfacing with the underlying hardware which are separate and distinct from the facilities for specifying the logical properties of a program. Consequently, in the eventuality the program is to be run on hardware different from that for which it was designed, the hardware-dependent parts can be readily identified and changed. These facilities also allow a program to accept hardware interrupts and control devices. For example, the declarations

```
PRINTER_BUFFER: CHARACTER;
for PRINTER_BUFFER use at 8#177566#;
```

allow the memory location 8#177566# (written in octal notation), representing the printer buffer, to be accessed via the variable PRINTER_BUFFER, which is of type CHARACTER.

As another example, consider the declarations

```
task INTERRUPT_HANDLER is
    entry DONE;
    for DONE use at 16#40#;
end INTERRUPT_HANDLER;
```

which associate an interrupt (at address 16#40#) with the entry DONE (U.S. Department of Defense, 1983). Occurrence of this interrupt causes the generation of a call to the entry DONE.

I was able to write device drivers easily because once the device interface was defined, i.e., association of device registers with program variables and interrupts with entries, writing the rest of the driver was like writing any other program.

10 GENERIC FACILITIES

Generic subprograms (packages) are subprograms (packages) that can be parameterized to accept the types and subprograms as parameters. Generic programs result in reduced programming effort and more manageable programs because fewer program units have to be written. Moreover, they lead to higher level of abstraction and portability of programs across types (Gehani, 1983a).

As an example, consider a generic sort procedure SORT whose specification is given below:

```
generic
   type ELEM is private;
   type VECTOR is array(INTEGER range <>) of ELEM;
   with function ">"(A, B: in ELEM) return BOOLEAN;
   procedure SORT(A: in out VECTOR);
```

A normal sort procedure is derived from the generic procedure SORT by instantiating it with three generic actual parameters—the element type, the array type and the comparison function ">". The index type of the array type must be an integer subtype (specified by INTEGER range <>).

The body of SORT looks like

```
procedure SORT(A: in out VECTOR) is
   I, J: A'RANGE;
   T: ELEM;
      .
      .
      .
begin
      .
      .
      .
end SORT;
```

where variables I and J were declared to be of the same type as the index type of A.[14]

Assuming that appropriate declarations have been given, sorting routines for arrays with elements of type INTEGER, BOOLEAN and EMPLOYEE can be instantiated as

---

[14] Characteristics of entities in the Ada programs can be examined by means of attributes. For example, attributes A'FIRST, A'LAST and A'RANGE of an array variable A yield the lower bound of its index, the upper bound of its index and its index type. The use of attributes can lead to programming ease and flexibility, e.g., the bounds of an array parameter do not have to be passed explicitly as parameters—they can be determined by using appropriate attributes (just as in PL/I).

```
procedure INTEGER_SORT is new
    SORT(ELEM => INTEGER, VECTOR => INTEGER_ARRAY,
        ">" => ">");

procedure BOOLEAN_SORT is new
    SORT(ELEM => BOOLEAN, VECTOR => BOOLEAN_ARRAY,
        ">" => ">");

procedure EMPLOYEE_SORT is new
    SORT(ELEM => EMPLOYEE, VECTOR => EMPLOYEE_ARRAY,
        ">" => GREATER_THAN);
```

where GREATER_THAN is a programmer defined function that compares two values of type EMPLOYEE and returns TRUE if the first value is greater than the second (according to some programmer-defined criteria) and FALSE otherwise. Note that binary functions can be passed as generic actual parameters for generic formal parameters that are binary operators. Binary operators can be similarly passed for binary functions.

Not only can SORT be instantiated to sort arrays of different types, but the sorting order can be reversed by supplying a different comparison operator:

```
procedure DECREASING_INTEGER_SORT is new
    SORT(ELEM => INTEGER, VECTOR => INTEGER_ARRAY,
        ">" => "<");
```

Generic facilities save the programmer much clerical work. However, in the above example it was a nuisance to have to pass both the array and element type.

11 CONCLUSIONS

Ada is a good programming language. Unlike any other major language, the Ada language incorporates many of the advances in programming language design resulting from the research of the 1970s. The Ada programming language has widened my programming horizon[15] by providing facilities to write a variety of programs, such as concurrent programs, device drivers and real-time programs.

The Ada language represents the first concrete realization of many recent advances in programming language concepts. The design of the Ada language has stimulated much interest and new research in programming language design. It has been an educational experience for the computer science community as a whole. One consequence of this education has been that the criticism of the Ada language has become more subtle and intelligent—the design of the Ada language spawned its own criticism!

---

[15] Professor Ellis Horowitz, in the preface to his book *Fundamentals of Programming Languages* (1983), writes

> As I studied the language, I began to incorporate it into my classes. Now I observe that many of my examples come from Ada. My main justification is because Ada is one of the very few languages which has included, in some way, all of the features I wish to discuss.

By pointing out problems and deficiences in the Ada language, I am not suggesting that they be remedied by any major additions to the language. On the contrary, I feel that some of facilities in the Ada language should be left out or redesigned. Facilities that have not been tried out in practice, and have not been proven to be useful and correct, should not have been included in a programming language intended for such widespread use. In particular, I feel that a string type should have been included, derived types should have been left out[16] and the concurrent programming facilities modified to eliminate the problems cited.

The inclusion of a string type will make it easier for the programmers to manipulate strings and make the Ada language more attractive for applications such as text processing.

Derived types are an unnecessary source of complexity. Moreover, the use of derived types results in verbosity, inconvenience and inelegance (because of the associated overloading that may be necessary) which may discourage a programmer from using derived types—perhaps to the point of avoiding them altogether (Gehani, 1983b).

The concurrent programming facilities in the Ada language are novel and have never been tried out in any programming language. My understanding of concurrent programming has benefited a great deal from understanding and using the facilities in the Ada language. Within a short time, I was able to write concurrent programs with ease—even device drivers—because interrupts are treated like entry calls. Although these facilities are suitable for the producer-consumer type concurrent programming problems, they are not so appropriate for other kinds of problems, e.g., numerical computation. Many of the deficiences in concurrent programming facilities in the Ada language are a direct result of the lack of experience in using such facilities.

Despite its shortcomings, I would prefer the Ada programming language to the other languages that are widely used today,[17] e.g., FORTRAN, Pascal and C. My preference for the Ada language is based on the assessement that it is at least as good as, if not much better than, any of these languages. The Ada programming language provides facilities for many advanced concepts that are not provided in these languages; its shortcomings are in some of these facilities. Many of these concepts (e.g., programming-in-the-large and concurrent programming) are so important that facilities for each one of them alone would make me prefer to use the Ada language instead of the others.

Finally, let me reiterate that in my opinion, Ada is a good programming language incorporating, to a greater extent than any other language in wide use, many recent advances in programming language design. However, its design is not perfect and it is not the ultimate programming language (if such a language exists!). The conclusion that Ada is not a perfect programming language is based, in part, on the new knowledge and insights gained by its design. However, I do feel that the Ada language represents a considerable improvement over existing languages.

---

[16] Units of measure should be considered as an alternative to derived types but only after confirming their utility by incorporating them in an experimental programming language.

[17] Provided production quality Ada compilers are available.

ACKNOWLEDGMENTS

I am grateful to A. R. Feuer, D. D. Hill, J. O. Limb, R. H. McCullough, M. D. McIlroy, C. S. Wetherell and the referee for their comments. Alan Feuer and Charlie Wetherell gave good advice on the organization of the paper. Doug McIlroy offered many constructive suggestions and comments—both technical and stylistic. Charlie's in-depth knowledge of Ada's nuances and suggestions have been an invaluable resource—both here and elsewhere. He has always had time to comment constructively on my manuscripts.

LANGUAGE CRITICISMS

Three of the four papers in this section are pointed criticisms aimed at C and Pascal, and one paper is a response to a criticism of Pascal. Unlike the assessments in the preceding section, these criticisms concentrate mainly on the weak points of the languages. And the sparks do fly!

Among other things, the papers in this section illustrate that some criticisms of a language reflect the different tastes of the designer and the critic; other criticisms reflect different programming styles and backgrounds. Over time, one hopes that a consensus emerges as to what is right and what is wrong in a programming language.

The Habermann and Lecarme–Desjardins papers are an illustration of point-counterpoint as applied to programming languages. In "Critical Comments on the Programming Language Pascal," Habermann criticizes Pascal, at that time a young language, on several fronts:

- Some useful constructs are missing such as own variables, dynamic arrays, and conditional expressions.
- Some concepts in the language are ill founded, such as the treatment of subranges.
- The standard reference manual is inaccurate and incomplete.

In response, Lecarme and Desjardins, in "More Comments on the Programming Language Pascal," classify Habermann's criticisms into four categories: clearly refutable (most of them); debatable (most of the rest); valid (a few); and misunderstandings and minor errors.

The next two papers take aim at Pascal and C, respectively. In "Why Pascal Is Not My Favorite Programming Language," Kernighan, an important contributor to C, tells of his experience in rewriting the popular book *Software Tools*. The book was originally written with program examples in the language Ratfor. This paper catalogs specific problems encountered in translating the Ratfor programs into Pascal. Kernighan states his case firmly: "Pascal is not adequate for writing real programs."

In "Type Syntax in the Language C" Anderson takes C's unusual notation for specifying types to task. He claims that "the syntax of [types in] C is irregular and messy." To illustrate his point, Anderson translates some arcane C type declarations into a more understandable Pascal-like notation.

A. N. HABERMANN
Dept of Computer Science, Carnegie-Mellon University, Pittsburgh, Pennsylvania

Critical Comments on the Programming Language Pascal

1 INTRODUCTION

The design of the programming language Pascal was based on the combination of two principal aims: to create "a language suitable to teach programming as a systematic discipline," but at the same time a language that can be implemented as a reliable and efficient programming system (Wirth, 1971).

Pascal is supposed not to contain the features and constructs of other languages that are hard to explain and are said to be an "insult to minds trained in systematic reasoning." Contrary to this statement we will see that on the one hand some useful constructs of other languages that are not hard to explain have been left out of Pascal, whereas Pascal, on the other hand, has features that are hard to explain and hinder the user in systematic programming.

We argue first that some useful and well understood constructs have not been incorporated in Pascal. Secondly we go through a simple programming exercise which shows that using Pascal as a teaching tool causes problems similar to the ones caused by using any other language. Subsequently, we discuss the major inadequacies of the language which are found in labels and **goto** statements, in confusing ranges, types and structures, and in procedures, functions and parameter passing. Finally, we examine the presentation of the syntax definition and the description of the semantics in the Revised Report (Wirth, 1972).

2 USEFUL CONSTRUCTS NOT INCORPORATED IN PASCAL

2.1 Block Structure

A sound programming principle is to declare a variable at the place where it is used. In a sorting program, for instance, a certain part of the program can be understood as "merge two ordered sections of length p and q into one ordered section of length $p + q$." The merging process needs some local pointers to carry out the ordering. Programming such a sorting problem in a constructive and systematic way requires that the action of merging two sections can be written as a module that fits in an environment to which only the external specification of that module is relevant. The internal structure (to which the declaration of such pointers clearly belongs) ought to be of no concern (and definitely not accessible) to the environment. The notion of a program block as defined in ALGOL 60 (Naur, 1963) is a clean and well-understood construct that is very useful for this purpose.

Runtime overhead of block entry and exit is sometimes mentioned as an argument against block-structure. Such overhead, however, is very small if erratic changes of control through **goto** statements are not possible. Moreover, there is no need for any overhead in the absence of dynamic arrays because space for local blocks can be fixed, overlaying parallel blocks, at procedure entry.

2.2 Dynamic Arrays

Changing the bounds of an array in Pascal implies recompilation of the program. It was conjectured that a resulting gain in execution speed would more than compensate for this inconvenience. Not only is this argument very doubtful, but the implications are much farther reaching than such a statement suggests.

It is well known that execution time for accessing array elements exceeds by far the time needed for processing an array declaration. Since the former hardly depends on whether or not an array can have variable bounds, a significant gain in execution speed is not to be expected.

The true reason for not incorporating dynamic arrays in Pascal is probably the fact variable subranges can hardly be treated as a type.

The absence of dynamic arrays causes other inconveniences as well. Suppose we program a function LENGTH that computes the length of a vector.

```
type A=array [0 ··· 63] of real; B=array [0 ··· 100] of real;
var p: A; q: B;
function LENGTH (u: ··· ; n: integer): real;
  var sum: real;
begin sum:=0;
  for i:=0 to n do sum:=sum+u[i]*u[i];
  {Pascal has no operator for exponentiation}
  LENGTH:=sqrt (sum)
end
```

The problem with the definition of function LENGTH is that we *must* choose between specifying the formal parameter as either type *A* or type *B* and as a result the function can operate only on one of the two types. Thus, instead of one uniform function LENGTH for all vectors, we are forced to define as many different functions LENGTH as there are vectors with different numbers of elements. The choice of the procedure statement example Transpose (*a*, *n*, *m*) (Section 9.1.2) and of the function declaration Max (Section 11) suggests by lack of any further explanation that Pascal is in this respect as powerful as ALGOL 60. [*Ed. note*: All section cross-references refer to the Revised Report (Wirth, 1972).] This is an unfair presentation of Pascal's reality.

2.3 own *Variables*

There are not many implementations of ALGOL 60 in existence that allow dynamic own arrays. If those are not implemented, storage allocation can be restricted to a mere stack discipline, whereas a heap in the ALGOL 68 sense is needed otherwise requiring considerable overhead at runtime for storage allocation and garbage collection (van Wijngaarden, 1969). But this is not to say that the concept of **own** is entirely useless. On the contrary, it serves the objective of writing well-structured programs and it can easily be defined as to allow an efficient implementation. The idea of specifying a named object as **own** is to make the name known only to the local environment, but in such a way that the last assigned value of the named object is retained across two successive activations of that local environment. Consider for instance the storage maintenance policy that uses the first fit algorithm as discussed in Knuth (1968). Storage consists of "free" and "used" blocks. When a request arrives for a free block of size *s*, the allocation agent searches for the first free block that is larger than *s*. Knuth observes that, if the agent starts at the beginning of the list of free blocks every time a request arrives, free blocks of small sizes tend to accumulate at the beginning of the list. But this can easily be avoided by resuming the search for a free block that is large enough at the very place where the search halted last time. The pointer that indicates this place is typically an object that should have been declared as an **own** variable of the allocation agent. Its value should not get lost in between two activations of the allocation agent, but the variable is of no concern to the environment in which the agent operates.

One can easily think of useful generalizations of the **own** concept to names that are shared by certain modules of a program, but which are inaccessible to other modules including the environment in which the former modules operate. It gives a module its private (or shared) section of global space. Observe that this **own** concept is basic to the structure and understanding of co-routines and concurrent processes.

Initialization of an **own** object is rather inconvenient in ALGOL 60. This inconvenience can easily be eliminated by incorporating the initialization in the declaration and placing the latter as a prefix of the environment in which the **own** object is used.

2.4 Conditional Expressions

ALGOL W has two sorts of conditional expressions, one of the form **if** *BE* **then** *e*1 **else** *e*2 and one of the form **case** *IE* **of** (expressionlist). It is conceivable that a teacher does not discuss these constructs when he goes through a first pass over a language with beginning programmers. But they do certainly make sense to a more advanced programmer who is concerned about a clear structure of his program. The statement

i:= **if** *i*=7 **then** 1 **else** *i*+1

expresses more clearly that a value is assigned to *i* than the statement

if *i*=7 **then** *i*:=1 **else** *i*:=*i*+1

in which it is more or less incidental that both alternative statements assign to *i* and do nothing else.

3 AN EXERCISE IN PROGRAMMING IN PASCAL

A typical problem for an introductory programming course is the sieve of Eratosthenes, an algorithm for computing the prime numbers less than a given number *N*. The idea of Eratosthenes' algorithm is to place the numbers 2 to *N* in a row and then repeat the action of finding the leftmost number in the row followed by erasing it and all its multiples still left in the row. A prime number is found every time that the leftmost number in the row is determined.

The row of numbers 2 to *N* is naturally represented as an array *A*. Since the array bounds must be fixed, let us choose an arbitrary number for *N*, e.g., *N* = 1999. The elements of *A* are initialized with the value of their index. Erasing a number from the row can be implemented by assigning a zero to the corresponding element in *A*. Thus, a natural start of the program is:

```
begin var A: array [2 ··· 1999] of integer; i: 2 ··· 1999;
    for i:=2 to 1999 do A [i]:=i
```

The innocent student in programming, for instance the one who studied program structuring as presented in Dijkstra (1971), may think that the **for** statement could be replaced consistently by a **while** or **repeat** statement. But an unexpected difficulty shows up if *i* is declared of subrange type 2 ··· 1999, because

```
begin var A: array [2 ··· 1999] of integer; i: 2 ··· 1999;
    i:=2; repeat A [i]:=i; i=i+1
        until i>1999
```

results in an error indication at the operator +. Section 8.1.3 is clear at this point: it requires that both operands of an addition are of type integer or real and there are reasons to assume that a phrase as "or subrange thereof" has not accidentally been omitted. For, Section 8.1.4 mentions subrange type explicitly in a similar place; furthermore, subrange type is not an instance of sclar type (see Section 6.1); finally, a type can hardly be associated with the result of an addition of two operands of subrange type.

It seems as if the problem can be avoided by writing $i:=succ(i)$ instead of $i:=i+1$. But now the test $i>1999$ fails at the very moment that the repeat statement is about to terminate, because $succ(i)$ is undefined when $i=1999$ (Section 11.1.4). The proper solution is to declare variable i as integer instead of as subrange type. (A clever programmer will of course use the trick of declaring i of subrange $2 \cdots$ 2000 and not use element A [2000]).

However, the use of i as index expression is strictly speaking illegal when i is declared of type integer, because the type of i does not match the index type of array A (Section 6.2.1). If this were true, there is hardly a way around applying a trick as mentioned above. But the report is sufficiently vague at this point as to allow a different interpretation. The crucial phrase used in the report is that index expression and index type must "correspond" (Section 7.2.1), whereas in similar situations the phrasing "same type" or "identical type" is used (Sections 6.2.1, 8, 9.1.1, 9.2.3.3). The correct interpretation of the word "correspond" seems to be that at runtime the evaluated expression must happen to be in the subrange as determined by the array type definition. It will interest advocates of compile time checks to find out that this interpretation implies at least as much checking at runtime as when ranges are not considered as types.

Our previous experience suggests that we program the search for prime numbers by means of a **for** statement.

> **for** $i:=2$ **to** 1999 **do**
> **if** $A[i]\neq 0$ **then**
> **begin** $PRINT$ (i); erase all multiples of i **end.**

A new difficulty arises when we program "erase all multiples of i." We would like to go through array A in steps of i, but Pascal provides only a fixed step element of one or minus one. We can, of course, create a range that can be stepped through in steps of one and compute the index value into array A as a function of the successive elements of this range. We then get:

> **for** $k:=1$ **to** 1999 **div** i **do** $A[k*i]:=0$.

Programming "erase all multiples of i" this way incurs paying the price of an integer division and a multiplication that is repeatedly evaluated. We can avoid the latter at the cost of an additional variable that holds the value of the index expression. The declaration of this variable must be added to the program heading and it turns out that a subrange type cannot easily be used as type for any of the variables for which this would make sense.

A simpler program is obtained, after all, if "erase all multiples of i" is programmed as a **while** statement. We won't pursue, however, the details any further, because the program is not really important here. The purpose of the exercise was merely to show that a teacher who uses Pascal cannot avoid discussion of language peculiarities just as he would when he used another programming language.

4 LABELS AND goto STATEMENTS

It is surprising that in the design of a tutorial language the issue of programming without **goto** statements is totally ignored. This does not seem to be very much in the spirit of structured programming as presented in Dijkstra (1972). But even so, the secondary aim of Pascal to provide a fast language system should have prevented inclusion of the **goto** statement because of the trouble it causes in a compiler, especially in a one pass compiler. An example of the difficulties a one pass compiler has to cope with because of labels and goto statements is sketched below.

```
procedure P; label 1;
    procedure Q;
        procedure R; begin — goto 1; — goto 1; — end {R};
        begin — goto 1; — goto 1; — 1: end {Q};
    begin — goto 1; — goto 1 — 1: end {P};
```

A non-local label requires a forward declaration as in procedure P. It seems as if the **goto** statements in procedures Q and R refer to that label. However, the label at the end of Q definitely changes the interpretation of the goto statements in Q.

At this point we may conclude that the program is in error because label 1 should have been declared as global in the heading of procedure Q (Section 10). But further scanning leads ultimately to a label defined at the end of procedure P for which a global definition certainly makes sense, so the conclusion may be that no mistake was made after all. If the **goto** statement should be incorporated, it probably ought to be restricted to local labels. A separate provision can be made for jumping to error handling procedures that cause an automatic change of scope.

The Revised Report is sometimes vague and probably mistaken in other places about labels and the consequences of **goto** statements. First, it is doubtful whether or not a label in front of the statement part of a procedure declaration is considered as "in the procedure" or not (see Section 9.1.3). We assume it is, because otherwise the problem arises that control could be transferred to such a labelled statement without activation of the procedure. Second, in the Revised Report, the scope of a label is defined to be the procedure within which it is defined (Section 9.1.3). We assume that it is a mistake that functions are not mentioned in the scope rule for labels, because it seems at least as strange to jump into a function as into a procedure. Finally, the change in scope definition from compound statement, as in the original Report, to procedure and the absence of block structure together cause the notorious problem of jumping into a **for** statement. There is nothing in Pascal that prevents this and it seems hard to impose this restriction gracefully given the definition of Pascal.

The Revised Report resolves the ambiguity of labels and case labels as it existed in the original Report by using comma as separator between case labels, by using colon as separator between the rightmost case label and the statement label, and by restricting the number of statement labels to one.

The statement

```
4: case i of
    1, 2: 3: goto 3;
        4: goto 4;
    5: 6: goto 5;
    6: 5: goto 6
   end
```

is then correct according to the Revised Report, but realize that the first alternative is the only one that, once selected, repeats merely itself.

5 SUBRANGES, TYPES, AND STRUCTURES

The most unsatisfactory aspect of the Pascal language is the artificial unification of subranges, types and structures. This has a negative effect on the tutorial qualities of the language, it conveys a narrow view on types as merely ordered sets of values and it causes problems for the programmer as will be shown below.

It turns out that subranges cannot consistently be treated as types and vice versa. E.g., using scalar types as subranges legalizes the declaration

var A: **array** [*real*] **of** *integer*.

The program exercise in the preceding section presented several examples of the difficulties that arise if subranges are strictly treated as types with respect to expressions, control ranges and index expressions. Such problems of interpretation are not just restricted to subranges of type integer as is shown in the example below.

```
case succ (d) of
    Tuesday, Thursday, Friday: S1;
    Wednesday, Saturday: S2
   end
```

Suppose variable d is declared of subrange type workday, which is defined as subrange Monday . . . Friday. The case expression $succ(d)$ is also of type workday if we hold on to the strict interpretation, so the statement contains a type conflict because of label Saturday (Section 9.2.2.2). Another question is how $succ(d)$ should be interpreted when $d =$ Friday, because Friday has no successor in type workday.

The idea of treating subranges as types is completely abandoned in case of assignment statements, because the type of the variable is even allowed to be a subrange of the type of the expression to be assigned (Section 9.1.1). One may expect that the same rules apply to value parameters, although nothing is said about subranges in Section 9.1.2.

Instead of considering subranges as types, the following rules should apply

1. The type of an object in Pascal declared of subrange type, *st*, is the type of the super-range of which *st* is a section.
2. Ranges are evaluated and tested at runtime. It would be feasible to consider Pascal subrange declarations as type declarations with a range attribute for runtime checks.

Consider subsequently the treatment of structures as types. The Pascal language has four fixed structuring rules indicated by the word delimiters **array, record, set** and **file.** A useful rule in Pascal is the composition of array and record structures such as

> **type** $R =$ **record** *vec*: **array** [1 . . . 10] **of** integer **end;**
> $A =$ **array** [1 . . . 10] **of array** [1 . . . 10] **of** R; **var** *s*:A

Although the Revised Report contains only one trivial example of accessing such structures or their components (Section 7.2.2), a Pascal compiler test showed that all useful constructs are accepted on the left hand side of an assignment statement: *s, s*[*i*], *s*[*i*][*j*], *s*[*i*][*j*].*vec* and *s*[*i*][*j*].*vec*[*k*].

However, the composition rule is not enough to justify the idea of treating structures as types. It turns out that in all relevant language constructs, except assignments, structures are, or ought to be, treated differently from simple type objects or pointers in Pascal. One has access to elements of a structure, but (of course) not to the structure of a simple typed object or pointer. Structured objects cannot be used as operands in algebraic expressions and should not be used as index expressions. The default parameter passing rule for simple types and pointers is by value, but the default rule for structures should be by reference. Range expressions in array declarations and control statements such as for statements or case statements can be of certain simple types, but should not be structures. So, the similarity of treatment in assignment statements does apparently not carry over to any other language construct.

The notion of simple type attempts to distinguish somewhat between types and structures, but, unfortunately, structures sneak in again by means of type identifiers. The declaration *v*:A parses variable *v* as being of simple type (Section 6.1), so the declaration

> **var** *p*: **array** [A] **of** *v*

is legal in a procedure. Observe that this declaration is legal irrespective of how type A is defined! It could be defined as array or file or even a composition of those.

A useful distinction between types and structures is based on two principles: (1) a typed object is treated as an atomic entity, i.e., the type definition hides the structure of the objects, whereas elements of a structure can be accessed anywhere within the scope of existence; (2) the major constituent of a structured type definition is the set of operations that can be performed on the objects of the type, whereas

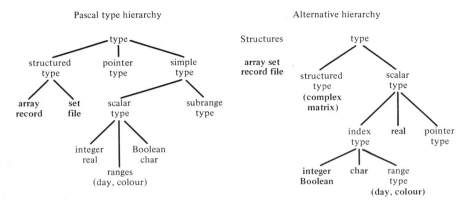

Figure 1

changes of structures are solely accomplished through operations on the elements.

Array and record are examples of structures, matrix and complex are examples of types. The representation of the latter can be changed radically without affecting the use of the typed objects.

The type hierarchy of Pascal is compared with the proper type hierarchy in Figure 1.

6 PROCEDURES, FUNCTIONS, AND PARAMETERS

In the original version of Pascal an attempt was made to avoid side-effects in functions by means of the rule that assignments to non-local variables were not allowed. This attempt failed, of course, because a side-effect could also be caused by a procedure call or by the use of pointer variables. The restriction has therefore been left out of the Revised Report (of which fact no notice is given in Section 11 in which functions are defined).

The difference between procedure and function is now so marginal that it is really not worth keeping. If it were useful to distinguish the two in the compiler in order to check whether or not an assignment to the function identifier occurs, the compiler could easily do so by means of the presence or absence of a function type identifier in the heading. A distinction, as in BLISS, between function and routine seems much more useful, because it serves two purposes, that of improving clarity of program structure and that of efficiency during compilation and execution (Wulf et al., 1971).

We argued before that the default case of passing an array, file, set or record ought to be by reference, because call by value implies that a complete copy of the structure must be passed across to the procedure or function activation.

A concept that leads to much inefficiency, particularly at runtime, is the formal procedure or function parameter. *Example*:

```
procedure P (procedure F);
   var p, q, r: integer; x, y, z: real;
begin — F (x, y, z); — F (p, q, z); — end;
procedure A (b, c, d: integer); begin — end {A};
procedure B (u: real; v: ↑R; w: f);
   begin — end {B};

   P(A); — P(B); —
```

It is hardly possible to perform all the necessary type checking at compile time and therefore code must be generated to check the types at runtime. One solution is to require full specification of the formal procedure or function with respect to its type and the types of its parameters. This would be consistent with the requirement for full specification of any other formal. It would have made much more sense if attention had been paid to this kind of consideration and simple forms of procedures or functions than to eliminating side-effects or creating an artificial distinction between procedures and functions.

7 THE REVISED REPORT

The description of the semantics is rather inaccurate and incomplete at times. Some of the changes have been indicated, but several major revisions remain unmentioned. E.g., the scope rules for labels in Section 9.1.3, the removal of the assignment restriction in functions, several type productions in Section 6.

The definition of ⟨base type⟩ is an example of the inaccuracy of the Report. The semantics of Section 6.2.3 describe ⟨base type⟩ as being not structured type. From the production ⟨type⟩ at the beginning of Section 6 we conclude that ⟨base type⟩ apparently goes to ⟨simple type⟩ or ⟨pointer type⟩; but the production in Section 6.2.3 for ⟨base type⟩ excludes ⟨pointer type⟩. And there are many more. The general experience is that one can start at an arbitrary point in the Revised Report on Pascal and will inevitably find a little mistake or a not precisely described notion after a while. A constant has no type; yet, the definitions of subrange and case statement depend on the type of constants. What are we to think of undefined notions as "corresponding types," "operations," "outside a procedure" etc.? Right at the beginning the notation { } is introduced. Yet, when it should be applied for the first time, the superfluous symbols * and ⊕ are used. First we learn that the functions *succ* and *pred* apply to arguments of scalar type. When subranges are introduced, nothing is said about these functions in spite of the fact that subrange type is not included in scalar type (Section 6.1). Yet in Section 11 we find that the functions *succ* and *pred* apply to both types. All these flaws, omissions and inconsistencies demonstrate that it may not be so easy to achieve precision and consistency in an informal description as was suggested in the introduction of the original Report (Section 1).

8 CONCLUSION

The result of designing the Pascal language is disappointing in view of the high spirits and strong statements in the introduction of the original Report. It is nice that a programmer can define types, but a type should not merely be viewed as a value range. We saw that subranges can hardly be treated as types, while structures and types do not allow a similar treatment in any language construct except, apparently, in assignments.

Paying attention to tutorial qualities of a language is laudable, but unacceptable in this regard are the confusion of subranges, types and structures, the inclusion of **goto** statements and the inferior presentation of the language in the Revised Report. It is worthwhile to strive for a language that can be supported by an efficient programming system, but this objective should not have led to the exclusion of some well-defined concepts present in other languages, whereas it should have resulted in better specification and substitution rules for parameters and a useful distinction between functions and procedures.

It would be regrettable if Pascal is going to be fixed in its present state, as the introduction of the Revised Report seems to do. There are still many fundamental language design issues to be discussed in general. Among the practical points are:

- Grouping of statements by means of bracket pairs or control delimiters
- Initialization in declarations
- Simple assignment operations of the sort "add to variable"

Among the major issues are:

- Type definitions as a template for structured objects [cf. mode and operation definitions ALGOL 68 (van Wijngaarden, 1969) and the class concept in SIMULA 67 (Dahl et al., 1967)]
- Structure definitions as a description of the access algorithm to elements of an instance of a structure
- Control statements and rules for leaving scopes of control

A small language of the Pascal sort can, of course, provide only limited capabilities with regard to these major issues. It is therefore acceptable that Pascal has fixed structuring rules, but viewing subranges and structures as types is a deplorable oversimplification. The value of the Pascal design and implementation effort is in stimulating research and development of language constructs in view of the present state of the art of programming. However, the language will defeat its purpose if it is going to be consolidated in its present form with all its flaws and inconsistencies for the sake of compatibility. Instead of presenting a particular language as **the** solace, we had better continue a discussion on language issues and analyze their impact on programming systems.

ACKNOWLEDGMENT

Comment by Profs. D. Gries and J. J. Horning has been most helpful to improve the presentation of this study.

O. LECARME
Laboratoire d'Informatique, Université de Nice, Nice, France

P. DESJARDINS
Départemente d'Informatique, Université de Montréal, Montreal, Canada

More Comments on the Programming Language Pascal

1 INTRODUCTION

We read with much interest and some miscontentment the paper "Critical comments on the programming language Pascal" by A. N. Habermann (1973). The interest was instigated by our current involvement with this language, and the miscontentment occasioned by the (sometimes unduly) strong attacks the paper makes on a language we like. We like it because, for three years now, we have been using it intensively, with complete success, as a support for teaching introductory and advanced courses in computer science (a first course on programming, and courses on data structures, compilers and operating systems design), and as an implementation tool for a compiler writing system (Lecarme and Bochmann, 1974) and for another Pascal compiler (Desjardins, 1973).

The aim of the present reply is to correct the unfavourable impression that readers, without any knowledge of Pascal, could get from Habermann's criticisms. We will not follow his argumentation point by point, but rather classify the subject matter into four parts: clearly refutable points, points which are at least debatable, valid criticisms and finally misunderstandings and minor errors. Although this plan may occasionally cause some problems to the reader who tries to go through Habermann's paper simultaneously, we believe it to be the only logical one. Thus, we strongly urge the reader to go through the whole of Habermann's paper first, so that he can see the debate in the proper perspective.

Since all the key texts on Pascal can now easily be obtained, we encourage the reader to mould his own opinion by reading Hoare and Wirth (1973), Jensen and Wirth (1974), and Wirth (1971b). One should notice, however, that Habermann

157

based his paper exclusively on the first version of the Revised Report (Wirth, 1974a) and only it (the Revised Report is now a part of Jensen and Wirth (1974)). The Axiomatic Description (Hoare and Wirth, 1973) was not available at the time he wrote his comments; this would allow for certain misinterpretations.

2 REFUTABLE POINTS

In this section, we deal with points which are, in our opinion, clearly refutable, i.e. criticisms which resulted from a misinterpretation of the basic aims of Pascal or a misunderstanding of some major aspects of the language itself. It is possible that some people might have preferred a different repartition of points between this section and the following one.

2.1 Useful Constructs Not Included in Pascal

Habermann suggests four such constructs, but it would be very easy to continue adding constructs to the language indefinitely: Pascal does not contain all the constructs which may be considered useful, nor even all those present in other programming languages. This is because creation of an endless list of constructs is clearly not the right direction to follow for the development of better programming languages. The most unfortunate attempt in this direction is that of PL/I (PL/I language specifications, n.d.), and even its most irreclaimable addicts and most enthusiastic eulogists always seem to find more constructs to incorporate in it (Dijkstra, 1972a; Holt, 1973; Sykes, 1972).

In fact, one of the principal strengths of Pascal is that it is a simple and concise language, including only what is vital for reaching its aims. We remind the reader that there are only two of them: to allow the teaching of programming as a systematic discipline, and at the same time to be implementable in a reliable and efficient way. These objectives are precisely the most difficult ones to reach when using languages which try to incorporate all "useful constructs." The author of Pascal has therefore severely restricted the number of facilities, and it is quite sure that almost everyone will find missing certain of his favourite constructs. Consequently, we find not valid as a whole the criticism that Pascal does not contain some feature or other. The individual importance of the specific "left out" constructs Habermann regrets constitutes yet another point, less decidable, which is deferred until Section 3.

2.2 An Exercise in Programming in Pascal

The simple exercise worked out for the reader by Habermann is supposed to prove that Pascal is a poor tool for teaching programming. All that such an example demonstrates is simply that it is possible to misuse Pascal, which is of course true for any tool. Consequently, we prefer to rework the part of the example which is given, to show that in actual Pascal no difficulties arise.

The problem is to compute prime numbers using the sieve of Eratosthenes. A comparison of the different algorithms available, even superficially, should be useful before trying to put down a solution (Dijkstra, 1972b; Wirth, 1974b), but this precise algorithm is not so bad, and it has been particularly well investigated by Dijkstra (1972b), Hoare (1974a), and Wirth (Jensen and Wirth, 1974; Wirth, 1973).

Habermann chooses to represent the numbers between *2* and *n* by an array of integers, in which every element contains its own index: to remove a number from the sieve, one assigns a zero to the corresponding element. Although using the set structure of Pascal should be far better (Hoare, 1974a; Jensen and Wirth, 1974), we shall use simply a Boolean array, not only because it seems more natural but because we will encounter the same problems with indexes as Habermann did. A natural way to start-off the program is:

```
const n=1999;
type index=2 . . n;
var A:array [index] of Boolean; i:index;
begin for i:=2 to n do A [i]:=true
```

The constant and type declarations for *n* and *index* are not mandatory but very useful: they contribute to the clarity of the program; the number *1999* textually appears in only one place; a modification of the program to deal with *3000* or *200* numbers would require modification of the constant declaration only.

Using as pretext the ideas of Dijkstra (1971), Habermann then proposes to replace the **for** statement by a **repeat** statement. This modification is completely useless, since the **for** statement is perfectly adapted to situations where the number of iterations is known before entering the loop. Moreover, the program could become less efficient, and surely be less clear. But the modification brings forth an interesting point: in a **repeat** or **while** loop simulating a **for** loop, the control variable needs to take on one more value than in the **for** loop. This is not inherent to Pascal but to the meaning of these statements. The natural solution in Pascal is to declare *i* on a subrange longer by one than the index type of *A*:

```
const n=1999;
type index=2 . . n; extendedindex=1 . . n;
var A: array [index] of Boolean; i: extendedindex;
begin i:=1;
    repeat i:=i+1; A [i]:=true
    until i=n
```

Furthermore, there is no problem in using the operator $+$, since all operators which are defined on integer operands also accept operands whose type is a subrange of the type *integer*. This is quite obvious; otherwise, there would have been no point in defining subrange types. Furthermore, all the above is clearly stated in the Axiomatic Description of Pascal (Hoare and Wirth, 1973), as we shall see in Section 2.3. Habermann deserves credit for having pointed out the problem, without ever having read the Axiomatic Description. Similarly, there would be no problem if we choose to write $i:=succ(i)$ instead of $i:=i+1$: as a general rule the *succ* function does not depend on whether or not its argument was declared to be of a scalar type or of a subrange of that type. So in the case of $succ(i)$ when $i=1999$, the successor value is defined since *1999* does have a successor in the base type *integer*. Finally, the fact that the index type of *A* is not the same as the type of *i* is no problem either; both have the same base type, i.e. *integer*, and the only validity condition for array references is that index values fall within array bounds, as in all programming languages. Of course, if the programmer wishes to forego the advantages obtained by using subrange types—namely the implicit checks upon assignment—he may also declare *i* to be of type *integer*.

The next section of the program deals with the search for prime numbers, and is straightforward. Add a variable *k* of type *0 . . n* (which can, for the sake of simplicity, serve also for *i*) then:

```
for i:=2 to n do
if A[i] then
begin write (i);
      {erase all multiples of i:}
      k:=0;
      while k≦n−i do
      begin k:=k+i; A[k]:=false end
end
```

Habermann's example stops here, consequently so does ours. The conclusion derived by Habermann was that "a teacher who uses Pascal cannot avoid discussion of language peculiarities just as he would when he used another programming language." We have already said at the beginning of the present section that one can, without proving anything, misuse any language. What seems more serious to us is that this section, as well as the remainder of Habermann's paper, places criticisms of the style of the Report, and criticisms of the language itself, on the same level, and incorrect interpretations which may result from the former are used to try to discredit the latter, by systematically using its possibilities at the wrong time.

2.3 Subranges and Types

One of the most original aspects of Pascal is the whole notion of type. To use the same terminology as Habermann, this one notion unifies different concepts which may be named "type" (the manner in which bit patterns must be interpreted), "range" (the set of possible values for a variable of the given type) and "structure" (a template for storing data). It is our intention to put off the discussion on structured types until Section 3.5, and to tackle here the rest of the question.

One must not fear that declaring a variable of subrange types makes that variable lose all the properties of the base type from which the subrange is taken. On the contrary, this variable inherits all the properties of the base type, plus the possibility of having run-time checks performed whenever values are assigned to that variable and also the property of possibly taking up less space in memory. Another most important point to understand is that the type of an expression is not always the same as the types of variables in it. This is true even in FORTRAN or ALGOL 60: for example, in ALGOL 60, *1/2* is of type *real* while its operands are of type *integer*, and 1 < 2 is of type *Boolean*. The Axiomatic Description of Pascal is perfectly clear on the matter. Given a scalar type T and a subrange type S extracted from T, if a and b are variables of type S and $\otimes$ an operator defined on type T, then the expression $a \otimes b$ is legal, and yields a result of type T. The assignment statement is handled in a similar way, but assignment of a value of type T to a variable of type S is not always legal.

Of course it is true that most of the validity checks involved in subrange types must be made at run time, but it is an easy thing to have them performed only when the user requests so (or better still, always have them made, unless the user explicitly says otherwise); moreover, they constitute an invaluable security device. It would be best to view such a dynamic check as nothing but application of the type transfer function into the subrange type, a function which happens to be only partial. Subranges have other important qualities. Their mnemonic and descriptive value is such that a well-written Pascal program generally does not contain integer variables: they are replaced by variables whose type is a subrange of type integer. Another important aspect is that they allow the user to control the space occupied by a variable of subrange type, for example when he includes one as an element of a packed structured type; this is much more general than the *long* and *short* attributes of *real* and *int* types in ALGOL 68 (van Wijngaarden et al., 1969).

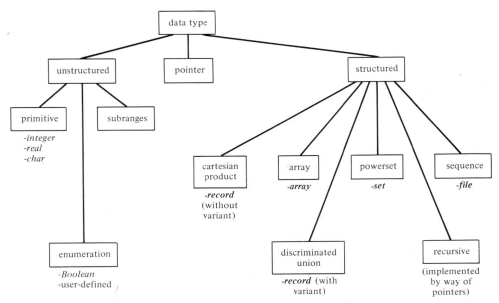

Figure 1

Section 5 of Habermann's paper concludes with a tree diagram supposed to represent the type hierarchy in Pascal. A more correct version of this diagram appears in Figure 1. It uses Hoare's terminology (1972), since Pascal implements most of the ideas presented in this paper. Of course, this hierarchy is not the "proper" one, but only that of Pascal.

2.4 Miscellaneous

In Section 2.2, Habermann writes in an example the expression $u[i]*u[i]$, and adds as comment that Pascal has no operator for exponentiation. Precisely to cover this case, Pascal offers the function $sqr(x)$, which squares its argument (*real, integer* or subrange thereof). For most compilers, the generated code for a multiplication would be better than the one for $u[i]\uparrow 2$, which would probably require evaluation of a logarithm and an exponential. More generally, the exponentiation operator was not made a part of Pascal for the sake of simplicity and clarity. If one tries to completely describe it, for all valid and invalid combinations of operand types, signs and precisions, one inevitably obtains several pages of complicated explanations and tables (PL/I (F) reference manual, n.d.). Moreover, the ground rule that the type of all results must be evident at compile time would be violated in the case $i\uparrow j$, at least if one insists that it be *integer* if $j \geqq 0$.

Another clearly refutable suggestion is the one which Habermann makes in Section 6, to have a default passing mode for structured values in procedure calls. Such a proposal would only introduce an incoherent particular case into the language, making programs less clear. The example of PL/I clearly shows the danger of default options which depend on context and on the nature of objects, especially in parameter passing. One of the basic principles of Pascal is to hide nothing from its user, and to do nothing in his place, as would be the case if a parameter was supposed to be variable simply because it was a structured one. The precise choice of the best suited passing mode is another problem, which must be decided by the user himself, taking into account the type of the parameters and their utilization within the procedure.

3 DEBATABLE POINTS

In this section, we deal with points on which reasonable people can disagree in all honesty. Generally, the direction chosen in Pascal is clearly not the only reasonable one, and a different approach would surely have its qualities. However, the solutions taken for Pascal generally fit well in the whole philosophy of the language, especially as to clarity and simplicity.

3.1 Block Structure

Pascal does not provide a block structure in exactly the same sense as ALGOL 60 (Naur, 1963), since all declarations are made at the procedure level, the program itself being a degenerate procedure. Therefore, it is not possible to open a block in the middle of another, simply by introducing some declarations after the **begin** symbol. However, it is important to clearly distinguish between the different possibilities given by the block structure of ALGOL 60, and to see which possibilities Pascal lacks because of its different approach. Both languages provide dynamic storage allocation of variables, as well as the notion of locality of declarations. Only ALGOL 60 offers the possibility of including two disjoint blocks within a single other one, thus saving storage by assigning variables of both blocks to the same area. In Pascal, this economy is only possible at the procedure level.

The advantage of the approach taken in Pascal is, once more, that of simplicity. Declarations are clearly separated from instructions, being grouped between the heading and the body of procedures (and functions). The **begin** symbol has only one purpose, which cannot be modified by what follows it. Another source of difficulty is the fact that the introduction of a declaration at the beginning of a compound statement changes the scope of every label defined within this construct.

In fact, the resulting simplification and clarification in Pascal has not proven to be disadvantageous, and our experience tends to show that for a program built in a modular and systematic way, the need for disjoint blocks which are not procedures seldom occurs. When it does, the price to pay is not heavy: define two procedures without parameters, one for each block, and call them in place of the blocks. The block then becomes a particular case of a more general construct. To define as procedures the modules used during program design is more general and natural than to replace them with disjoint blocks. In fact, it is a logical consequence of top-down design, which is one of the bases of structured and systematic programming. Habermann argues that the block of ALGOL 60 allows better locality of declarations, which is of course true. But what he fails to mention is that this type of structuring concept can also have harmful effects (Shaw and Wulf, 1973). One intermediate solution could be a syntactic device similar to the monitor (Hoare, 1974b), which Brinch Hansen proposes to implement in Pascal (Brinch Hansen, 1974).

3.2 Dynamic Arrays

The bounds of an array declared in Pascal must be known at compilation time, so changing these bounds implies recompilation of the program. Although generations of programmers have submitted daily to this constraint when using FORTRAN, it is true it is an inconvenience. However, it is worth examining the magnitude of this inconvenience, and to see whether it is not compensated by some advantages. The problem of array parameters is yet another issue, the discussion of which is deferred until Section 4.1.

It is true that the cost of dynamic local arrays is quite small on machines with displacement addressing and good integer multiplication. Nevertheless it is also true that in this case, the compiler has to generate code in order to check that the index expression in $a[3]$ is within bounds; that compilers working on computers having immediate-type instructions cannot make use of those time-saving instructions in code sequences involved with array bounds checking.

One of the most important aspects to be considered is the consequences involved in allowing dynamic arrays as components of other arrays, records or files: in a language striving to be both general and simple, the added complexity in the behaviour of such structures would certainly not be helpful to the user. Furthermore, the implementor would have the choice either to ignore the special case of fixed bounds and thus deteriorate performances of all programs, including those not using dynamic arrays, or to try to optimize when possible, obtaining an optimizing compiler hampered with bulkiness, unreliability and consequently higher maintenance cost (Wirth, 1974c).

The facilities for constant and type declarations in Pascal make it extremely easy to simultaneously change the bounds of one or several arrays, subrange declarations, limits of loop and any other points regarding the arrays involved; see for example the partial programs in Section 2.2. Moreover, to be able to choose array bounds at run time frequently leads the programmer to leave the user with the responsibility of choosing sufficient limits, checking that they are not overflowed, and even of counting his data by hand.

3.3 Conditional Expressions

Habermann judges that the statement $i:=$**if** $i=7$ **then** 1 **else** $i+1$ expresses more clearly than the statement **if** $i=7$ **then** $i:=1$ **else** $i:=i+1$ that a certain value is assigned to i. This point seems to be at the very least debatable, and our experience suggests that ALGOL 60 programmers use almost exclusively the second form, which has the advantage of allowing the replacement of either of the two assignments by a compound statement without modifying the other. Of course, there exist some other ALGOL 60 styles, à la Lisp, which use a great deal of embedded constructs, but readability rapidly becomes a problem.

ALGOL 60 gives an intermediate and quite acceptable solution, but with the inconvenience that the same basic words have different syntactic functions. The only way to allow full generality in that sense would be (depending on the chosen point of view) to unify or to confuse the notions of statement and expression, yielding an expression language like ALGOL 68 (van Wijngaarden et al., 1969) or Bliss (Wulf et al., 1971). The consequences of such a decision for the language structure and for its compilation are very complex, and exceed by far the doubtful advantage quoted before. As may be seen in several examples in van Wijngaarden et al. (1969) or Wulf et al. (1971), the normal use of an expression language may yield formulas which are much too deeply parenthesized (be it explicitly or not) to be easily understandable. Just as the human mind can manage only small amounts of program at a time (Dijkstra, 1972b), it seems to have a mental stack of a very limited depth. This may be a more important reason for the lack of understandability of APL programs than the plethora of different operators, and it is another case of the situation where generality is contradictory with simplicity (Wirth, 1974c).

3.4 Labels and Goto Statement

This point is the most characteristic of those aspects of programming languages about which reasonable people may disagree in all honesty, as may be seen in Leavenworth (1972). Knuth is even able to disagree with himself on this issue (Knuth, 1974)!

However, let us remark that Pascal restricts the use of labels severely. They are not at all manipulable objects, they must be declared in all cases, and the effect of jumping from outside of a structured statement into that statement is not defined (although compilers will not necessarily indicate an error) (Jensen and Wirth, 1974), and so on. Since you cannot prevent the users from writing bad programs if they like to do so, and since a **goto** exiting a procedure is the simplest way to handle error cases where the structure of the program must be irreparably broken (Hoare, 1973a), the choice to maintain labels and **goto**'s in Pascal is as well defensible as the other solutions currently proposed (Leavenworth, 1972; Wulf et al., 1971).

3.5 Structured Types

As we said in Section 2.3, the notion of type in Pascal includes three different concepts, which we call type, range and structure, to use the same terminology as Habermann. The decision to name "type" that information which is used by compilers to determine a storage template, is indeed debatable, but the important question is not the appropriateness of the particular labels chosen. More important is the fact that a structured object can, in all sensible situations, be handled as an unstructured one. For example, an array may be a component of a file or another array, or a field of a record; assignments are valid for almost all objects, provided that the left-hand and right-hand sides have the same type, consequently one can in a single statement copy a record (without variant) or an array; some operators may have structured operands, for example the comparison operators for packed arrays of characters (called "strings").

The result of the approach chosen in Pascal is that the whole notion of a data type is simple and coherent, as may be seen in the tree diagram at the end of Section 2.3 (Figure 1). In this schema, all structured types are made from other types, which can themselves often be structured, but ultimately lead to unstructured types, and from there to either primitive types or enumeration-defined types. Of course, compilers may enforce some restrictions to facilitate implementation, for example they may forbid files as components of other structures, especially files of files.

The set of primitive types could indeed be extended to include, for example, complex numbers, but they have no counterpart in most hardware, and may be simulated at a very small cost using the data structuring tools offered by Pascal, with the important restriction that functions cannot return a structured result. We do not think that the lack of distinction between types, ranges and structures, by labelling all of them as type, is a source of confusion, although it may hinder somewhat the understanding and explanation of subrange type particularities.

3.6 Side-Effect in Functions

While the original Report on Pascal (Wirth, 1971a) recommended that a function make no modification to non-local variables (but did not pretend that they could not), the Revised Report does not say anything on the matter, which is regrettable. In fact, to enforce such a restriction would be extremely difficult and costly, if not impossible, unless one forbids variable parameters and procedure calls within the body of a function. This is another instance of the situation where you cannot prevent the user from writing silly programs, unless you prevent him from writing any program at all. Moreover, the Revised Report allows declaration and call of a parameterless function, which is of no use if it cannot modify any non-local variable. Such functions **are** useful in some cases, and several standard functions have (or sometimes have) no parameter.

4 VALID CRITICISMS

This section deals with points which are indeed deficiencies in Pascal, and should perhaps be changed in a future version of the language (if possible). The brevity of this section is in itself a good argument in favour of Pascal.

4.1 Array Parameters

Since the bounds of an array are part of its type (or, more exactly, of the type of its indexes), it is impossible to define a procedure or function which applies to arrays with differing bounds. Although this restriction may appear to be a severe one, the experiences we have had with Pascal tend to show that it occurs very infrequently. The reason is probably that, because array bounds are static, different arrays which have components of the same type and which have to be handled in the same way generally have the same bounds, not exactly fitted to the set of data during a particular run. However, the need to bind the size of parametric arrays is a serious defect in connection with the use of program libraries.

4.2 Variable Initialization

Pascal does not presently allow initialization of variables at compilation time, at least in its official version. The richness of data structuring tools makes such a possibility very difficult to define. A possible solution would be to define constructors for structured data types (Hoare, 1972), as in the following example:

```
type r = record
            name: packed array [1 . . 10] of char;
            age: integer;
            male: Boolean
         end;
var x:r;
begin x: = r ('B. Pascal', 42, true);
```

4.3 Parametric Procedures

Pascal presently contains, in one respect, a lack of rigorous specification which either leads to a certain inefficiency, if one wants to do all the necessary checks, or to a certain insecurity if they are not all done. In the specification of a function or procedure passed as a parameter (we shall say "parametric procedure"), the type and number of parameters are not specified at all, so it is generally impossible to easily detect at compile time the following error (this example is ours):

> **procedure** P (**procedure** Q); **begin** $Q(1, "A")$ **end**;
> **procedure** R (x:*Boolean*); **begin** *write*(x) **end**;
> **begin** $P(R)$ **end**

Although Pascal, in this respect, strictly adopted the rules of ALGOL 60, some restrictions have already been made to the use of parametric procedures: a parametric procedure was at first not allowed to have procedure of function parameters (Wirth, 1971a), and now it cannot have variable parameters either (Jensen and Wirth, 1974), leaving only value parameters. While useful and not constricting, these restrictions do not suffice to ensure complete security, and they are not made explicit in the syntax. However, it is easy to make the simple syntactic modification which appears below, redefining the non-terminal ⟨*formal parameter section*⟩ in Section 10 of the Revised Report.

> ⟨*formal parameter section*⟩::=⟨*parameter group*⟩|
>   **var** ⟨*parameter group*⟩|
>   **function** ⟨*procedure skeleton*⟩:⟨*type identifier*⟩
>   {, ⟨*procedure skeleton*⟩:⟨*type identifier*⟩}|
>   **procedure** ⟨*procedure skeleton*⟩ {, ⟨*procedure skeleton*⟩}
>   ⟨*procedure skeleton*⟩::=⟨*identifier*⟩|
>   ⟨*identifier*⟩ (⟨*type identifier*⟩ {, ⟨*type identifier*⟩ })

With this modification, the restrictions quoted before appear explicitly in the syntax, and the heading of our procedure P must be either

> **procedure** P(**procedure** Q(*integer, char*))

which will allow detection of an error when P is called with R as a parameter, or

> **procedure** P(**procedure** Q(*Boolean*))

which will allow rejection of the call to Q in the body of P. The verification of compatibility between formal and actual parameters of parametric procedures can thus be made completely (and cheaply) at compile time, even with a one-pass compiler, if it adopts the convention of pre-declaring procedures (see Wirth, 1974a, Section 13).

5 MISUNDERSTANDINGS AND MINOR ERRORS

We shall consider in this section only the misunderstandings and errors made by Habermann which may lead the reader to a false idea of Pascal. We shall ignore many obvious points, which any serious reader can easily rectify by himself.

5.1 Syntactic Errors in Examples

In Pascal, all declarations precede the body of a procedure or of the program. Thus, in both examples of Section 3 of Habermann's paper, **begin** should occur after the declarations. Similarly, a **begin** should be placed in front of the last line of the example in Section 6. In Section 2.2, however, this is done correctly.

One error is repeated consistently throughout the whole paper: the lower and upper limits of a subrange (in a type declaration or as an index type) should be separated by ". ." instead of ". . .".

In fact, when it is said in Section 3 that a program "results in an error indication at the operator +", an actual Pascal compiler would have indicated four errors before encountering this operator (**begin** before declarations; ". . ." in a subrange, twice; and $i=i+1$ instead of $i:=i+1$), and none at that point.

5.2 Errors Concerning the Notion of Type

At the beginning of Section 5, it is said that, since scalar types are subranges, the declaration

> **var** A: **array** [*real*] **of** *integer*

is legal. Of course, this is false: the type *real* constitutes a singular case of scalar type, since the number of values of this type is unknown. This however, is not clearly stated in the Revised Report.

Similarly, it is said near the end of the same section that, since a simple type may be represented by a type identifier, a file or array type may serve as index for an array. This is patently absurd, and it is evident that a type identifier does not always represent a simple type.

In Section 7, it is said that "a constant has no type." This is obviously false, and the Report clearly specifies in Section 4 the type of the value represented by each kind of constant.

5.3 Miscellaneous Errors

In the middle of Section 4, a question is asked "whether or not a label in front of the statement part of a procedure declaration is considered as 'in the procedure' or not." The answer is that a label is forbidden in such a place, as the Report clearly states.

6 CONCLUSION

The main point to note in conclusion of this reply is that the Report on Pascal is aimed to serve both as a defining document and as a manual and tutorial for programmers. Such a paper must necessarily rely on some natural good will on the part of the reader, unless it is to grow into PL/I-like dimensions (PL/I language specifications, n.d.; PL/I (F) reference manual, n.d.) or ALGOL 68 unreadability (van Wijngaarden et al., 1969).

The second point is that the Report has an indispensable complement and companion, the Axiomatic Description (Hoare and Wirth, 1973), which defines in a rigorous manner all the semantics of Pascal and occupies only nine printed pages. Moreover, it is quite readable.

ACKNOWLEDGMENTS

Our colleague Neil Stewart was most helpful in improving the style of this paper. Jim Horning was particularly helpful by strongly criticizing the emotional and technical contents of a first version. Finally, we must thank Dave Gries and the referee for pertinent suggestions and thorough study of our argumentation.

BRIAN W. KERNIGHAN

Bell Laboratories, Murray Hill, New Jersey

Why Pascal Is Not My Favorite

Programming Language

1 GENESIS

This paper has its origins in two events—a spate of papers that compare C and Pascal (Feuer and Gehani, 1982; Mateti, 1979; Springer, 1979) and a personal attempt to rewrite *Software Tools* (Kernighan and Plauger, 1976) in Pascal.

Comparing C and Pascal is rather like comparing a Learjet to a Piper Cub— one is meant for getting something done while the other is meant for learning—so such comparisons tend to be somewhat farfetched. But the revision of *Software Tools* seems a more relevant comparison. The programs therein were originally written in Ratfor, a "structured" dialect of FORTRAN implemented by a preprocessor. Since Ratfor is really FORTRAN in disguise, it has few of the assets that Pascal brings— data types more suited to character processing, data structuring capabilities for better defining the organization of one's data, and strong typing to enforce telling the truth about the data.

It turned out to be harder than I had expected to rewrite the programs in Pascal. This paper is an attempt to distill out of the experience some lessons about Pascal's suitability for programming (as distinguished from learning about programming). It is *not* a comparison of Pascal with C or Ratfor.

The programs were first written in that dialect of Pascal supported by the Pascal interpreter *pi* provided by the University of California at Berkeley. The language is close to the nominal standard of Jensen and Wirth (1978), with good diagnostics and careful run-time checking. Since then, the programs have also been run, unchanged except for new libraries of primitives, on four other systems: an interpreter from the Free University of Amsterdam (hereinafter referred to as VU, for Vrije Universiteit), a VAX version of the Berkeley system (a true compiler), a compiler purveyed by Whitesmiths, Ltd., and UCSD Pascal on a Z80. All but the last of these Pascal systems are written in C.

Pascal is a much-discussed language. A recent bibliography (Moffat, 1980) lists 175 items under the heading of "discussion, analysis and debate." The most often cited papers (well worth reading) are a strong critique by Habermann (1973) and an equally strong rejoinder by Lecarme and Desjardins (1975). The paper by Boom and De Jong (1980) is also good reading. Wirth's own assessment of Pascal is found in Wirth (1975). I have no desire or ability to summarize the literature; this paper represents my personal observations and most of it necessarily duplicates points made by others. I have tried to organize the rest of the material around the issues of

> Types and scope
> Control flow
> Environment
> Cosmetics

and within each area more or less in decreasing order of significance.

To state my conclusions at the outset: Pascal may be an admirable language for teaching beginners how to program; I have no first-hand experience with that. It was a considerable achievement for 1968. It has certainly influenced the design of recent languages, of which Ada is likely to be the most important. But in its standard form (both current and proposed), Pascal is not adequate for writing real programs. It is suitable only for small, self-contained programs that have only trivial interactions with their environment and that make no use of any software written by anyone else.

2 TYPES AND SCOPES

Pascal is (almost) a strongly typed language. Roughly speaking, that means that each object in a program has a well-defined type which implicitly defines the legal values of and operations on the object. The language guarantees that it will prohibit illegal values and operations, by some mixture of compile- and run-time checking. Of course compilers may not actually do all the checking implied in the language definition. Furthermore, strong typing is *not* to be confused with dimensional analysis. If one defines types *apple* and *orange* with

> **type**
>> apple = integer;
>> orange = integer;

han any arbitrary arithmetic expression involving apples and oranges is perfectly legal.

Strong typing shows up in a variety of ways. For instance, arguments to functions and procedures are checked for proper type matching. Gone is the FORTRAN freedom to pass a floating point number into a subroutine that expects an integer; this I deem a desirable attribute of Pascal, since it warns of a construction that will certainly cause an error.

Integer variables may be declared to have an associated range of legal values, and the compiler and run-time support ensure that one does not put large integers into variables that only hold small ones. This too seems like a service, although of course run-time checking does exact a penalty.

Let us move on to some problems of type and scope.

2.1 The Size of an Array Is Part of Its Type

If one declares

    var arr 10 : array [1 . . 10] of integer;
        arr 20 : array [1 . . 20] of integer;

then *arr10* and *arr20* are arrays of 10 and 20 integers respectively. Suppose we want to write a procedure *sort* to sort an integer array. Because *arr10* and *arr20* have different types, it is not possible to write a single procedure that will sort them both.

The place where this affects *Software Tools* particularly, and I think programs in general, is that it makes it difficult indeed to create a library of routines for doing common, general-purpose operations like sorting.

The particular data type most often affected is *array of char*, for in Pascal a string is an array of characters. Consider writing a function *index (s, c)* that will return the position in the string *s* where the character *c* first occurs, or zero if it does not. The problem is how to handle the string argument of *index*. The calls *index ('hello',c)* and *index('goodbye',c)* cannot both be legal, since the strings have different lengths. (I pass over the question of how the end of a constant string like 'hello' can be detected, because it can't.)

The next try is

    var temp : array [1 . . 10] of char;
    temp := 'hello';
    n := index(temp,c);

but the assignment to *temp* is illegal because 'hello' and *temp* are of different lengths.

The only escape from this infinite regress is to define a family of routines with a member for each possible string size, or to make all strings (including constant strings like 'define') of the same length.

The latter approach is the lesser of two great evils. In *Tools,* a type called *string* is declared as

    type string = array [1 . . MAXSTR] of char;

where the constant *MAXSTR* is "big enough," and all strings in all programs are exactly this size. This is far from ideal, although it made it possible to get the programs running. It does *not* solve the problem of creating true libraries of useful routines.

There are some situations where it is simply not acceptable to use the fixed-size array representation. For example, the *Tools* program to sort lines of text operates by filling up memory with as many lines as will fit; its running time depends strongly on how full the memory can be packed. Thus for sort, another representation is used, a long array of characters and a set of indices into this array:

type charbuf = **array** [1 . . MAXBUF] **of** char;
          charindex = **array** [1 . . MAXINDEX] **of** 0 . . MAXBUF;

But the procedures and functions written to process the fixed-length representation cannot be used with the variable-length form; an entirely new set of routines is needed to copy and compare strings in this representation. In Fortran or C the same functions could be used for both.

As suggested above, a constant string is written as

'this is a string'

and has the type **packed array** [*1 . . n*] **of** *char*, where *n* is the length. Thus each string literal of different length has a different type. The only way to write a routine that will print a message and clean up is to pad all messages out to the same maximum length:

error('short message   ');
error('this is a somewhat longer message');

Many commercial Pascal compilers provide a string data type that explicitly avoids the problem; strings are all taken to be the same type regardless of size. This solves the problem for this single data type, but no other. It also fails to solve secondary problems like computing the length of a constant string; another built-in function is the usual solution.

Pascal enthusiasts often claim that to cope with the array-size problem one merely has to copy some library routine and fill in the parameters for the program at hand, but the defense sounds weak at best (Lecarme and Desjardins, 1975, p. 239):

> Since the bounds of an array are part of its type (or, more exactly, of the type of its indexes), it is impossible to define a procedure or function which applies to arrays with differing bounds. Although this restriction may appear to be a severe one, the experiences we have had with Pascal tend to show that it tends to occur very infrequently. [. . .] However, the need to bind the size of parametric arrays is a serious defect in connection with the use of program libraries.

This botch is the biggest single problem with Pascal. I believe that if it could be fixed, the language would be an order of magnitude most usable. The proposed

ISO standard for Pascal (Addyman, 1980) provides such a fix ("conformant array schemas"), but the acceptance of this part of the standard is apparently still in doubt.

2.2 There Are No Static Variables and No Initialization

A *static* variable (often called an *own* variable in ALGOL-speaking countries) is one that is private to some routine and retains its value from one call of the routine to the next. *De facto,* FORTRAN variables are internal static, except for COMMON;[1] in C there is a static declaration that can be applied to local variables.

Pascal has no such storage class. This means that if a Pascal function or procedure intends to remember a value from one call to another, the variable used must be external to the function or procedure. Thus it must be visible to other procedures, and its name must be unique in the larger scope. A simple example of the problem is a random number generator: the value used to compute the current output must be saved to compute the next one, so it must be stored in a variable whose lifetime includes all calls of the random number generator. In practice, this is typically the outermost block of the program. Thus the declaration of such a variable is far removed from the place where it is actually used.

One example comes from the text formatter described in Chapter 7 of *Tools*. The variable *dir* controls the direction from which excess blanks are inserted during line justification, to obtain left and right alternately. In Pascal, the code looks like this:

```
program formatter ( . . . );
var
   dir : 0 . . 1;      { direction to add extra spaces }
   :
procedure justify ( . . . );
begin
   dir := 1 − dir;      { opposite direction from last time }
   . . .
end;

   . . .

begin { main routine of formatter }
   dir := 0;
   . . .
end;
```

The declaration, initialization and use of the variable *dir* are scattered all over the program, literally hundreds of lines apart. In C or FORTRAN, *dir* can be made private to the only routine that needs to know about it:

---

[1] Strictly speaking, in FORTRAN 77 one must SAVE to force the static attribute.

```
    . . .
main( )
{
    . . .
}
    . . .
justify( )
{
    static int dir = 0;
    dir = 1 − dir;
    . . .
}
```

There are of course many other examples of the same problem on a larger scale; functions for buffered I/O, storage management, and symbol tables all spring to mind.

There are at least two related problems. Pascal provides no way to initialize variables statically (i.e., at compile time); there is nothing analogous to FORTRAN's DATA statement or initializers like

```
int dir = 0;
```

in C. This means that a Pascal program must contain explicit assignment statements to initialize variables (like the

```
    dir := 0;
```

above.) This code makes the program source text bigger, and the program itself bigger at run time.

Furthermore, the lack of initializers exacerbates the problem of too-large scope caused by the lack of a static storage class. The time to initialize things is at the beginning, so either the main routine itself begins with a lot of initialization code, or it calls one or more routines to do the initializations. In either case, variables to be initialized must be visible, which means in effect at the highest level of the hierarchy. The result is that any variable that is to be initialized has global scope.

The third difficulty is that there is no way for two routines to share a variable unless it is declared at or above their least common ancestor. FORTRAN COMMON and C's external static storage class both provide a way for two routines to cooperate privately, without sharing information with their ancestors.

The new standard does not offer static variables or initialization.

2.3 Related Program Components Must Be Kept Separate

Since the original Pascal was implemented with a one-pass compiler, the language believes strongly in declaration before use. In particular, procedures and functions must be declared (body and all) before they are used. The result is that a typical

Pascal program reads from the bottom up—all the procedures and functions are displayed before any of the code that calls them, at all levels. This is essentially opposite to the order in which the functions are designed and used.

To some extent this can be mitigated by a mechanism like the #**include** facility of C and Ratfor: source files can be included where needed without cluttering up the program. #**include** is not part of standard Pascal, although the UCB, VU and Whitesmiths compilers all provide it.

There is also a **forward** declaration in Pascal that permits separating the declaration of the function or procedure header from the body; it is intended for defining mutually recursive procedures. When the body is declared later on, the header on that may contain only the function name, and must not repeat the information from the first instance.

A related problem is that Pascal has a strict order in which it is willing to accept declarations. Each procedure or function consists of

label	*label declarations, if any*
const	*constant declarations, if any*
type	*type declarations, if any*
var	*variable declarations, if any*
procedure and **function** *declarations, if any*	
begin	
	body of function or procedure
end	

This means that all declarations of one kind (types, for instance) must be grouped together for the convenience of the compiler, even when the programmer would like to keep together things that are logically related so as to understand the program better. Since a program has to be presented to the compiler all at once, it is rarely possible to keep the declaration, initialization and use of types and variables close together. Even some of the most dedicated Pascal supporters agree (Welsh et al., 1977):

> The inability to make such groupings in structuring large programs is one of Pascal's most frustrating limitations.

A file inclusion facility helps only a little here.

The new standard does not relax the requirements on the order of declarations.

2.4 There Is No Separate Compilation

The "official" Pascal language does not provide separate compilation, and so each implementation decides on its own what to do. Some (the Berkeley interpreter, for instance) disallow it entirely; this is closest to the spirit of the language and matches the letter exactly. Many others provide a declaration that specifies that the body of a function is externally defined. In any case, all such mechanisms are non-standard, and thus done differently by different systems.

Theoretically, there is no need for separate compilation—if one's compiler is very fast (and if the source for all routines is always available and if one's compiler has a file inclusion facility so that multiple copies are not needed), recompiling everything is equivalent. In practice, of course, compilers are never fast enough and source is often hidden and file inclusion is not part of the language, so changes are time-consuming.

Some systems permit separate compilation but do not validate consistency of types across the boundary. This creates a giant hole in the strong typing. (Most other languages do no cross-compilation checking either, so Pascal is not inferior in this respect.) I have seen at least one paper (mercifully unpublished) that on page n castigates C for failing to check types across separate compilation boundaries while suggesting on page $n+1$ that the way to cope with Pascal is to compile procedures separately to avoid type checking.

The new standard does not offer separate compilation.

2.5 Some Miscellaneous Problems of Type and Scope

Most of the following points are minor irritations, but I have to stick them in somewhere.

It is not legal to name a non-basic type as the literal formal parameter of a procedure; the following is not allowed:

procedure add10 (**var** a : **array** [1 . . 10] **of** integer);

Rather, one must invent a type name, make a type declaration, and declare the formal parameter to be an instance of that type:

type a10 = **array** [1 . . 10] **of** integer;

. . .

procedure add10 (**var** a : a10);

Naturally the type declaration is physically separated from the procedure that uses it. The discipline of inventing type names is helpful for types that are used often, but it is a distraction for things used only once.

It is nice to have the declaration **var** for formal parameters of functions and procedures; the procedure clearly states that it intends to modify the argument. But the calling program has no way to declare that a variable is to be modified—the information is only in one place, while two places would be better. (Half a loaf is better than none, though—FORTRAN tells the user nothing about who will do what to variables.)

It is also a minor bother that arrays are passed by value by default—the net effect is that every array parameter is declared **var** by the programmer more or less without thinking. If the **var** declaration is inadvertently omitted, the resulting bug is subtle.

Pascal's **set** construct seems like a good idea, providing notational convenience and some free type checking. For example, a set of tests like

if (c = blank) **or** (c = tab) **or** (c = newline) **then** . . .

can be written rather more clearly and perhaps more efficiently as

if c **in** [blank, tab, newline] **then** . . .

But in practice, set types are not useful for much more than this, because the size of a set is strongly implementation dependent (probably because it was so in the original CDC implementation: 59 bits). For example, it is natural to attempt to write the function *isalphanum(c)* ("is c alphanumeric?") as

```
{ isalphanum( c ) -- true if c is letter or digit }
function isalphanum (c : char) : boolean;
begin
   isalphanum := c in ['a' . . 'z', 'A' . . 'Z', '0' . . '9']
end;
```

But in many implementations of Pascal (including the original) this code fails because sets are just too small. Accordingly, sets are generally best left unused if one intends to write portable programs. (This specific routine also runs an order of magnitude slower with sets than with a range test or array reference.)

2.6 There Is No Escape

There is no way to override the type mechanism when necessary, nothing analogous to the "cast" mechanism in C. This means that it is not possible to write programs like storage allocators or I/O systems in Pascal, because there is no way to talk about the type of object that they return, and no way to force such objects into an arbitrary type for another use. (Strictly speaking, there is a large hole in the type-checking near variant records, through which some otherwise illegal type mismatches can be obtained.)

3 CONTROL FLOW

The control flow deficiencies of Pascal are minor but numerous—the death of a thousand cuts, rather than a single blow to a vital spot.

There is no guaranteed order of evaluation of the logical operators **and** and **or**—nothing like && and | | in C. This failing, which is shared with most other languages, hurts most often in loop control:

while (i <= XMAX) **and** (x[i] > 0) **do** . . .

is extremely unwise Pascal usage, since there is no way to ensure that *i* is tested before *x[i]* is.

By the way, the parentheses in this code are mandatory—the language has only four levels of operator precedence, with relationals at the bottom.

There is no **break** statement for exiting loops. This is consistent with the one entry-one exit philosophy espoused by proponents of structured programming, but it does lead to nasty circumlocutions or duplicated code, particularly when coupled with the inability to control the order in which logical expressions are evaluated. Consider this common situation, expressed in C or Ratfor:

```
while (getnext( . . .) ) {
    if (something)
        break
    rest of loop
}
```

With no break statement, the first attempt in Pascal is

```
done := false;
while (not done) and (getnext( . . . ) ) do
    if something then
        done := true
    else begin
        rest of loop
end
```

But this doesn't work, because there is no way to force the "**not** done" to be evaluated before the next call of *getnext*. This leads, after several false starts, to

```
done := false;
while not done do begin
    done := getnext( . . . );
    if something then
        done := true
    else if not done then begin
        rest of loop
    end
end
```

Of course recidivists can use a **goto** and a label (numeric only and it has to be declared) to exit a loop. Otherwise, early exits are a pain, almost always requiring the invention of a Boolean variable and a certain amount of cunning. Compare finding the last non-blank in an array in Ratfor:

```
for (i = max; i > 0; i = i − 1)
    if (arr(i) != ' ')
        break
```

with Pascal:

```
done := false;
i := max;
while (i > 0) and (not done) do
  if arr[i] = ' ' then
    i := i - 1
  else
    done := true;
```

The index of a **for** loop is undefined outside the loop, so it is not possible to figure out whether one went to the end or not. The increment of a **for** loop can only be + 1 or − 1, a minor restriction.

There is no **return** statement, again for one in-one out reasons. A function value is returned by setting the value of a pseudo-variable (as in FORTRAN), then falling off the end of the function. This sometimes leads to contortions to make sure that all paths actually get to the end of the function with the proper value. There is also no standard way to terminate execution except by reaching the end of the outermost block, although many implementations provide a **halt** that causes immediate termination.

The **case** statement is better designed than in C, *except* that there is no default clause and the behavior is undefined if the input expression does not match any of the cases. This crucial omission renders the **case** construct almost worthless. In over 6000 lines of Pascal in *Software Tools in Pascal*, I used it only four times, although if there had been a default, a **case** would have served in at least a dozen places.

The new standard offers no relief on any of these points.

4 THE ENVIRONMENT

The Pascal run-time environment is relatively sparse, and there is no extension mechanism except perhaps source-level libraries in the "official" language.

Pascal's built-in I/O has a deservedly bad reputation. It believes strongly in record-oriented input and output. It also has a look-ahead convention that is hard to implement properly in an interactive environment. Basically, the problem is that the I/O system believes that it must read one record ahead of the record that is being processed. In an interactive system, this means that when a program is started, its first operation is to try to read the terminal for the first line of input, before any of the program itself has been executed. But in the program

```
write( 'Please enter your name: ');
read( name );
      . . .
```

read-ahead causes the program to hang, waiting for input before printing the prompt that asks for it.

It is possible to escape most of the evil effects of this I/O design by very careful implementation, but not all Pascal systems do so, and in any case it is relatively costly.

The I/O design reflects the original operating system upon which Pascal was designed; even Wirth acknowledges that bias, though not its defects (Wirth, 1975, p. 196). It is assumed that text files consist of records, that is, lines of text. When the last character of a line is read, the built-in function *eoln* becomes true; at that point, one must call *readln* to initiate reading a new line and reset *eoln*. Similarly, when the last character of the file is read, the built-in *eof* becomes true. In both cases, *eoln* and *eof* must be tested before each read rather than after.

Given this, considerable pains must be taken to simulate sensible input. This implementation of *getc* works for Berkeley and VU I/O systems, but may not necessarily work for anything else:

```
{ getc -- read character from standard input }
function getc ( var c : character ) : character;
var
   ch : char;
begin
  if eof then
     c := ENDFILE
  else if eoln then begin
     readln;
     c := NEWLINE
  end
  else begin
     read( ch );
     c := ord( ch )
  end;
   getc := c
end;
```

The type *character* is not the same as *char*, since ENDFILE and perhaps NEWLINE are not legal values for a *char* variable.

There is no notion at all of access to a file system except for predefined files named by (in effect) logical unit number in the program statement that begins each program. This apparently reflects the CDC batch system in which Pascal was originally developed. A file variable

var fv : **file of** *type*

is a very special kind of object—it cannot be assigned to, nor used except by calls to built-in procedures like *eof, eoln, read, write, reset* and *rewrite*. (*reset* rewinds a file and makes it ready for re-reading; *rewrite* makes a file ready for writing.)

Most implementations of Pascal provide an escape hatch to allow access to files by name from the outside environment, but not conveniently and not standardly. For example, many systems permit a filename argument in calls to *reset* and *rewrite*:

    reset (fv, filename);

But *reset* and *rewrite* are procedures, not functions—there is no status return and no way to regain control if for some reason the attempted access fails. (UCSD provides a compile-time flag that disables the normal abort.) And since *fv*'s can not appear in expressions like

```
reset( fv, filename );
if fv = failure then . . .
```

there is no escape in that direction either. This straightjacket makes it essentially impossible to write programs that recover from mis-spelled file names, etc. I never solved it adequately in the *Tools* revision.

There is no notion of access to command-line arguments, again probably reflecting Pascal's batch-processing origins. Local routines may allow it by adding non-standard procedures to the environment.

Since it is not possible to write a general-purpose storage allocator in Pascal (there being no way to talk about the types that such a function would return), the language has a built-in procedure called *new* that allocates space from a heap. Only defined types may be allocated, so it is not possible to allocate, for example, arrays of arbitrary size to hold character strings. The pointers returned by *new* may be passed around but not manipulated: there is no pointer arithmetic. There is no way to regain control if storage runs out.

The new standard offers no change in any of these areas.

5 COSMETIC ISSUES

Most of these issues are irksome to an experienced programmer, and some are probably a nuisance even to beginners. All can be lived with.

Pascal, in common with most other ALGOL-inspired languages, uses the semicolon as a statement separator rather than a terminator (as it is in PL/I and C). As a result one must have a reasonably sophisticated notion of what a statement is to put semicolons in properly. Perhaps more important, if one is serious about using them in the proper places, a fair amount of nuisance editing is needed. Consider the first cut at a program:

```
if a then
    b;
c;
```

But if something must be inserted before *b*, it no longer needs a semicolon, because it now precedes an **end**:

```
if a then begin
    b0;
    b
end;
c;
```

Now if we add an **else**, we *must* remove the semicolon on the **end**:

```
if a then begin
    b0;
    b
end
else
    d;
c;
```

And so on and so on, with semicolons rippling up and down the program as it evolves.

One generally accepted experimental result in programmer psychology is that semicolon as separator is about ten times more prone to error than semicolon as terminator (Gannon and Horning, 1975). (In Ada (Ichbiah et al., 1979), the most significant language based on Pascal, semicolon is a terminator.) Fortunately, in Pascal one can almost always close one's eyes and get away with a semicolon as a terminator. The exceptions are in places like declarations, where the separator vs. terminator problem doesn't seem as serious anyway, and just before **else**, which is easy to remember. C and Ratfor programmers find **begin** and **end** bulky compared to { and }.

A function name by itself is a call of that function; there is no way to distinguish such a function call from a simple variable except by knowing the names of the functions. Pascal uses the FORTRAN trick of having the function name act like a variable within the function, except that where in FORTRAN the function name really is a variable, and can appear in expressions, in Pascal, its appearance in an expression is a recursive invocation: if f is a zero-argument function, $f := f + 1$ is a recursive call of f.

There is a paucity of operators (probably related to the paucity of precedence levels). In particular, there are no bit-manipulation operators (AND, OR, XOR, etc.). I simply gave up trying to write the following trivial encryption program in Pascal:

```
i := 1;
while getc( c ) <> ENDFILE do begin
    putc( xor ( c, key[ i ] ) );
    i := i mod keylen + 1
end
```

because I couldn't write a sensible *xor* function. The set types help a bit here (so to speak), but not enough; people who claim that Pascal is a system programming language have generally overlooked this point. For example (Welsh et al., 1977, p. 685),

> Pascal is at the present time [1977] the best language in the public domain for purposes of system programming and software implementation.

seems a bit naive.

There is no null string, perhaps because Pascal uses the doubled quote notation to indicate a quote embedded in a string:

'This is a " character'

There is no way to put non-graphic symbols into strings. In fact, non-graphic characters are unpersons in a stronger sense, since they are not mentioned in any part of the standard language. Concepts like newlines, tabs, and so on are handled on each system in an *ad hoc* manner, usually by knowing something about the character set (e.g., ASCII newline has decimal value 10).

There is no macro processor. The **const** mechanism for defining manifest constants takes care of about 95 percent of the uses of simple *#define* statements in C, but more involved ones are hopeless. It is certainly possible to put a macro preprocessor on a Pascal compiler. This allowed me to simulate a sensible error procedure as

#define error(s) **begin** writeln(s); halt **end**

halt in turn might be defined as a branch to the end of the outermost block. Then calls like

error('little string');
error('much bigger string');

work since *writeln* (as part of the standard Pascal environment) can handle strings of any size. It is unfortunate that there is no way to make this convenience available to routines in general.

The language prohibits expressions in declarations, so it is not possible to write things like

const   SIZE = 10;
type   arr = **array** [1 . . SIZE + 1] **of** integer;

or even simpler ones like

const   SIZE = 10;
              SIZE1 = SIZE + 1;

6 PERSPECTIVE

The effort to rewrite the programs in *Software Tools* started in March, 1980, and, in fits and starts, lasted until January, 1981. The final product (Kernighan and Plauger, 1981) was published in June, 1981. During that time I gradually adapted to most of the superficial problems with Pascal (cosmetics, the inadequacies of control flow), and developed imperfect solutions to the significant ones (array sizes, run-time environment).

The programs in the book are meant to be complete, well-engineered programs that do non-trivial tasks. But they do not have to be efficient, nor are their interactions with the operating system very complicated, so I was able to get by with some pretty kludgy solutions, ones that simply wouldn't work for real programs.

There is no significant way in which I found Pascal superior to C, but there are several places where it is a clear improvement over Ratfor. Most obvious by far is recursion: several programs are much cleaner when written recursively, notably the pattern-search, quicksort, and expression evaluation.

Enumeration data types are a good idea. They simultaneously delimit the range of legal values and document them. Records help to group related variables. I found relatively little use for pointers.

Boolean variables are nicer than integers for Boolean conditions; the original Ratfor programs contained some unnatural constructions because FORTRAN's logical variables are badly designed.

Occasionally Pascal's type checking would warn of a slip of the hand in writing a program; the run-time checking of values also indicated errors from time to time, particularly subscript range violations.

Turning to the negative side, recompiling a large program from scratch to change a single line of source is extremely tiresome; separate compilation, with or without type checking, is mandatory for large programs.

I derived little benefit from the fact that characters are part of Pascal and not part of FORTRAN, because the Pascal treatment of strings and non-graphics is so inadequate. In both languages, it is appallingly clumsy to initialize literal strings for tables of keywords, error messages, and the like.

The finished programs are in general about the same number of source lines as their Ratfor equivalents. At first this surprised me, since my preconception was that Pascal is a wordier and less expressive language. The real reason seems to be that Pascal permits arbitrary expressions in places like loop limits and subscripts where FORTRAN (that is, portable FORTRAN 66) does not, so some useless assignments can be eliminated; furthermore, the Ratfor programs declare functions while Pascal ones do not.

To close, let me summarize the main points in the case against Pascal.

1. Since the size of an array is part of its type, it is not possible to write general-purpose routines, that is, to deal with arrays of different sizes. In particular, string handling is very difficult.

2. The lack of static variables, initialization and a way to communicate non-hierarchically combine to destroy the "locality" of a program—variables require much more scope than they ought to.

3. The one-pass nature of the language forces procedures and functions to be presented in an unnatural order; the enforced separation of various declarations scatters program components that logically belong together.

4. The lack of separate compilation impedes the development of large programs and makes the use of libraries impossible.

5. The order of logical expression evaluation cannot be controlled, which leads to convoluted code and extraneous variables.

6. The **case** statement is emasculated because there is no default clause.
7. The standard I/O is defective. There is no sensible provision for dealing with files or program arguments as part of the standard language, and no extension mechanism.
8. The language lacks most of the tools needed for assembling large programs, most notably file inclusion.
9. There is no escape.

This last point is perhaps the most important. The language is inadequate but circumscribed, because there is no way to escape its limitations. There are no casts to disable the type-checking when necessary. There is no way to replace the defective run-time environment with a sensible one, unless one controls the compiler that defines the "standard procedures." The language is closed.

People who use Pascal for serious programming fall into a fatal trap. Because the language is so impotent, it must be extended. But each group extends Pascal in its own direction, to make it look like whatever language they really want. Extensions for separate compilation, FORTRAN-like COMMON, string data types, internal static variables, initialization, octal numbers, bit operators, etc., all add to the utility of the language for one group, but destroy its portability to others.

I feel that it is a mistake to use Pascal for anything much beyond its original target. In its pure form, Pascal is a toy language, suitable for teaching but not for real programming.

ACKNOWLEDGMENTS

I am grateful to Al Aho, Al Feuer, Narain Gehani, Bob Martin, Doug McIlroy, Rob Pike, Dennis Ritchie, Chris Van Wyk and Charles Wetherell for helpful criticisms of earlier versions of this paper.

BRUCE ANDERSON
Man-Machine Laboratory, Department of Electrical Engineering Science, University of Essex
Colchester, Essex, England

Type Syntax in the Language C: An Object Lesson in Syntactic Innovation

The systems implementation language C (Kernighan and Ritchie, 1978; Ritchie et al., 1978) is now widely used, mainly because of the popularity of UNIX (Ritchie and Thompson, 1974), on the PDP-11, Interdata 8/32 and VAX machines, but also in implementations for other operating systems (RSX-11, RT-11) and processors (8086, PDP-10, IBM/370, Honeywell 6000). Fundamentally it is BCPL-like, but with explicit records and a sort of type structure. Types are built up out of basic types with type operators as in ALGOL-68 or Pascal. (The exception is that procedure declarations need give only the result type, and not that of the arguments.) While the semantics of the types are of some interest, we concentrate here on the syntax. In general the syntax of C is irregular and messy, as evidenced by

1. The difficulty of writing a formatter.
2. The large number of user errors, even amongst experienced programmers.
3. The difficulty of writing syntax analyzers for it—no two compilers accept the same syntax.
4. The lack of a definition of the syntax anywhere—even the published book admits to being only a rough guide! The type syntax is no exception.

There are three places where types are written down:

- **Declarations:** associating a type with a name, as in declaring external variables, or the formals of a procedure
- **Definitions:** associating a value (and a type) with a name, as in defining a procedure

· **Casts:** when asking for the representation of an object as of another type, as in obtaining the value of a character as integer

Corresponding examples are:

```
extern char x;
    /* x is an external of type character */
char x;
    /* x is of type character, and storage should be allocated for it here */
(int x)
    /* give the integer representation of x */
```

Here we refer only to the basic types *int* and *char*, but as mentioned above more complex types are built up by type-constructing operators. What then does

```
char (*x1( ))[ ];
```

mean? The answer is that *x1* is a function returning a pointer to an array of characters. While this example is perhaps enough for a syntactician (or cryptographer?) to deduce the notation, it seems more appropriate here to give a short tutorial! The key is that the type declaration of an object has the syntactic form of the *use* of that object. The operators, which are thus used both in describing types and in constructing C expressions, are:

*	follow pointer (i.e., the RV operator)
( )	apply function
[ ]	access array

and the * operator binds more loosely than the others. Thus if *x1* has a type as declared above:

```
(*x1(99))[7]
```

is of basic type *char*; that is, apply *x1* to 99, dereference the pointer to obtain an array, then take element 7 to obtain the character. We will now use an ALGOL 68-meets-Pascal notation (i.e., "ref" means "pointer to") in order to explain the C convention in a less cryptic fashion.

```
int x
=>      x: int
int *x
=>      *x: int =>              x: ref int
int x[ ]
=>      x[ ]: int =>           x: array of int
int x( )
=>      x( ): int =>           x: proc( ) int
```

i.e., *x* is an integer, a pointer to an integer, an array of integers, and function returning an integer, respectively.

Two classic cases are

int *x[ ]
=>   *x[ ]: int =>   x[ ]: ref int
=>   x: array of ref int

i.e., *x* is an array of pointers to integers, and

int (*x)[ ]
=>   (*x)[ ]: int =>   *x: array of int
=>   x: ref array of int

i.e., *x* is a pointer to an array of integers. Note the use of parentheses to defeat the operator precedence. Similarly for functions

char *x( )
=>   *x( ): char =>   x( ): ref char
=>   x: proc( ) ref char
char (*x)( )
=>   (*x)( ): char =>   *x: proc( ) char
=>   x: ref proc( ) char

i.e., *x* is a procedure returning a pointer to a character, and a pointer to a procedure returning a character, respectively.

int x[ ]( )
=>   x[ ]( ): int =>   x[ ]: proc( ) int
=>   x: array of proc( ) int

so *x* is an array of procedures returning integers. This case is actually "semantically" excluded, as discussed below; we are allowed arrays of pointers to functions, but not arrays of functions themselves, so we should use

x: array of ref proc( ) int
<=   x[ ]: ref proc( ) int <= *x[ ]: proc( ) int
<=   (*x[ ])( ): int <=   int (*x[ ])( )

As a more complex example, if *x* is a function returning a pointer to an array of pointers to functions returning characters, we get

x2: proc( ) ref array of ref proc( ) char
<=   x2( ): ref array of ref proc( ) char
<=   *x2( ): array of ref proc( ) char
<=   (*x2( )) [ ]: ref proc char
<=   *(*x2( )) [ ]: proc( ) char
<=   (*(*x2( )) [ ]) ( ): char
<=   char (*(*x2( )) [ ]) ( )

We have used this alternative notation as an explanatory technique, but it turns out to be needed in practice, i.e., in order to make declarations of any complexity one needs to write something down from which to compute the C declaration! There are two reasons for this:

1. It is much more natural to think in the conventional notation, because it reflects the structure itself rather than just one of its uses. Thus one might want to know the type of

   (*x2( )) [ ]

   in some context, and this is not easily extracted from the C declaration! It is in fact a pointer to a function returning a character. [*Ed. note*: Actually, *x2* is a function returning a pointer to an array.] With more complex structures the problem is worse.

2. The mix of prefix and postfix operators with different binding power is confusing.

This last point is well brought out by the incorrect syntax for function definitions given in the manual, which includes the equations.

〈function-definition〉 ::=
   〈type-specifier〉〈function-declarator〉〈function-body〉
〈function-declarator〉 ::=
   〈declarator〉( ) |
   〈declarator〉(〈parameter-list〉)

i.e., even the author naturally expects the *last* pair of parentheses in a function definition to contain the argument list, but in fact it doesn't if the function itself returns a (pointer to) a function. So the declaration

extern char (*x( )) ( );

requires a corresponding definition of the form

char (*x(i)) ( ) { /* body */ }

so that the parentheses following the name of the function are the ones that will contain the argument list. If the syntax in the manual were correct, then functions could never return functions, even though this is well within the punning power of C. Luckily (!) the compilers all accept a definition syntax in line with the one for declarations, rather than the documented one.

    We said above that we would restrict this note to syntactic matters, so this is not the place to discuss C's confusion over names, objects and values, or its monstrous coercions, but a brief semantic skirmish is needed to cover some further points. It's clear that, pragmatically, composite objects such as arrays and functions must all be represented by their addresses when being manipulated, e.g., as parameters. Depending on the language's view of values, one might expect to see either

int useon6(x) int x[ ]; { return(x[6]); }
int thex[10];
useon6(thex);

or

```
int useon6(x) int (*x)[ ]; { return ( (*x)[6]; }
int thex[10];
useon6(&thex);              /* "&" is the LV operator */
```

though the first is conventional, and is in fact what C requires. Unfortunately this does not follow from a semantics, but is explained as a sort of coercion: ". . . a reference to an array is converted by the compiler to a pointer to the beginning of the array" (Kerninghan and Ritchie, 1978, p. 94). Functions are not so lucky, and require a mixture of these two views, so the corresponding sequence is

```
int useon6(x) int (*x) ( ); { return( (*x) (6) ); }
int thex( ) . . . ;
useon6(thex);
```

i.e., the two declarations of the function parameter, as formal (x) and actual (*thex*) are different! The call uses an address implicitly on the calling side but explicitly on the called side. The confusion is compounded by the fact that explicit "conversion" overrides implicit, so that x and $\&x$ are essentially synonymous if x is a function or array! Even for arrays this "conversion" is not done consistently, hence the rule that functions may not return arrays (or functions) but instead pointers to them. As an example of such illegal types, consider:

```
char (w ( ) [ ] ) ( );        /* very illegal */
char (*x ( ) [ ] ) ( );       /* illegal */
char ( (*y ( ) ) [ ] ) ( );   /* illegal */
char (*(*z ( ) )[ ] ) ( );    /* legal */
```

w is a function returning an array of functions, i.e., is doubly illegal; z is the correct version, a function returning a pointer to an array of pointers to functions; x and y are intermediate cases. Experiments show (!) that the compiler allows all these to be declared as external, allows only y and z to be used, but (correctly!) allows only z to be defined. In no case do the error messages refer to an illegal type.

The final use of types is in casts, with yet another syntax but at last we have true type-expressions, i.e., a definition of a type *not* intimately bound up with a name. They "work" because we can see where the identifier *would* go if it were inserted, if the constraint that (⟨empty⟩) is never used is obeyed. Type-expressions do have advantages:

1. It's easier to see that two objects are being declared as the same type, as one can have

    ⟨name 1⟩, ⟨name 2⟩: ⟨type⟩

    rather than C's

    ⟨basic type⟩ ⟨declarator 1⟩, ⟨declarator 2⟩

    where the declarators are identical apart from the embedded names.

2. One has the immediate possibility of defining new types, even if this is implemented only by textual substitution, without any new syntax

#define snumber ref int
x, y: snumber

The original C (Ritchie, 1974) had no mechanism for this, but recently (Kernighan
and Ritchie, 1978) a type defining facility has been introduced, so that

typedef int *IP;
IP x;

is equivalent to

int *x;

This is known technically as "beating about the bush!"

C's types seem quite strict, and unsuitable for a SIL in the same way that
Pascal's are; surely we need generic types and so on? In place of this *flexibility*
(which is of course not easily achieved!), we have *slackness*, i.e., typechecking is
not at all thorough, especially of agreement between function definitions and their
use, and we can pass pointers to various different things and get away with it. The
extent of this is not clear and is *certainly* not written down; it leads to great confusion.

This is not the place to go into details of other infelicities in C's syntax, nor
indeed further into the problems of its type structure, but it will be clear to users
of UNIX, or even to readers of its documentation, that the designers and implementors
of C have a lax attitude to syntax and semantics, and it's interesting to speculate
on the seeming paradox of the widespread and successful use of such a vaguely-
specified and implemented language!

APPENDIX: SIMPLIFIED TYPE SYNTAX

⟨declaration⟩	::=	⟨type-specifier⟩⟨declarator⟩
⟨type-specifier⟩	::=	char | int | . . .
⟨declarator⟩	::=	⟨identifier⟩ |
		(⟨declarator⟩) |
		*⟨declarator⟩ |
		⟨declarator⟩( ) |
		⟨declarator⟩[ ]
⟨definition⟩	::=	⟨function-definition⟩ |
		⟨data-definition⟩
⟨function-definition⟩	::=	⟨type-specifier⟩⟨function-declarator⟩
		⟨function-body⟩

⟨function-declarator⟩ ::=   ⟨declarator⟩( ) |
                              ⟨declarator⟩(⟨parameter- list⟩)
⟨data-definition⟩   ::=   ⟨type-specific⟩⟨declarator⟩
⟨type-name⟩   ::=   ⟨type-specifier⟩⟨abstract-declarator⟩
⟨abstract-declarator⟩   ::=   ⟨empty⟩ |
                              (⟨abstract-declarator⟩) |
                              ∗⟨abstract-declarator⟩ |
                              ⟨abstract-declarator⟩( ) |
                              ⟨abstract-declarator⟩[ ]
⟨cast-expression⟩   ::=   (⟨type-name⟩ ⟨expression⟩)

METHODOLOGY FOR COMPARING AND ASSESSING LANGUAGES

Papers in the previous sections were case studies of programming language comparisons and assessments. In this the final section of the book, the discussions are more general in nature in that they step back to remark on the process of comparison and assessment itself.

The first paper, "A Methodology for Comparing Programming Languages" by Feuer and Gehani, concentrates on the process of comparing languages. It presents an outline of the topics and a discussion of the criteria that one might use in conducting a comparison. The topics provide a good starting point for anyone embarking on a language comparison or assessment.

The next two papers illustrate particular methodologies for comparing languages. They have been extracted from more comprehensive papers that go on to discuss languages outside the scope of this book.

Shaw, Almes, Newcomer, Reid, and Wulf, in their paper "A Comparison of Programming Languages for Software Engineering," present a method for comparing languages based on a subset of the features of each language which they call the *core* of the language. They argue that the core of a language is representative of the design philosophy for the language and that the rest of the language is likely to adhere to this philosophy of design. They concentrate on identifying the *mind set* induced by the language philosophy and then look at how the mind set affects programming *in the small* (i.e., at the statement level) and *in the large* (i.e., at the procedure and module level).

The next paper addresses the important issue of language implementations, which is largely ignored in the other papers. A language, no matter how good its facilities are, will not be a contender for practical applications if it cannot be implemented efficiently and reliably. Boom and De Jong, in "A Critical Comparison of Several Programming Language Implementations," directly address the issues of comparing particular compilers. They raise such issues as:

- How closely does the language implemented by the compiler match the current standard?
- How does the implementation help to create reliable programs?
- Is the documentation readable, precise, complete, and easily available?

They go on to evaluate four languages with regard to the implementation issues raised. Although we have kept their evaluation of a Pascal compiler in full, we have eliminated their evaluation of the other compilers since the languages implemented by them are outside the scope of this book.

In the final paper, "Programming Languages: What to Demand and How to Assess Them," Wirth, the prolific language designer, presents his view of why some modern languages are superior to older ones. He suggests criteria for language design, documentation, and implementation that should be looked for in programming languages. He goes on to show how Pascal meets these criteria and concludes by giving a collection of Pascal programs to illustrate its versatility and performance.

ALAN R. FEUER AND NARAIN H. GEHANI
Bell Laboratories, Murray Hill, New Jersey

A Methodology for Comparing Programming Languages

1 INTRODUCTION

As society becomes more and more dependent on computer systems, their reliability and flexibility becomes more critical. One consequence of this growing dependence is an increasing concern about the quality of software products and the ability to produce them quickly and to modify them easily. The programming language used for a project is a critical determinant of the speed of development, the ease of maintenance, and the portability of the software to other systems.

In response to the increasing importance of software, computer scientists have designed programming languages to address various aspects of software use, such as efficiency, portability, reliability, and maintainability. The resulting proliferation of languages has made choosing a programming language for a particular application all the more difficult. Although many language comparisons (Anderson and Shumate, 1982; Feuer and Gehani, 1982; Shaw et al., 1981; Tanenbaum, 1977; Wichmann, 1980) and evaluations (Anderson, 1980; Dijkstra, 1978; Habermann, 1973; Lecarme and Desjardins, 1975) have appeared, little has been written about *how* to compare and assess languages.

In this paper we present a methodology for comparing programming languages. The main part of the paper is structured around a list of topics on which to base a language comparison and assessment. The topics have been chosen with procedural languages in mind, such as Pascal, C, and Ada. Associated with each of the topics are questions one might ask to characterize a language. In addition, for each topic we suggest criteria that can be used in judging a language once it has been characterized. Throughout the paper we give examples of how the criteria might be applied.

197

Our methodology is presented in three sections. In the first section are topics to be addressed at the outset of a comparison study. Next are the topics that are used to characterize each language. Finally we suggest a strategy for assessing a language for particular programming domains.

2 PRELIMINARY CONSIDERATIONS

Much like writing a computer program, the comparison will be easier to do and be more successful if it is designed in advance. The topics in this section address the overall goals and procedures of the comparison.

2.1 Purpose

What is the purpose of the comparison?

Is it primarily academic interest or is it for pragmatic reasons such as selecting a language for a project or advocating a change in language?

Being clear about the motivation for the comparison will help to determine which of the topics in the comparison are most important. For example, if the motivation is to produce an academic study, then issues such as the philosophy and structure of the languages are important. On the other hand, in a comparison aimed at choosing a language for a particular project, issues like suitability, availability, performance, reliability, and cost become paramount.

2.2 Audience

Who is the audience for the comparison?

What is their familiarity with the languages being compared and with underlying language concepts?

Knowing the audience will help determine what level of detail is appropriate (e.g., whether each language feature must be described before it can be discussed) and what terms can be used without definitions.

2.3 Approach

What style will the comparison take?

How many people will be involved?

There are two basic ways to approach the comparison—we label them cooperative and advocatory. In the *cooperative approach*, the topics of the comparison are collected into groups (e.g., data types, control structure) and one person examines the same groups for each language. With the *advocatory approach*, each language has an advocate. For each topic in the comparison, the advocates argue in favor of their languages.

Of course, the approach taken depends upon the number of people involved, their skill, and their personalities.

2.4 Authorities

What will be the definitive source of answers to questions about each language?
How much of a language and its environment will be examined?

Throughout the comparison, questions about the fine points of the languages will arise. Authorities are needed to resolve questions about language syntax and semantics, language usage, and designer intent. Examples of authorities are

- *A defining document*: The reference manual for the language is essential. Other documents, such as a user guide, may prove helpful by expanding upon and clarifying statements in the reference manual.
- *A formal definition*: While a formal definition is potentially the ultimate defining document, the underlying assumptions of the definition must be noted. For example, the language defined by the formal definition may be only a subset of the language defined in the reference manual.
- *A reference compiler*: When the language definition is not complete, the syntax and semantics of a feature may be discovered by using a reference or "standard" compiler for the language.

The scope for the comparison depends upon the purpose of the comparison and upon what is comparable. Comparing the cores of languages is reasonably straightforward; comparing facilities for input/output, dynamic storage manipulation, and concurrency becomes progressively messier because these facilities are often implemented in the environment rather than in the language itself. The environment for a language tends to be less well defined than the language itself and is more open to change.

3 COMPARING THE LANGUAGES

There are two basic ways to characterize and compare languages—by feature and by function. For languages that are similar in nature, e.g., procedural languages, either a by-feature or a by-function comparison is appropriate. If the comparison is between basically dissimilar languages, e.g., a procedural language and an applicative one, then a functional comparison is more suitable. In a functional comparison, a few problems are programmed in each language and the resulting programs are contrasted. Depending upon the motivation for the study, the problems may be chosen to illustrate differences in the approaches of the languages or to be indicative of the kind of tasks the language will be used for.

As mentioned earlier, the methodology presented in this paper is oriented towards procedural languages. This section contains topics for a feature-by-feature comparison.

3.1 History and Philosophy

For whom and for what purpose was the language designed?

A brief history of each language will put the comparison in perspective. Most languages are designed with some class of applications in mind, even though the language may be suitable for other applications. Knowing the intent of the designers and their design philosophy often makes it easier to see and understand the structure of a language.

For example, C was designed for system programming; one of the guiding design principles was that the language provide a convenient, efficient, and flexible way to control the underlying machine. With that background, it is understandable that C includes operations on the bits in a word but not on data types like sets and strings.

3.2 Syntax

Are programs in the language readable?
Is the syntax consistent?
Is it concise yet sufficiently expressive?
Is the syntax dangerous?

Although it is easy to comment on syntax, objective evaluation is difficult. Personal taste is the ultimate judge of syntax. However, there are a few criteria on which an assessment of syntax could be based:

- *Consistency*: Inconsistency in the syntax of a programming language makes the language difficult to learn and the programmer prone to errors. Two examples of inconsistency are the use of the same symbol for different things in different contexts and arbitrary restrictions such as allowing expressions in some places but not in others.
- *Redundancy of constructs*: A language with redundant or overlapping constructs has multiple ways of writing the same operation. With better partitioning, the number of concepts in the language could have been reduced. Redundant constructs also lead to idiosyncracies in programming—different programmers using different idioms to do the same thing.
- *Expressiveness*: A well-written program reflects the structure of its underlying algorithm. The more expressive a language, the easier it is for a programmer to match the solution to the problem.
- *Wordiness and safety*: There is an informal guideline that all routines ought to fit on a single page; long programs are more difficult to read than short

ones. A verbose language can turn short algorithms into long programs. On the other hand, cryptic syntax is not desirable either. Syntactic correctness is an easy thing for a compiler to check; syntax errors are the first protective barrier against programming and typing errors. In a language that is too concise, i.e., with little redundancy, many errors are not detectable because the resulting program is still (syntactically) correct (Horning, 1979).

3.3 Type Philosophy and Data Types

What primitive types does the language support?

Can new types be created?

How are user-defined types treated in comparison with the built-in types?

How strict is the language in its treatment of types?

Recent developments in programming language design have emphasized the treatment of data types. In many ways, the style of programming in a language is a direct result of the type philosophy. Organizing data has been recognized as an important aspect of programming.[1] In addition, types play a key role in automatic error checking and program readability.

Given its importance, the characterization and assessment of the type philosophy for a language is a crucial, though complex, part of any comparison. The next few paragraphs introduce some aspects of data types and some criteria on which to judge the type philosophy of a language.

Most languages provide at least a few types such as integer, real, and character. Built-in types are usually more convenient to use than user-defined types since a type definition does not have to be written. A language oriented towards a specific programming domain should have types that facilitate programming in that domain, e.g., extended precision reals for scientific computing.

Most languages also provide facilities for structuring data such as arrays, records, and sets. Two important qualities of a data structuring facility are flexibility and safety.

One reason flexibility is important is that, for many problems, a programmer has the choice of trading execution speed for memory used and vice versa. The choice often depends on being able to create and use a particular kind of data structure. Some examples are the tight packing of data, using table look-up in place of computation, and using ragged arrays instead of rectangular ones.

The safety of accessing data is a primary contributor to program reliability. Dangerous practices include the uncontrolled use of pointers (leading to stray pointers and dangling references) and uncontrolled representation viewing by using variants or by breaching type checking.

Type checking is an important aspect in the automatic detection of errors.

---

[1] See, for example, the essays by Dijkstra and Hoare in the classic book *Structured Programming* (Dahl et al., 1972).

The more strongly a language is typed, the more discipline it enforces in the use of types. Liskov (1976) argues for very strong typing, claiming that implicit conversions from one type to another of any kind are bad. Gries and Gehani (1977) moderate this by saying that only those implicit conversions that make sense mathematically and do not result in any loss of information should be allowed (e.g., from integer to real).

Facilities for type creation range from the ability to create a synonym for an existing type identifier to being able to define the representation and operations of a new type. Including a facility to define a new type completely, i.e., a facility to create abstract data types, was a key development in programming language design during the 1970s.

3.4 Operators and Assignment

Do the built-in operators complement the primitive data types?
Are the operators well-defined?
Are the precedence rules straightforward?
Do they encourage the use of side-effects?

Built-in operators are those that are provided by the language. The semantics of built-in operators are frequently based either on a mathematical or a machine operation. Built-ins may be more efficiently implemented than user-defined operations since they can take advantage of specialized hardware instructions. Analogously to data types, a language designed for a specific application should have operators tailored for that application.

The operator precedence rules of a language are fairly important. A language with unconventional operator precedence invites miscoding and misreading of programs. Having a reasonable number of precedence levels is also important. Too many precedence levels may put an unnecessary burden on the programmer to remember them, while too few levels may lead to awkward construction of expressions.

The question of side effects is another important issue. Relative to operators, a language embraces side effects if it has assignment expressions rather than assignment statements; that is, if assignment is treated as an ordinary operator. It is commonly argued that programs with side effects are less reliable and readable than programs without them (Horning, 1979) although they may be more compact.

3.5 Control Flow

Does the language support structured programming?
Are exceptions handled in a controlled way?

With respect to sequential control flow, programming in a structured way has come to mean programming using only sequence, and iteration.

Selection implements the control abstraction of a multi-way switch. Questions to ask about a selection construct are: Are the branches mutually exclusive or do they flow into one another? What are the restrictions on the expression that selects a branch? Does the construct allow an "if all else fails" branch?

Loops appear in a few different basic forms. Questions to ask are: Are n-time loops easy to express? What about $n \frac{1}{2}$ loops (Knuth, 1974)? What happens to loop control variables when the loop exits (both normally and by exception)? What are the restrictions on the controlling condition for the loop?

A program exception is a break from the normal flow of control. Exceptions are used to handle errors and other special conditions. A wide range of mechanisms has been invented to handle exceptions. Some are general in that they can be used to handle a large class of exceptions; others are more specific, limited perhaps to just handling arithmetic overflow or hardware interrupts.

3.6 Routines and Scope

Is a distinction made between functions and procedures?

Is the parameter passing mechanism safe?

Is it efficient?

Can generic routines be written?

Is there a restriction on return values?

Are there levels of scope?

Can routines be called recursively?

A function extends a language by creating a new operation while a procedure extends a language by creating a new type of statement. Thus ideally, functions return values and have no side effects while procedures return no values and may have side effects. Some languages distinguish between functions and procedures as an aid to program clarity.

There are several ways to pass parameters to a routine, some designed for safety (e.g., value and value-result) and some for runtime efficiency (e.g., reference). Depending on the use of a routine and the types of the parameters, stressing either safety or efficiency may be appropriate. Thus, a language should support both.

A generic routine is one which can be applied to arguments of a variety of different types. The routine performs a conceptually similar operation across all argument types. A typical example is a *sort* procedure that can sort arrays of integers, reals, and strings. Generics can reduce the amount of code and programming effort required for a project. There are a number of ways to implement them: by passing procedures as parameters, by overloading procedure names, by passing types, or by being able to determine the type of an object dynamically.

It is generally considered good programming practice to define variables in the narrowest scope required (Wulf and Shaw, 1973). There are a variety of mechanisms for controlling scope: block structuring, packages, files, labeled common. There are also mechanisms for bypassing the scope rules: equivalences, pointers, call-by-reference.

3.7 Concurrent Programming Facilities

Is the concurrent programming facility integrated into the language?

Is it a high or a low level facility?

How do processes communicate?

Does the facility support real-time programming?

A concurrent program consists of parts that can be executed in parallel. These parallel parts, frequently called *processes,* interact to synchronize their flow of control and to exchange information.

There are two primary reasons for supporting concurrent programming (Hoare, 1978):

1. Some algorithms (e.g., operating systems, simulations) are inherently concurrent. A concurrent programming facility allows the algorithms to be specified concurrently, thus preserving the structure of the algorithm.
2. On hardware with more than one active unit (e.g., two processors or a processor and smart peripherals), concurrent programs may be executed more efficiently.

Some computer scientists argue that concurrent programming facilities belong in programming languages so that concurrent programs may be portable across systems (Hoare, 1978). Including concurrency in the language also leaves open the possibility of scheduling optimization by the compiler (Pratt, 1982). And by including concurrent control flow statements in a programming language, some paradigms for interprocess communication can be written more easily and securely than if the paradigm had to be implemented via subroutines.

Others argue that concurrency is better left to the operating system and accessed via system calls (Ritchie et al., 1978). If concurrency is defined in a programming language, it locks programmers into one particular concurrent programming model, which may poorly match a particular operating system.

A variety of concurrency mechanisms has been invented, some lower level than others. For example, semaphores and signals are primitive operations that require careful programming to use properly. Higher level mechanisms like monitors and rendevous are less prone to misuse.

3.8 Input/Output

Is simple input/output simple to write?

Is input/output sufficiently flexible to talk to disks as well as terminals?

Does it work equally well for batch and interactive programs?

Can files be accessed randomly?

Even though virtually every program uses the input/output (I/O) facilities of a language, I/O is frequently designed with less thought than other features. I/O routines can be tricky to implement since, to be easy to use, they must be able to accept a variable number of arguments of arbitrary type. In addition, the output routine must be flexible enough to write formatted text as well as control information for arbitrary devices. Being able to read and write from files as well as terminals with the same code is always a challenge. For example, standard Pascal has well known problems with reading from a terminal (Feuer and Gehani, 1982).

3.9 Independent Compilation

Can routines be compiled independently?

Is type consistency enforced across independently compiled routines?

The ability to link together object modules resulting from different compilations is important for all but the smallest programs. The ability to link to libraries of precompiled modules is important even for small programs.

Passing arguments of the wrong type to a routine is one of the most common programming errors (Boehm et al., 1978). Having the ability to detect this kind of error when the called and calling routine are compiled independently is a great asset.

3.10 Access to Routines in Other Languages and to the Hardware

Can subroutines written in another language be called?

Is there an escape to assembly language?

Is there high-level access to physical addresses and devices?

Depending upon the operating environment, linking to other high-level languages may be a function of the link editor rather than the compiler. In any case, there are issues of calling sequences, parameter passing, and the representation of data that need to be agreed upon for routines in the two languages to communicate.

Occasionally, a program may need access to a special machine instruction or to a particular location in memory. If a higher-level language provides access to low-level operations such as these, it can reduce the need for assembly language.

3.11 Practical Considerations

There are a large number of practical issues that can render the technical issues moot. Here are a few:

Does a reliable and efficient compiler exist? Is it supported (who fixes it if it breaks)?

Is there a standard for the language?

Is the documentation adequate? What about training? Consulting?

What is the development environment like? Are there debugging aids and project management tools?

4 DRAWING CONCLUSIONS

The questions in the previous section are used to characterize the languages being compared and to assess their relative merits from a technical viewpoint. It is possible that a language that is technically superior overall may not be the best choice for a particular programming domain. For example, although Pascal is technically superior to COBOL, for typical business applications COBOL is the better choice since it was designed explicitly with business programming in mind.

We propose a three-step procedure to select a programming language for a particular application. First, characterize the application by placing it in a programming domain. It is not unusual for an application to span more than one domain. For example, an accounting program may have a forecasting subsection that is more like scientific than business programming. Here is a list of some common programming domains:

- Scientific programming—numerical software
- Business programming—database access, report generation, accounting
- Machine dependent systems programming—access to the hardware
- Machine independent systems programming—concurrency
- Text processing—string manipulation
- Expert systems—dynamic data structures
- Real time programming—scheduling control

Next, identify the features of a programming language essential or important for effective programming in the domain of interest. If the application spans more than one domain, identify the features for all of the domains. Here is a partial list of language features for scientific programming (Feuer and Gehani, 1982):

- Extended precision arithmetic
- Array operations
- Complex data type
- Availability of a large number of mathematical functions
- Input/output of binary files
- Parameter passing by value and reference
- Separate or independent compilation

- Ability to pass routines as parameters
- Non-zero lower bounds for arrays

Finally, determine the suitability of each programming language for the application by asking the following questions for each feature listed:

- Is the feature provided in the language?
- If not provided, can the feature be easily implemented in the language?

The answers to these questions should provide a good framework for making an informed choice of a language.

5 OUR EXPERIENCE

We conducted a thorough comparison of C and Pascal. The intent of the comparison was to spark serious discussion about the programming languages used at Bell Laboratories—at the time, C was in wide use at Bell to the exclusion of most other languages. The comparison was presented in two papers. The first contained a feature-by-feature description and comparison. It was targeted for a technical population unfamiliar with one or both of the languages. The second paper considered properties of programs written in each language and the suitability of the languages for a variety of programming domains. Here we assumed that the reader was familiar with the features of the two languages.

 We used the advocatory approach during the comparison—one of us argued for C and the other for Pascal. This approach worked well for us since, in our initial biases, one of us favored Pascal and the other C. With experience we evolved a set of rules for settling disputes. We sought to compare the standard version of each language and thus relied almost exclusively on the reference manuals augmented by the appropriate user manuals. Where the manuals were incomplete, we resorted to other available authorities including the formal definition for Pascal and the UNIX compilers for C. There was a constant temptation to attribute features to the languages not described in the manuals but commonly found in current compilers. This was particularly true for C, since we were well aware of the continuing evolution of the language.

 Evaluating the languages did not prove as pacific as describing them. Here we relied on patience, supporting documents from the literature, and occasionally a third party to help us focus on the issue at question.

 The study lasted considerably longer than we had at first estimated. We spent more time than expected designing the form of the comparison: how much detail about each language to include, how to partition the topics we wanted to cover, what was *really* the definition of each language. Once these issues were settled, the comparison proceeded more quickly.[2]

---

[2] In this paper these issues are discussed in Section 2, Preliminary Considerations.

6 SUMMARY

We have presented a methodology for comparing and assessing programming languages. The approach consists of two primary parts. First, each language is characterized by describing its treatment of important topics. Then the facilities in each language are compared with the requirements for programming in specific application domains.

The method presented should be viewed as a starting point for a comparison; trim and embellish it as befits the situation.

ACKNOWLEDGMENTS

We are grateful to John Linderman and Charles Wetherell for their helpful comments.

**MARY SHAW, GUY T. ALMES, JOSEPH M. NEWCOMER,
BRIAN K. REID, AND WILLIAM A. WULF**
Computer Science Department, Carnegie-Mellon University, Pittsburgh, Pennsylvania

A Comparison of Programming Languages for Software Engineering

1 INTRODUCTION

This report is a comparison of four programming languages in the light of modern ideas of good software engineering practice. We include three existing languages (FORTRAN, COBOL, Jovial) and the proposed DoD standard for programming embedded computer systems.[1]

At least some of the acrimony that surrounds the discussion of the relative merits of various programming languages arises from a failure to draw a proper distinction between *comparison* and *evaluation*. In a comparison, the analysis is directed at distinctions and similarities of the languages, and possibly at the relative merits of particular features under certain circumstances. An evaluation, on the other hand, is aimed at making a judgment, hopefully in terms of a set of clearly-defined objectives. We wish to emphasize that our primary goal in this report is a *comparison* of languages. Our comparison focuses on those dimensions that bear on modern notions of program structure and good software engineering practice.

In preparing this report we first addressed the problem of language comparison itself. After an examination of existing language comparisons, we felt that a new approach was needed. Thus, to replace the customary exhaustive feature-by-feature comparative evaluation, we have devised a "language core" technique; this technique is described in detail below. We believe it to be a substantive improvement in language-comparison methodology.

One of the reasons for evaluating programming languages is to help select one

---

[1] This language has been variously called DoD-1, "Strawman," "Woodenman," "Tinman," and "Ironman." The final version of the language will be named Ada.

for use in a particular project or organization. This selection process often engenders bitter debate, as typically there are no clear goals or unified interests. The results frequently depend on the prior language experience of the evaluators rather than on any objective criteria.

We believe, however, that objectivity in the comparison process is possible, and we have based this report on that assumption: rational and objective comparisons can be made. An evaluation combines comparison with judgments about particular objectives and methods; it must be accomplished with clear goals and proper information. This report can provide the language-dependent part of the information needed to make a rational evaluation in a given context.

1.1 Comparison Methodology

There have been a substantial number of "evaluations" of various programming languages (Goodenough, 1976; Higman, 1967; Nicholls, 1975). Generally these comparisons or evaluations have been based on a detailed analysis of the *features* available in each of the languages under study. Because our goal is more specific, namely comparison only with respect to the use of the language in conjunction with modern notions of software engineering, we have chosen a different approach.

Our approach is based on three closely-related premises about programming languages:

1. The designers of each language had a strong image of how programs are, or ought to be, written—and that they designed the language accordingly.
2. The designers' image is strongly and consistently reflected throughout the language. Moreover, once a language is defined, it tends to acquire an independent identity. Extensions and revisions tend to continue in the original style, thus remaining true to the original image of program construction.
3. This reflected image is a major factor in determining how the language will actually be used. That is, we believe that the language designer's philosophy of program construction dominates the language so strongly that it dictates (at least to a first approximation) a "mind set" which, in turn, strongly impacts how programs will be structured.[2]

If our goal is the comparison of languages with respect to the way they support software engineering, a consequence of these premises is that we should compare the central images of the languages and the programming paradigms embodied by those designs. We propose to do just that, albeit in a somewhat indirect manner. Our comparison methodology has two steps:

---

[2] A programmer who learns one programming language or who predominantly uses one language may mentally program in that language and transliterate into another which he uses less frequently. In such cases his use of the second language will not conform to the argument above; however, we are primarily concerned with the primary impact of language and not with secondary effects.

1. Capturing the designer's image with a definition of the central core of each language
2. Comparing these core languages

The remainder of this section elaborates these two steps and the rationale for this approach.

Language cores.   As stated above, we believe that the language designers' image of the programming paradigm is a major factor in determining the structure of programs written in the language. It would be ideal to compare these images directly and possibly to discuss the extent to which each language really does support its image. In most cases, of course, we have little or no direct evidence of the designers' intent. In fact, we do not believe that this image was necessarily explicit. The notion of a "core language" is our attempt to express what we infer to have been their intent.

Since we believe that the designers' image of the programming paradigm is strongly and consistently reflected throughout the language—both in the choice of features and in the way the features are composed into programs—it is generally not necessary to examine the entire language in order to see this image. In other words, it is possible to isolate a subset of the language that captures the image; we call such a subset a *core* of the language.

Thus our language comparisons begin with the definition of each of the language cores. We shall compare (only) these cores since they were designed to capture the attributes we wish to compare.

In general, a core of a language will not be unique; for example, it may be possible to select any of several features to capture some single aspect of the image. Since small cores are easier to compare than large ones, a core will usually omit much of a language and, in principle, need not be complete.[3] Moreover, the selection of which aspects to include or exclude from the core of a particular language will be solely a property of that language; one is not entitled to expect corresponding features, even when they exist, to appear in the cores of two languages being compared. Such features may contribute to the unique flavour of a language in one case but not another.

Comparison of languages.   Although we realize that focusing the comparison on the cores of the languages in question has some obvious shortcomings for certain purposes, we also believe it has significant advantages over attempts at more comprehensive comparisons. These advantages are all, in one form or another, assertions that it is possible to do a more complete, intellectually tractable, and scientifically honest comparison of a small number of things than a large number. More precisely:

1. We assert that the design philosophy of a language pervades all programs written in that language. Indeed, we believe that this has a far more important impact on program construction than the presence or absence of specific features. Since,

---

[3] That is, it is not necessary for the core to be capable of expressing an arbitrary computation.

by design, the core language captures the language design philosophy, comparison of the cores captures the first-order effects in program composition.

2. We believe that comparison of (only) the cores avoids a whole raft of silly, finger-pointing arguments—those arguments of the flavour ". . . in MY language there is an *X* construct" . . . "Well, in MY language there isn't an explicit *X*, but you can do the same thing with a *Y*. . . ." Such discussions may be interesting to some language designers, but they shed little light on the real merits of either language. To avoid such silly discussions,

   a. We should accept the premise that all languages are computationally complete; that is, all are adequate for describing all computations. One language will undoubtedly be more convenient than another for particular isolated examples; but the reverse will usually be true for other examples. Thus these isolated cases serve little purpose.

   b. We should recognize that all languages tend to accrete features to compensate for their most glaring initial deficiencies. Genuinely important facilities will migrate into all languages in some form. The way in which these facilities are included, however, is important: in nearly all cases they enter the language in a style consistent with the original design philosophy.

   c. We should recognize that the simple presence of features is not a good indication of the worth of a language. A large collection of *ad hoc* features, patched together without thought to uniformity or elegance, will not produce a usable language.

   The core language approach responds directly to each of these points.

3. The core language is probably "solid" with respect to its semantics. Even though all the languages in question have strong portability goals, from practical experience we know that the less-exercised features of a language are likely to be implemented incompatibly. By staying within the centre of the language we avoid disagreements about the semantics of strange cases.

4. Most importantly, we believe that the "core language" approach is intellectually manageable. Any "more complete" treatment would, of necessity, involve a lengthy enumeration of comparisons. It would then be difficult to determine (a) what the most important comparisons are and (b) whether crucial comparisons are missing.

1.2 Dimensions of Comparison

Having established the value of comparison over evaluation, and having outlined the ideas behind our comparison strategy, we now describe the actual comparisons to be used.

One of the most important but least tangible factors in the programming process is the "mental set" of the programmer: his view of the strengths, weaknesses, peculiarities and proper use of the programming tools that he uses. Many factors are involved in the evolution of a particular programmer's mental image of the programming process; we shall try to isolate the ones that are affected by language.

When a programmer learns a language and continues to use it, his mind set is largely determined by that language. When a programmer learns to program in one language and then switches to another, his mind set is a juxtaposition of the two, and to a certain extent he will be programming mentally in one language and translating into the other as the code is written down. For our purposes, then, the mental language is much more important than the actual language.

We shall compare the effects that language-induced mind sets have on programming "in the small," that is, on the use of individual statements, statement-groups, loops, procedures or even programs. For example, we compare how the language syntax and lexical structure shape the code that is written. We examine how the data abstractions that are built into the language affect the programmer's choice of representation and how the control structures provided by the language impact the grouping and local flow of the finished program.

We shall then compare the effects that languages have on programming "in the large," that is, the composition of individual programs and program segments into whole systems. Thus, we examine the ways a language can affect our ability to segment a task into independent subproblems, to assemble independent components into a system, and to maintain such a system once it exists.

Not all of these questions are meaningful to ask of all languages, and not all of the dimensions of comparison are relevant for all languages. But it is with these techniques and their implied goals that we examine the various language cores.

1.3 Scope of Project

We have undertaken only a comparison of languages. To use this comparison in a language selection process, one must consider many other factors of the programming environment. Although these aspects are often regarded as part of the language, they in fact result from almost independent decisions and consequently must be treated separately.

We have specifically *excluded* two major categories of potential comparison criteria from our study: compiler- or system-specific features and problem-domain issues. Thus, for example, we removed the Environment Division from our COBOL core because it is completely system-specific, and in some operating systems its functions have been subsumed by the job control and file system interface. Similarly, although we have discussed language features that affect modularity, we have not discussed nonlinguistic problems of separate compilation and program linkage. Finally, such important, but problem-domain specific facilities as COBOL's formatting facilities or FORTRAN's access to a scientific subroutine library are not considered.

The omission of these issues from this report is *not* to imply that we regard them as unimportant. On the contrary, in many contexts they may be *more* important than the issues considered here. They are omitted simply because they are outside the scope of the current study.

The original objectives of this study were:

1. To identify language features currently in use, and to evaluate them in terms of their specification and scope of effects, their use in practice, the provability of program correctness, and their suitability to programmers' needs

2. To enumerate language features conducive and detrimental to good program structure, and to identify small variations that may have significant impact

As the study proceeded, it became apparent that overall program organization and the way language features are used have a much greater impact on the quality of a program than does the selection or non-selection of individual features. We therefore adopted the "language-core" methodology described above. Evaluations of language features appear throughout the report, but we have made no attempt to construct exhaustive lists. Indeed, we believe that such lists would detract from the major results of the study.

2 DEFINITIONS OF CORE LANGUAGES

In this section we define the "cores" of the four languages under investigation. A section is devoted to each; except for Ironman, the definitions of the cores are structured similarly. The common organization is:

Philosophy
Core properties
    Lexical and syntactic issues
    Data and data-structure issues
    Control structure issues
    Other issues
Definition of a core
    Syntactic definition
    Semantic comments
    Example program

The section on "Philosophy" examines some of the contextual information surrounding the language definition. In many cases the essential flavour of a language derives from such information as the nature of the problem domain, the state of compiler technology at the time of the language definition, the typical mode of computer usage, and so on. This section attempts to capture those aspects of the context which strongly affected the language.

The section on "Core properties" isolates those properties which *every* core of the language should contain. These are the features and policies that give the language its identity. The description of these properties is intentionally terse and hence depends to some extent upon the general knowledge of the reader.

The final section, "Definition of a core," defines one possible core which reflects the properties outlined in the previous section. This core is defined syntactically, semantically, and by example. The syntactic definition uses an extended BNF notation. The semantic definition is in prose; it is not intended to be complete, but rather to emphasize those aspects of the semantics which are most relevant to the subsequent comparison sections. The example program is an implementation of the same simple algorithm in each of the core languages. The primary purpose of the example is to illustrate that the cores do indeed capture the essence of the language.

[*Material Deleted*]

3 COMPARISONS OF CORE LANGUAGES

3.1 Comparison of Philosophies

Language designers, we believe, make a number of fundamental philosophical decisions which significantly affect the nature of the language they produce. While these decisions are not always explicit (they may be the result of historical or other contextual factors), they tend to have an enormous impact. Thus, we shall begin our comparison by examining some of these issues for the four languages in question.

The issues we shall consider are:

- **The designer's view of the problem**: The designer's image of the nature of the problem domain is undoubtedly the most important of all influences on the language. The distinction between numeric computations, data processing, and command-and-control is the most obvious manifestation of this view. In addition, however, whether the designers perceived solutions to problems as consisting of single programs, sets of single programs, or large systems is a major factor.
- **Selection vs. synthesis**: There is a spectrum of approaches to providing "power" in a programming language. At one end of this spectrum is the selection, or menu, approach: to anticipate every possible need in the form of specific features, thus making the programming task one of simply selecting the right option for a given problem. The other extreme of this spectrum is the synthetic approach: to supply a small set of basic mechanisms together with a flexible means of composing them into larger units, thus making the programming task one of constructing the proper substructure in which ultimately to state the solution to a problem.
- **The degree of permissiveness**: Another important spectrum in language design is the degree to which it *enforces*, *encourages*, *permits* or *prevents* various programming practices. In software, just as in other technologies, powerful tools are often dangerous. Precisely the same language features which are touted as powerful are often subject to misuse. The enforcement spectrum, then, expresses the degree of permissiveness in the language relative to the use of these powerful, but dangerous mechanisms. A given language generally takes a stand at some point on this spectrum and then must respond by either (a) imposing restrictions on the power of the language and then permitting controlled circumvention of its own restrictions, or (b) providing powerful but dangerous features and allowing conventions to be imposed on their use.

Not all combinations of these philosophical positions make sense, nor are any of the languages in question completely consistent in their positions on these issues.

Nevertheless, observing the way the languages respond to these questions provides insight into their actual use.

[*Material Deleted*]

3.2 Programming in the Small

This set of comparisons deals only with language features of the cores and with the impact of these features on the construction of individual procedures or small programs. The features addressed here affect the ease with which algorithms and data structures can be described, they affect the programmer's ability to construct "well structured programs," and thus they affect the legibility of the resulting code. They do not necessarily seriously impact the organization of large program systems (although there are some features which impact both).

Syntax issues.   The grammar rules of a language affect the programmer's ability to read and write the language fluently. It is important for a programmer to be able to think about the problem and algorithm; he should not waste energy worrying about how to express the algorithm. Thus, the uniformity, expressiveness, clarity, and size of the language are of major significance. If the language definition is large, as those for FORTRAN and COBOL are, a programmer may not be able to know the entire language and, as a result, may code in a private sublanguage. Abstraction mechanisms can also help readability in particular by focusing the text on appropriate details.

Regularity of Grammar.   The grammars of the languages under comparison have different degrees of regularity—that is, they reuse definitions of substructure to a greater or lesser extent.

[*Material Deleted*]

We have used the word "regularity" where others have used "involution," "orthogonality" and "symmetry." All of these words are intended to connote the desirable property that the programmer need only learn a small number of concepts that may then be used in any of a large number of contexts. It seems clear that FORTRAN, Jovial, and Ironman form a spectrum of increasingly regular syntax, and that within this spectrum, greater regularity is better. COBOL, however, is interesting in that it rejected the idea that uniformity is an inherent "good," and chose instead to adopt a specialized, "natural" syntax for each of its constructs.

Readability and Intelligibility.   A language is *readable* to the extent that the form and style of programs in the language simplify the mechanical aspects of reading. A program is intelligible to the extent that what is read can be understood. Generally a program must be readable in order to be intelligible; the proper choice of comments, mnemonic identifiers, consistent indentation and so on all contribute to the understandability of a program. These factors are under the control of the programmer, not the language, and are usually more important than language-dependent factors.

[Material Deleted]

We recommend that the interested reader examine Weissman's study (1973) of the effect of various factors that are commonly thought to affect the intelligibility of programs, e.g., indentation, mnemonic identifiers, etc. The overall impression given by this study is that intelligibility is affected less by language features than one might expect. Thus, again, we emphasize that the above discussion must be tempered by the realities of its actual import.

Synonyms or Aliasing.   The ability to generate synonyms, or aliases, will impact large program organization as well as local readability. If there are two or more naming paths by which the same storage location can be addressed simultaneously, we say that synonyms, or aliases, exist for that location. Most aliasing arises in one of the following ways: (1) a global variable is passed as a parameter to a subroutine, so the subroutine can name the variable as both the formal parameter and as the global itself, (2) the same variable name is passed to a subroutine in two parameter positions, so the subroutine can name it with either formal name, (3) the language supports a "reference," or "pointer" data type, and two references to the same variable can be created and (4) an explicit "remapping" operation (or declaration) can appear in the language (e.g., EQUIVALENCE in FORTRAN).

In some cases, the ability to create synonyms can increase the readability of a program. Often, however, it can lead to subtle, but profound, interactions and hence to obscure programs.

[Material Deleted]

It seems clear that completely unconstrained aliasing is incompatible with modern software engineering practice, and it certainly precludes any possibility of program verification. The practicalities of the situation are unclear, however. No language that prohibits all aliasing has yet been used to construct a significant piece of software.

Abstraction Facilities.   The readability of even small sections of program text is affected by the kind and amount of detail exhibited in the text. An abstraction mechanism is one which permits the programmer to define all the details of the implementation of a conceptual entity in one, localized place. The most familiar abstraction mechanism is, of course, the subroutine. Subroutines, however, provide only operational (i.e., algorithmic) abstractions; modern programs also require data and control abstractions.

[Material Deleted]

Data issues.   Since the primary purpose of most programs is to transform data from one form to another, the data types and organizations provided by the language have a profound effect on the resulting programs. The important aspects of a language's data structuring facilities include its view of data types, the mechanisms for defining non-scalar structures, the degree of user control over data organization and representation, and the interaction between types and operations.

Language View of Type.   The fundamental view of typing in a language emerges through the set of primitive types provided and the degree of enforcement of type rules (that is, the "strength" of type checking).

[*Material Deleted*]

The extent of the influence these type selections have on the programmer is impacted by the degree to which type associations are enforced. That is, languages that check type correspondences under all circumstances force the programmer to be more attentive to his data than do those in which the type declaration means little more than a comment. The impact of type checking is also affected by the richness of the underlying type structure; if this is lean, information that might be carried in the types may have to be encoded in data. Enumerated types, for example, are superior to explicit integer encoding, even when they result in identical object code.

The strength of type checking is intimately related to the amount of coercion (i.e., automatic type conversion) permitted by the language. Coercions occur when the data to be used in some context has a type other than that explicitly anticipated by the program text. Performing the conversion automatically can serve as a convenience to the programmer, but it can also produce unexpected effects without warning. Type checking can also be defeated through aliasing; since aliasing problems are discussed above we shall not repeat the discussion here.

[*Material Deleted*]

Definition and Representation of Data.   A user may exercise control over data definitions at two levels: at the language level by defining new abstractions and at the machine level by controlling the low-level representation on the hardware.

At the high level, we must further distinguish between data organizations provided by the language itself and facilities provided to the programmer for application-specific structures. These might be as simple as enumerated types or as complex as extensions to the basic type structure of the language.

[*Material Deleted*]

Access to the underlying physical representation of data is also important. It is of major concern to programmers who must interface with given constraints, either in time, space, or pre-existing data representations.

[*Material Deleted*]

Interaction between Data and Operations.   The contemporary view of data types holds that types are characterized by both a set of values and a set of operations on those values. Thus the kinds of operations a language provides on its primitive data and the consistency of those operations from one type to another strongly affect the tone of the language. We must consider what kinds of operations are available, whether they can be applied to aggregate structure or only to scalars, and the degree to which they are implicitly invoked.

[Material Deleted]

Control issues. We will consider separately the commands used to describe the flow of control within a subprogram and the facilities for inter-module control.

Local Control. The considerations of modern programming methodology have identified a number of control constructs whose use leads to more manageable, understandable programs. These constructs are:

1. A grouping syntax (for making compound statements or blocks)
2. Two flavours of alternatives, an **if** and a **case** (either an enumerated or an indexed multi-way alternative construct)
3. Two styles of loops, a **while** loop that iterates until a specified condition is satisfied, and a **for** loop which sequences through a specified set of values and assigning each value in the sequence to a "control variable."

[Material Deleted]

Despite the theoretical soundness of the arguments in favour of the "well-structured" command set, certain practical situations [notably processing (local) exceptions] are awkward to handle with those commands alone. Therefore, in addition to the 'well-structured' control set, all these languages [FORTRAN, COBOL, JOVIAL, and Ada, as well as C and Pascal, Eds.] provide an explicit **goto**. However, the particular flavour of any **goto** is coloured by the possible destinations of the jump as determined, for example, by the scope of the statement labels.

[Material Deleted]

Non-local Control. In addition to the local control commands described above, all the languages provide inter-module control in the form of subroutine calls. Although these constructs are primarily concerned with organizing the relations among groups of programs, they also impact local programming. The inter-module issues are discussed below; here we focus on the local issue.

The subroutine is the primary tool for defining (and isolating) abstractions in most traditional languages; as such we have come to rely heavily on its properties. The properties that are important for local programming are: (1) how the body is delimited, (2) parameter conventions and options, and (3) local variable conventions and options.

[Material Deleted]

Efficiency concerns. Despite the fact that the need for "efficiency at all costs" has decreased as hardware has become less expensive and faster, there are some ways, and some applications, in which the efficiency of a language significantly affects the way in which it is used. In particular, programmers will contort a program's organization in order to avoid constructs that are known to be inefficient; typically, for example, procedures (subroutines) are larger in PL/I programs because programmers are aware of the overhead associated with calling them. Similarly, programmers will warp the organization of a program in order to use those features that are known to be efficient—as in the extensive use of COMMON in FORTRAN programs.

The impact of efficiency concerns arises in both programming "in the small" and "in the large"; we have placed the discussion here because it was the first opportunity to do so. The reader should be aware that these remarks actually apply in both contexts.

The first paragraph of this section used the phrase "the efficiency of a language"; this phrase requires some explanation. The major factor in determining the efficiency of a particular program is generally the proper choice of data structure and algorithm for that program—factors outside the influence of the language. Usually the next most important factor is the quality of the particular implementation of the language— a factor beyond the control of the language designer. In addition, however, the language design may prevent highly efficient implementation. It is these factors that are of concern in a language comparison, and even then they are of concern only to the extent that they are likely to impact good program organization.

[Material Deleted]

3.3 Programming in the Large

The languages we are concerned with in this report are used to write (the components of) large programming systems. A language comparison must therefore address the support they provide for problems that arise when programs are thousands of lines long, when programs are in use for many years, or when several programmers are involved in the design, implementation, and maintenance of a program system.

There are a number of software engineering methodologies for dealing with large programs. They differ in details, but they share a common view: When a project involves long times and several people, it must be possible to:

1. Decompose the task into subtasks which can be worked on independently.
2. Assemble the resultant pieces into a coherent, operational whole.
3. Manage the requisite long-term maintenance and enhancement.

Support for the tasks of decomposition, assembly and maintenance must be provided in many ways, not just through the programming language. For example, when more than one person is involved in these activities a number of management and coordination problems arise. A tool, e.g., a language, cannot solve all of these problems, but it may facilitate their solution. Thus, in this section we shall consider those aspects of the languages under consideration that impact these issues.

Decomposition of the system.   A system may be decomposed along natural lines in any of several dimensions. Two obvious dimensions are functional and data-oriented, but there may be others and, of course, a single system may be decomposed along more than one dimension simultaneously.

We will discuss each of these dimensions presently; whatever the nature of the decomposition, however, the resulting pieces must correspond to "work assignments" (Parnas, 1972). That is, the decomposition is not useful unless it permits a portion of the original task to be performed by a person (or team) in relative isolation. As we shall see, the major impact of language issues on "programming in the large" is the degree to which a language permits or encourages such independence.

By a *functional* decomposition we mean one which emphasizes major algorithmic components of the system. Often such components are temporally related: First one component is applied to the data, then the next, and so on until the task is complete. This is the traditional view of program decomposition and is typified by elaborate and detailed specifications of the data structures which form the "interface" between the functional subunits.

By a *data-oriented* decomposition we mean one which emphasizes the major (abstract) data structures and the operations defined on them. This view of decomposition is more modern and, although not proven on a large number of systems, is gaining a great deal of favour. It is typified by careful, often mathematical, specifications of the abstract data structures in terms of their invariant properties and the operations which may be applied to them.

Since no practical decomposition is purely functional or purely data-oriented, the issues related to both become entwined in the following discussion.

Languages can affect the ability to decompose a system into modules in two important ways. We must first ask what kinds of modular decompositions are supported by the language; that is, we must examine the facilities for defining and using abstractions. We must then consider the extent to which they ensure the actual independence of separate work assignments.

Definition and Use of Abstractions.   Abstraction is one of the most important tools of the modern software engineer. The language designer's choices about abstraction facilities have a strong impact on the availability of functional or data-oriented abstraction. This, in turn, determines which system designs (i.e., decompositions) are practically feasible.

Almost all languages provide some methods for separating the definitions of isolable concepts from the use of those concepts: at a bare minimum, procedures will be available.

[*Material Deleted*]

Enforcement of Independence.   When a system is decomposed into isolated tasks that are created as independent work assignments, it is important that each programmer know *how* other program segments will depend on his. The most important term of support is clear specification of the interface, but that is (at present) not a language issue. Some language facilities do support this independence, however. The degree to which abstractions can be encapsulated (see preceding section) is important, as is the ability to avoid aliasing (see above). A third set of features affects the programmer's ability to control when and by whom his data may be accessed. These later features include scope and extent rules, allocation policies, and declarations.

The scope, extent and allocation rules for a variable determine the lifetime of the variable and the portions of the program in which it can be accessed. Scope and extent rules for a variable are usually, but not always, determined by its declaration. Allocation rules are generally inflexible; at most a small menu of allocation policies is available.

[*Material Deleted*]

Assembly of a system from components.   The task of assembling a number of independent modules into a coherent, operational system is usually regarded as a problem in integration and testing. As such, it is supported primarily by non-linguistic tools such as file librarians, linkers, debugging systems, and analysis packages. Although (as for decomposition) the language is not the dominant factor affecting the task, some properties of the language may be of substantial help or hindrance. These aspects of the language are concerned with the ways independently-developed units can be coupled and with the safety of the assembly process.

In the preceding section we discussed the ways a system can be separated into independent subproblems. In that discussion we were concerned with the *logical* separation of modules. However, if individuals or small teams are to work independently, it is extremely helpful to be able to separate the tasks *physically* as well. The degree to which the language supports the development of physically independent modules impacts the integration process and the testing style. The amount of support the language provides for making sure that interface assumptions are observed is also important.

Physical Independence of Modules.   The most common way to support physically independent module development is to provide a means for independently compiling the various modules of a system. This provides a boundary for protection of data; it may facilitate independent testing; and it may allow substantial savings in compilation time.

In order to establish a common context between separately-compiled modules, particularly in a functional decomposition, it is necessary to communicate both the structure and the location of the data that is being shared. This context may be established by linking separate code segments into a common address space, or it may be loosely coupled, with external data serving to carry the common information. In sharing, it is at least necessary to communicate the location of the code, and perhaps other properties as well (e.g., number and/or types of the parameters).

[*Material Deleted*]

Checking Module Linkages.   The only form of module specification provided in current languages takes the form of type and number checking of external declarations and parameters. External linkages were discussed in the previous section; we turn now to parameters.*

Parameter binding rules determine whether the actual parameter may be used for input or for output, whether it is re-evaluated each time it is used, and whether or not its value is dynamically updated during procedure execution. In addition, a language may or may not enforce type checking across procedure calls, particularly when separately compiled modules are involved.

[*Material Deleted*]

Maintenance and enhancement.   We have grouped together maintenance (repairing errors) and enhancement (adding features or improving performance) because they involve similar activities and are both done on "operational" systems. Experience, often bitter experience, suggests that these activities are both costly and error-prone, and hence deserve special attention in the design of the tools (e.g., languages) used.

The most outstanding characteristic needed in a maintainable system is *understandability*. The person responsible for maintaining a system is usually not one of its original authors—and even when it is, the interactions in large systems are usually subtle, complex, and easily forgotten. Thus the first problem of maintenance is to (re)understand the existing code well enough to design and implement the necessary changes.

Some aspects of understandability are discussed in the sections on programming in the small. However large programs introduce additional problems. It is no longer the case that the definition and use of each variable (or subroutine) will appear within a few pages of each other. One cannot simply "flip pages" to find how a variable was declared, whether it is ever used in particular ways, or whether certain properties of it are assumed by the code. Indeed the definition and uses of a variable (or subroutine) may not even be in the same module (or file), and responsibility for maintenance of the modules may reside with different people. Thus, while the ability to indent, to use nicely-structured control constructs, and so on, are helpful for understanding local parts of the system, they do not address some of the essential properties of large-system maintenance.

The preceding paragraph emphasizes one aspect of maintaining large systems— the need to be able to locate relevant information. The dual problem, which is even more important, is to hide irrelevant information. Humans are not well suited to coping with vast amounts of detail, and systems maintainers are no exception. The maintainer needs to be able to function with an abstract model of the components of the system—to be able to understand the components in terms of what they do rather than the details of how they do it. When errors are to be fixed or changes made he uses this model to guide him to the code to be modified—and, equally importantly, to suggest what code can be ignored as irrelevant to the current task.

There is a clear tension between these two aspects of making a large system understandable; some information must be easy to find, other information must be hidden. Modern methodology, of course, holds that systems can be structured, often hierarchically, so that at a given level there is a clear separation between what must be known and what must be hidden. We subscribe to that view but it must be remembered that: (1) it often takes an especially perceptive individual to devise a suitable structure for a given system, and (2) none of the existing languages was designed at a time when these issues were as clear as they now are.

[*Material Deleted*]

4 CONCLUSIONS

4.1 On Describing Languages through Cores

We developed the core approach to language comparison for much the same reason that motivates us to devise abstractions for our programs. Full language definitions contain an enormous amount of detail; most of it, however, is not significant for our goals. By concentrating on the essence of the languages, we are able to focus on the properties that in fact influence the way programs are written. It is these properties that should be compared to satisfy our goals, and the suppression of other information eliminates many distractions from the discussion. The resulting analysis is, we believe, more pertinent to the goal than a comprehensive comparison of details would have been.

The cores for the three existing languages are all short—the syntax definitions are about one page long—but they span the actual languages well. Indeed, we had to deviate from the core languages only slightly to write runnable versions of the example programs, and those deviations were primarily concessions to our operating system. Throughout the comparisons, we found that the cores included the aspects of the languages that our intuitions argued are pertinent to software engineering.

This is not to say that any subset of a language which is complete, or almost complete, can serve as a core for a study such as this. On the contrary, defining a representative core requires substantial sensitivity to language issues in general and to the languages under comparison in particular. It is easy, for example, to define a computationally complete subset of FORTRAN that fails to capture the flavour and power of the language. Once a representative core has been defined, however, it sharpens the issues and leads to more concrete comparison.[4]

4.2 Remarks on the Comparisons

The dimensions along which we compared the core languages were chosen to emphasize our view of software engineering. We see three major interactions between language design and software engineering practice. First, the language designer's implicit assumptions about programs and programming have subtle but important effects on the language and its usefulness as a tool. Second, the language is the primary tool for actually writing the algorithms that control computations. As such, its uniformity and expressive power has a strong impact on the programmer at those times when he is actually generating code. This is programming in the small. Third, all significant

---

[4] It is interesting to consider whether the core approach could serve as a training tool or an organizational principle for a course in language comparison. We are enamoured of the idea, but it is inappropriate to pursue it here.

systems are made up of many components and the choice of language affects both the decomposition of a system into components and the styles of communication among those components. These considerations impact multi-person projects—that is, programming in the large.

[*Material Deleted*]

[In addition to those references cited above, the following works were consulted in the preparation of this article: American Standards Association (1966, 1974, 1978), U.S. Air Force (1976a,b), and U.S. Department of Defense (1960, 1977).]

ACKNOWLEDGMENTS

We are particularly grateful to Carolyn Councill and Howard Wactlar for system support provided during the preparation of this report, and to Roy Weil (of Michael Baker, Jr., Inc) for his insightful comments on the use of the programming languages in practical contexts.

This research was supported by the Rome Air Development Center under Contract No. F30602–75–C–0218.

[*Material Deleted*]

H. J. BOOM AND E. DE JONG

Mathematisch Centrum, Amsterdam, The Netherlands

A Critical Comparison of Several Programming Language Implementations

1 INTRODUCTION

Around the end of 1974, it was decided to carry out a comparison of some of the programming language implementations available on the CDC Cyber 73 of the Stichting Academisch Rekencentrum Amsterdam (henceforth known as SARA). The intention was to provide some guidance to new users of this system. In order to limit the scope of this study, four languages were selected for which there was general interest within the Mathematical Centre (MC). These were ALGOL 60, ALGOL 68, FORTRAN and Pascal.

It soon became clear that running computer programs and measuring execution times and storage consumption would tell less than half of the story. For most programming projects, qualitative aspects of the language are far more important than quantitative ones. The varying facilities available in different languages strongly affect their suitability for different problems. Indeed, in recent years it has become generally known that assembly languages may not be the best tools to use on large systems programming projects, even if efficiency of execution is the most important criterion. The code generated by a good optimizing compiler can be better than that produced by a good assembly language programmer, if the program is large.

The scope of the study has therefore been extended to include various qualitative aspects.

Finally, we must mention that we have found this analysis to be far more difficult and time-consuming than we had originally expected. It may well be that errors have crept into this critique, perhaps because the systems were themselves being changed or replaced by new versions during the study. If so, we would appreciate hearing of them.

226

2 THE LANGUAGE IMPLEMENTATION

[Material Deleted]

But it is the implementation of a language that a programmer uses, and in his eyes the implementation becomes inseparable from the language. Each implementer makes his own impact on the user by various deficiences and extras. Little distinction will therefore be made in the rest of this paper between the implementations and the languages. The following implementations were studied:

Pascal
ALGOL 60:   CDC ALGOL 60 version 3
             CDC ALGOL 60 version 4
ALGOL 68:   CDC ALGOL 68 version 1.0.9
FORTRAN: CDC Extended FORTRAN

3 COMPATIBILITY

It is desirable to be able to export programs to other installations and to import programs from other installations. It is even more pleasant if those other installations can achieve reasonable communication even though the computing machinery they possess differs greatly from that locally available. Such "portability" significantly increases the market for any program one wishes to export, and makes it possible to avoid effort by importing a working program instead of writing one locally.

There are essentially two means of transporting programs. First, it may be possible to have them written in a generally available programming language. Second, it may be possible to have them clearly written in a language of such elegant semantics that it becomes very easy to translate them to one of the locally available languages by hand. Translating an existing program usually involves less work than writing a new one, *if* the original program is easy to understand.

The first approach seems quite attractive, and one must choose the language. It is important that

1. the language be standard,
2. an implementation be locally available, and
3. the implementation indeed implements the language.

If the language does not have a unique definition with some official status, it is extremely unlikely that implementations on different machines will be even slightly compatible. For example, although nearly every large computer has several implementations of Lisp, they differ sufficiently that it is not practical to use Lisp as a language for portable programming.

If an implementation of the language is not available, it is impossible to write debugged programs for export. Import is still possible if one is willing to convert the program by hand, but it is extremely tedious.

It is desirable that the local implementation implements *exactly* the standard. If it implements a subset of the standard, importing programs becomes difficult. If it implements a superset of the standard, it becomes impossible to be certain that a locally debugged program for export does not accidentally use a superlanguage feature. Such matters may be extremely subtle. An implementation may define some matter which the language definition leaves undefined, such as whether variables are initialized to any specific value. Initialization could be relied on without any explicit mention of the fact within the program.

If the implementation accepts some standard language features but assigns *different* semantics to them, it will be extremely difficult either to import or export programs. Compilers will not detect such language deviations in a program; the answers will merely be wrong.

Because of practical difficulties, it will usually be necessary to make some small changes in a program upon transportation even if a conscientious attempt was made to adhere to the standard language. It is then of great importance that the program be readable.

It may in some cases be easier to hand-recode a program written clearly but in a locally unavailable language than to alter a confusing program written in a slight variation on a locally available language.

3.1 Pascal

Pascal is defined by a defining Report (Jensen and Wirth, 1975). Different editions of this Report are, however, rumoured to differ on points such as heap storage allocation and freeing, and the Report is not at all clear about crucial matters such as data type equivalence. As a result, significant differences will appear among implementations even if the implementers have the best of intentions. The CDC implementation does appear to conform closely to the Report; it appears that other implementations are likely to do so too. Nonetheless, it is not clear to what extent the Pascal implementation for the Cyber is compatible with implementations on other machines. Other implementations are only now appearing, and reports of experience with them has not yet reached a general audience. The Report leaves ample room for implementers to use machine-dependent criteria such as the size of a machine word to determine a number of details. It would be reasonable if this extended to matters such as the precision of arithmetic, but at a number of points these limitations can be expected to affect program correctness severely. The following list contains important parameters:

- The number of significant characters in an identifier. (Extra ones are legal and ignored. This can be disastrous if one attempts to transport a program and finds that formerly distinct identifiers have become identical, or vice versa.)
- The size and coding of the character set.

- The number of elements permitted in a power set. (The CDC implementation permits 59. This means that a **set of** *char* is impossible, because 64 characters are recognized in the character set.)
- The number of characters in a value of type *alfa*.

Other implementations will probably find other ways to impose annoying qualitative restrictions by propagating low-level machine-dependencies to the level of the high-level language. Pascal provides high-level concepts, but restricts them so that the programmer has to think in machine terms.

Whether a program violates the above constraints is a matter that can easily be determined at compile-time. There seems to be no reason why the CDC compiler should not compile code for these prohibited cases anyway, perhaps by using more storage for larger objects, without impairing run-time efficiency one whit for the nonuser. The CDC compiler has set an example of unnecessary machine-dependent restrictions which we regret other implementers appear to be following.

[*Material Deleted*]

4 RELIABILITY

It is not sufficient that the programmer, with one finger on the language definition and one on the coding sheet, can write texts which resemble syntactically correct programs. He must also be able to run such a program on a real machine, correct any errors it might contain, and ascertain that it does then perform reliably.

The behaviour of the language and of the implementation has enormous influence on debugging. The implementation itself must reliably conform to specifications, the specifications must be clear, simple and useful, and the language and implementation must together prevent errors and clearly report those which do occur. We can distinguish a number of specific requirements.

The implementation itself must work, and be fully debugged. If a program fails, the programmer must be able to be certain that the fault lies with the program and not with the implementation. If there are implementation errors, they must be well publicized and swiftly repaired.

The language must actively help a programmer to structure his programs. This does not mean that it must straightjacket the programmer into one specific approved style of program construction; it must instead provide primitives that are of use in forming structure, and in detecting accidental violations of any structure the programmer himself imposes. The language must, furthermore, refrain from providing the unwary with traps.

There are more ways to structure a program than a man can shake a stick at.

One man's bug is another man's structure.

Traditional

The implementation must then help the programmer to find the errors remaining in the program. It must be possible for the implementation to catch all language violations. It must be highly likely that programmer errors lead to such language violations, preferably ones that are detected at compile time. It must be easy for the programmer to request such thorough checking. When an error is detected, it must be easy for the programmer to find it. The implementation should assist him, providing a reasonable amount of post-mortem information in a readable form. The implementation may not run amok, providing false or misleading messages or forcing the programmer to wade through octal or similar core dumps.

Complete checking has two virtues.

First, it can signal the presence of certain program bugs, to wit, those which cause the program to violate language restrictions. Even if checking were only 98 per cent complete, bug-detection would not be significantly impaired. A bug which fails to be detected by one possible but absent check will likely be caught by another.

Second, it can be used in finding the error. For example, suppose one wishes to know at which point in a program a variable receives an anomalous value. It is an enormous help to know that this cannot happen through the use of an out-of-bounds subscript in an apparently irrelevant assignment. The fact of complete checking can thus be used in logical deductive reasoning to reduce the search domain drastically. This property is completely lost if checking is only 98 per cent complete.

The fact of complete checking, together with a selective and readable post-mortem dump, is often more useful than run-time tracing of jumps, assignments to specific variables and the like. Complete checking, moreover, does not have to be planned in advance; whereas the more traditional traces must be carefully used in further runs after a bug has been detected.

4.1 Pascal

Until April 1975, errors were found in the Pascal compiler in use at SARA, and new releases appeared approximately every $1\frac{1}{2}$ to 2 months. The latest release was received in August 1975, and no errors in it have come to the authors' attention. [*Ed. note*: *The original version of this paper is dated April 1977.*] It thus appears to be of reasonably solid construction. This is perhaps because the current version of the compiler was itself written in Pascal. This makes reasonable clarity of code possible, and makes the compiler itself one of its own test cases. Unfortunately, when one examines the source code of the compiler itself, one finds it written in an unreadable and nearly comment-free style.

Identifiers may contain only 10 significant characters; extra characters may be coded, but are ignored without warning by the compiler. It is thus easy for a programmer to code two apparently different identifiers and have the compiler misinterpret the program by failing to recognize the difference. This can be catastrophic if the two identifiers are of the same type, since the error can then go completely undetected.

Syntactic error recovery is good; it is extremely rare to get two error messages for one single syntax error. However, missing or extra **begin**s or **end**s can cause the compiler to fail to properly identify identifiers, which can cause much trouble. Nonetheless, the compiler rarely loses all track of the intended syntactic structure, and therefore it is possible to remove syntactic errors in relatively few runs.

Run-time checking is incomplete. There are a number of points where program errors can lead to incomprehensible and undefinable chaos. Two serious problems are variants, and the parameters of parameters.

A Pascal record may have "variants," which means that at various times, different fields may be present in the record. (The record corresponds to the ALGOL 68 structure, and the variants to united modes.) Unfortunately, there is no built-in check to ensure, when a field of some variant is used, that the variant with that field indeed does reside in the record at that time. This can be used for intentional or unintentional punning. As Niklaus Wirth (1975) says, assembly language programmers delight in ingeniously misusing features provided with honest intentions to betray the language's very principles. The serious high-level language user must lament the lack of security and the resulting difficulty debugging.

When writing a procedure which accepts a procedure as a parameter, there is no way to specify the types of the parameters to the parameter, although these are usually known to the programmer. There is therefore no compile-time check on the compatibility of the parameter type checking in such cases. There appears to be no run-time check either.

Pascal does provide list processing, but does not provide a garbage collector. This means that storage allocation and freeing must be explicitly coded by the programmer, with the attendant risk of catastrophic error. Storage allocation is done using the procedures *new* for allocation and *dispose* for freeing. If the storage freed by *dispose* is reused by *new*, there is danger that the now reused storage is still pointed to by a pointer left over from its previous use. This can cause interactions between independent parts of a program that are extremely difficult to diagnose. If the storage is not reused by *new*, there is no sense in using *dispose* at all, and any serious attempt to do list processing will fail when memory becomes full of useless list cells that cannot be reused.

There seems to be no secure way of implementing the language defined by the Pascal report on conventional computers without going to the prohibitive expense of providing tag bits on every value for dynamic type checks. Without such a run-time mechanism, Pascal is not type-secure. A garbage collector is therefore not practical, and programmers will have to make do with an insecure language.

At program termination, Pascal provides a symbolic dump of the run-time stack, including the names of variables. Unfortunately, the elements of arrays and records are not printed, the records allocated by *new* are not printed and nothing at all sensible can be printed if the above-mentioned insecure use of pointers has seriously damaged the stack.

[Material Deleted]

5 ARITHMETIC

The hardware of the CDC Cyber is notorious for the poor quality of its arithmetic. It provides no immediate warning of overflow, underflow or serious loss of significance, and instead yields infinite, indefinite or nonsensical values and allows computation to continue. Such undetected faults can seriously impair the reliability of numerical results.

It must be granted that only a finite subset of all numbers can be represented on a computer. Operations cannot always be performed exactly, since their exact values may not belong to this finite subset. Nonetheless, it is reasonable to require a number of properties to hold on the operations as implemented by the hardware. For example, one might require:

1. If the exact result of an operation on specific operands is exactly representable on the machine, then a representation of that exact result must be produced by the machine operation.
2. If the mathematically exact operation is monotonically increasing (decreasing) over some range, then the implementation shall not be decreasing (increasing) over that range.
3. If there is no reasonable approximation to the exact result available, an error will be signalled in an effective manner.

Further conditions, and some discussion on their necessity, have been described by Kuki (1971). Such properties are, in fact, more important than that the computed values be "close" to the true values. Many iterative algorithms do not require high precision, but will fail if one of these requirements (such as monotonicity) is not satisfied.

The arithmetic on the CDC Cyber fails even the *first* of these requirements. What is even more amazing, it fails to satisfy it on *integer* arithmetic! The machine ostensibly provides 60-bit integers, 59 bits and a sign bit. It uses one's-complement arithmetic; there are therefore two representations for zero, a $+ 0$ and a $- 0$. Correct fixed point addition and subtraction operators are provided (except for overflow), but multiplication fails if the product exceeds 2^{48}. No error indication is provided; the answer is instead just wrong. There is no fixed point divide instruction; floating point division must be used instead, followed by truncation to integer. Division thus also fails on integers greater than 2^{48}.

Floating-point addition and subtraction produce an unnormalized result, which can be separately normalized by a normalize instruction. This implies that under some conditions the last (significant) bit of computed value is irretrievably lost.

The Cyber appears to satisfy the second requirement except when capacity constraints such as the above are exceeded, but does not satisfy the third one properly. Depending upon the operations performed, one may get a nonsensical result or a special value 'infinity' upon overflow. In some cases, special 'indefinite' values can be produced. If the result is nonsensical, computation can merrily continue, combining nonsense to beget more nonsense. If the result is infinite, an error interrupt is not signalled by hardware until an attempt is made to use the infinite values as an operand. Production of infinite or indefinite values is perhaps tolerable, since it is at least possible to see afterward that something has gone wrong, though it may no longer be easy to find out where. But getting nonsensical answers without warning, as happens when a fixed point multiplication goes out of range, is really inexcusable.

For reasonable reliability, a programming language implementation on the Cyber must find ways of compensating for these deficiencies. The results must be correct, not merely rapidly computed. Unfortunately, proper software compensation for these hardware faults is prohibitively expensive. The most that is usually done is to post warnings in manuals as to the limitations of the implemented arithmetic.

The reasons for the various code sequences generated by the Pascal compiler are discussed by Wirth (1972). The serious user of the CDC 6600 is strongly advised to read this paper, because its 'understanding may prevent him from certain pitfalls which are inherent in the use of the CDC 6600.'

[*Material Deleted*]

6 DOCUMENTATION

There must exist precise and readable documents describing the language and the implementation. There must be a rigorous definition of the language for reference, and there must be introductions for beginners. The implementation manuals must clearly describe the interface with the operating system, restrictions, extensions and other deviations from the standard language, and implementation decisions relating language features to the machine. All information necessary for use must be in the manual, and the user must not have to experiment to determine facts about language features. The documentation must be readily available, whether this be through bookstores or manufacturers' representatives.

6.1 Pascal

There is a user's manual and defining report (Jensen and Wirth, 1975). It appears to correspond closely to the implementation on the Cyber, and clearly distinguishes between the Standard Pascal language and implementation quirks. It is on sale to the public through normal channels.

It is usually clear and explicit, except for some guilty secrets involving datatype equivalence. Several violations of run-time security are mentioned in this paper in the section on "Reliability," but the manual nowhere mentions that the language misuse that leads to such insecurity is indeed unlawful. Apparently it hopes that failing to mention an unchecked restriction will prevent users from running into it by accident.

The discussion of separate compilation in the Pascal user's manual can only be called inadequate. A few hints are given, and the bright thinker who is familiar with the CDC Cyber and the way things work there is left to puzzle it out himself.

Wirth (1972) is essential if one wishes to know the limitations of the arithmetic as implemented. It is unfortunate that these limitations are not clearly presented in Chapter 13 of the Pascal user manual, which describes peculiarities of the Pascal 6000–3·4 implementation.

[*Material Deleted*]

7 EXPRESSIVE POWER

"Expressive power" is the most important (and most qualitative) aspect of programming language design. It refers to the interaction between the language, good patterns of thought and the domain of application. It is slowly becoming clear that one's programming languages determine one's patterns of thought, limit one's ability to see elegant methods of solving problems and limit the useful generality and flexibility of one's programs. In the linguistics of natural languages, the effect of language on thought is very difficult to distinguish from the effect of thought on language. This is different from computer linguistics for several reasons. First, a programming language is a relatively static entity, and does not change whenever a programmer discovers a new programming concept. A natural language usually responds instantly by acquiring a new word. Second, the class of programming language users is enormously larger than the class of language designers; a programmer has much less influence on his programming language than a speaker has on the natural language spoken in his circle of friends.

We shall examine expressive power from the viewpoint of structured programming and general purpose languages.

A programming language must be able to express the structure of programs written in it. The structure must be visible in the program, and not merely hidden in the mind of the programmer.

"General purpose" will be understood in the following sense. It must be possible to adapt the programming language to various purposes, perhaps by the definition of procedures and data types or by the choice of variable names. A large program usually contains collections of primitive routines that implement basic operations on those special kinds of objects that the program deals with. Such a collection of primitive routines in effect defines a specialized dialect of the programming language for the problem at hand. It must be possible to build such specialized dialects on a general purpose language. There are many possible dialects for many different applications. Nonetheless, it is possible to distinguish some "general purpose" features. These are features which occur in many different dialects, or which are necessary tools for constructing dialects. A general purpose language must possess such features. The language designer should keep them down to a small, easily understood set. Because, ultimately, all operations are carried out on a computer, machine operations common to many computers are usually included in general purpose languages.

It is not necessary, from the viewpoint of expressive power, that the features provided be easy to implement. It *is* important that they be easy to use and have simple properties. Many implementers unnecessarily complicate the properties of the primitive concepts of their language by propagating machine-dependent patterns of thought upwards. This can cause much agony to a programmer who finds himself required to think on two levels of abstraction at once—that of his dialect, and that of the machine hardware. These machine-dependent aspects often involve capacity constraints—limits on the size of a program, on the number of blocks or identifiers and so forth. Such limits are usually imposed because an implementation has chosen fixed size tables or has chosen to place certain information in main storage, which is limited in capacity. It is important that all such limits be soft. Other implementation techniques should be invoked automatically when the limits are exceeded. Excess table information can be placed on disc or extended core storage, excess object code can be handled by overlay techniques, etc. This will probably influence efficiency, but not (directly) possibility. The price can very well be worth paying if it makes it unnecessary to confusingly and perhaps catastrophically maim a program in order to trim it after a restriction has been encountered.

7.1 Pascal

At first sight, Pascal seems to be singularly free of the barnacles usually found encrusted on a programming language. Further inquiry, however, leads one to conclude that the ragged collections of extra features that other languages bear have been replaced by ragged and inconvenient restrictions.

The most important restriction in Pascal is that the sizes of all arrays are determined at compile time. It is therefore impossible to write many programs efficiently and clearly in such a way that they are independent of the amount of data to be processed. The only way to maintain a program library of, say, numerical routines is to keep it in source form. To use a routine in the library, the user must make a copy of the source code, tinker with the array bounds, and include it in his own program. If he wishes to call the library procedure several times, giving it arrays of different sizes, he must include multiple copies of the procedure, each with a separate name and a separate array size. In this respect, Pascal is more restrictive than even FORTRAN, which at least permits a subroutine to be told by its caller what the size of an array argument is. Needless to say, algorithms which rely on a procedure that recursively calls itself for subarrays or smaller arrays than the original parameters can not be cleanly expressed in Pascal.

It is possible to parameterize array sizes at compile time, using a manifest constant. If this is declared once, its name can thereafter be used in array declarations, and the compiler will find the appropriate actual size at compile time. This makes it possible to localize the dependency of a program on array sizes. Unfortunately, expressions such as $N + 1$, where N is a manifest constant, or even $3 + 1$ are not allowed as array bounds.

There are a host of restrictions on parameters and values yielded by procedures.

One can divide values into two classes: "normal" values and "second rate" values. Normal values are those which fit into one word on the CDC Cyber 73 (so much for machine independence), and second-rate values are those which do not. In the Pascal Report, when one reads through the various rules and restrictions, one finds that the second-rate values are records and arrays. There may be some sense in making such a distinction between elementary and compound values. On the other hand, Pascal presumably does not have double precision arithmetic because double precision values would have to be elementary but do not fit into a single machine word. By experimenting with the compiler one discovers that the type *alfa*, which is a packed array of characters, can often be used as if it were elementary after all! It does fit into a single word on the Cyber.

With the "normal" values, one can do anything one pleases. One can pass them to procedures as parameters, and one can return them as values. One cannot do this with the "second rate" values. As an example of the elegance of Pascal's data structures, the Pascal manual shows how complex numbers can be represented as records containing two real numbers each. It is clear, since Pascal does not have complex numbers built in, that one cannot use the usual operations +, −, *, and / on them, and procedures must be written. At this point the manual forgets about the example and goes on to other matters. One would expect to have to write functions *add*, *subtract*, *multiply* and *divide* to perform arithmetic, so as to be able to write an expression

add (*multiply* (*a, b*), *multiply* (*c, d*))

instead of $a*b + c*d$. Unfortunately (and here comes the catch), these procedures cannot be written either, since they would have to deliver second rate values as function values.

It is not clear what the language or the programmer gains from such inconvenience. It cannot be efficiency, since the programmer who needs these facilities is now required to go to complex circumlocutions to express what might have been simple. Since the compiler can easily distinguish between single-word values and multiple-word values at compile time, the non-user of multiple-word values should not need to suffer inefficiency for a feature he does not use.

"Power sets" are provided as one of the means of constructing new types from old. Given any scalar type (except *real*, which is a kludge), one can construct its power set type, whose values are sets of values of the original type. This is a very clean concept of wide generality. Unfortunately, power sets are classed as normal values and must therefore fit within one CDC machine word. This, in turn, makes it quite clear that the purpose of introducing power sets was not to make available a clean and elegant concept for program construction, but to provide access to the underlying hardware bit manipulation. A power set of characters, for example, would seem to provide an elegant way of classifying characters. Instead, it is useless, because the character set contains 64 characters, not merely 59. (Power sets are actually restricted to 59 bits instead of to 60 to avoid having to distinguish between positive and negative zero.)

A language design should not rule out "inefficient" features by imposing implementation restrictions, if this forces the programmer who needs them to go to even more inefficient circumlocutions to compensate. The only time that such a restriction can be excused is if the unrestricted feature would cause significant costs to non-users.

Pascal does provide something resembling COBOL and PL/I style record-directed input/output. A file consists of elements of some single data type; another file may have another data type. This type may be a record type, and it may be an array type. Each input or output operation transfers one value of the specified type, without formatting or conversion. Unlike CDC COBOL, Pascal does not use the Record Manager.

Special kludges are provided to graft page and line structure onto character files, and to provide a small amount of formatting on output. Unlike COBOL and PL/I, Pascal does not provide any types for decimal arithmetic, and therefore the record structure cannot be used to achieve formatting.

Here are some typical stupid restrictions:

1. Power sets may have only 59 elements.
2. These 59 elements must each be such that *ord* (*element*) is between 0 and 58, inclusive.
3. Strings may be compared only if their length is less than 10 or a multiple of 10.
4. Only the first 10 characters of an identifier are significant.

[*Material Deleted*]

8 LARGE PROGRAMS

When large programs are written, or when small programs become large (they inevitably do), serious logistic problems arise. The first difficulty is that the program itself becomes difficult to understand because of its complexity. At still greater size, it becomes difficult merely to deal with the amounts of text involved.

To deal with these problems, programming languages and their implementations have adopted various small-scale and large-scale structuring facilities and shoehorns. These may involve:

- pleasant control structures, such as the if-then-else of ALGOL 60 and loops
- the ability to break a program into modules, such as procedures or groups of declarations
- the ability to use textual layout to indicate program structure (e.g., indentation and pagination)
- the ability to restrict the scopes of names of those portions of the text where they are meaningful

- the ability to code large modules containing smaller modules
- the ability to compile modules separately, and to combine them later
- the ability to manage complicated file structures containing source and object code in an intelligent manner
- shoehorns (such as overlay mechanisms) to handle object code or data which is too large for the address space of the machine

Alas, any program management facilities that make vital use of the file system on direct access secondary storage have to be considered useless at SARA, because of the policy of scratching files after 4 days of inactivity.

It is important to be able to fragment programs into separate compilations without having planned it beforehand, and without extensive rewriting. An unexpected split may become necessary through slow and gradual growth of an originally small program, or through importing programs from a larger installation.

The use of separate compilation and other shoehorn mechanisms should not exclude the use of other implementation facilities, such as run-time debugging tools. It is precisely when a program is large that one needs all the debugging aids one can get.

8.1 Pascal

Two methods are available for managing large programs.

First, procedures can be declared within one another, subject to the usual nested name scope rules. Unfortunately, this block structure does not permit declarations within **begin-end** blocks. The only "blocks" for determining the scopes of names are procedures. Declarations can be made within each procedure and are then valid throughout the procedure. Such nested procedure structure is adequate up to a fairly large program. It tends to break down only when the program itself becomes physically hard to manage.

Secondly, groups of procedures can be compiled separately. It is possible (but not easy) to surmise from the Pascal manual how this is to be done. The details are instructively chaotic. The main program, which calls the procedures, is provided with dummy declarations of the separately compiled procedures. Such a dummy declaration is just like a normal declaration except that the body is replaced by the single reserved word **extern** or **Fortran.** If **Fortran** is coded, the separately compiled program is called using FORTRAN linkage conventions (and it can thus be a FORTRAN routine; see the section on escape for complaints) and if **extern** is used Pascal linkage conventions are used.

To compile the external routines, a program is compiled with the "$E+$" option. The object code for each procedure will then have an entry point name consisting of the first seven letters of the procedure name. If the dummy procedure in the calling program has the same name, contact is achieved.

When one attempts to use this mechanism, however, one begins to feel like a sneak thief, relying on his wits and good luck to keep things from going wrong.

First, the $E+$ option should normally not be used if one is not interested in separate compilation. If two procedures happen to have the same name (which is legal if they are in different ranges) they will get the same entry point, and the system loader will refuse to load more than one of them. All calls will be routed to this single one, regardless of the program block structure. Thus (as hinted in the manual) one must use the $E-$ option, whereupon "a unique symbol is generated by the compiler" for each procedure. This would seem clear. However, if one is concerned with separate compilation, new phenomena occur. If one compiles a group of procedures separately, one might expect that one can use $E+$ for some of them to make them available publicly and $E-$ for others in the group that are to be available internally (perhaps one of them is a local procedure within a larger public one). However, as soon as one attempts this, the compiler generates the same "unique" external names for every separate compilation.

The only way to avoid this is, despite the apparent block structure of Pascal, to give each procedure in the separate compilation a unique name and specify $E+$ for all of them. No checks are provided by the compiler for duplicate external names. It is even possible to confuse procedures in disjoint blocks, with different static nesting depths. Furthermore, none of these names may be of the form "PRCdddd," where each "d" stands for an octal digit. These are the unique names Pascal generates.

There is no check on parameter compatability between separately compiled procedures. The separate compilation method can, with care, be used in building large programs. However, it is virtually useless when building program libraries because of the array-bound restrictions. As lamented in the section "Expressive Power," all Pascal array bounds are fixed at compile time. It is therefore impossible to precompile array manipulation procedures for program libraries without knowing the users' array sizes (before the users have even thought of the problem they are going to use the library for).

The Pascal compiler is capable of compiling itself. It itself is a Pascal program of some 7000 lines.

Pascal does not have conditional expressions. This is unfortunate, since a conditional boolean expression is often needed in a **while**-loop.

[Material Deleted]

9 COMMUNICATION WITH THE OPERATING ENVIRONMENT

For a programming language to be useful for general use, it must have a decent operating system interface. This means that those options in the operating system which might reasonably be expected to match with language features must indeed interact harmoniously. The most important areas involve fault detection, input/output and interactiveness.

The implementation must cause errors detected by the operating system to be signalled to the programmer in a reasonable way. It must not give up on error recovery and readable post-mortem activity simply because the operating system has detected the error instead of the language implementation.

The implementation should be capable of accepting and producing the various kinds of files that the operating system supports. On the Cyber 73 under Scope 3.4, these supported file types are implemented by the "Record Manager." In addition, SARA provides an encoding for paper tapes as sequences of 12-bit characters. (Since line length is not always clearly defined on paper tape, it may be difficult to use the Record Manager for such files.) Furthermore, several other forms of 12-bit character files are recognized by some of the line printers and terminal drivers as representing a character set of more than 64 characters. The Record Manager understands 6-bit characters only; it can therefore be difficult to recognize 12-bit characters. Most of the languages discussed here do not.

The implementation must be able to produce object code that is suitable for interactive use. Many implementations have a buffering problem: in a question-answer sequence between a user and the program, some systems require the user to provide the next line of input before giving him the response to his previous line. Furthermore, an interactive system often has difficulty with programs using large amounts of memory or exhibiting poor locality of reference. Since the CDC Cyber has no paging mechanism, poor locality of reference cannot be a problem; on the other hand, large memory consumption can significantly reduce system performance. At SARA, there is a limit of 60,000 (octal) words of storage for an interactive program.

9.1 Pascal

All Pascal input/output files must reside on disk. Card reader and printer files are acceptable because the operating system, Scope, automatically spools them via disk. Magnetic tape files are not available to Pascal programs; they must first be copied to disk (and afterwards copied back) using a system utility. This causes the length of every tape record to be rounded upwards to a multiple of sixty bits, which may be tolerable on input, but probably not on output.

Pascal does not use the Record Manager. In one blow this eliminates most of the file types accepted by most other systems on the Cyber. Magnetic tapes would probably have been available if the Record Manager had been used: the problem is one of buffer length and the Record Manager is willing to manage its own buffer length correctly.

The Pascal implementation recognizes two kinds of files: "character files" and "other files." Character files have the type "**file of** *char*" the other files have the type "**file of** *othertype*," where "*othertype*" stands for some other type. Conceptually, Pascal sees these files as sequences of values of the given type, without arbitrary boundaries. On the other hand, character files are used for character input/output from the card reader and printer and this imposes further structure on them. Now and then, between otherwise normal characters, an "end of line" or an "end of page" may occur. On output files for the line printer, the operating system requires the program to prefix a carriage-control character to each line to indicate whether it is to appear at the top of the page. This responsibility is faithfully handed over to the programmer by Pascal, forcing him to treat print files differently from other character files. (End of line already makes character files different from other files.) There is an obscure procedure called "*new-page*" mentioned in the Pascal manual, which is supposed to cause further output to begin on a new page; it is not clear how it interacts with the programmer-supplied carriage-control character.

It is possible to get Pascal to read every bit of a disk file. To do this, one declares the file to be of a type which fills entire words evenly, for example:

file of packed array [0 . . . 59] **of** *bool*
file of packed array [0 . . . 4] **of** 0 . . . 4095

Other types are of course possible (subject to a number of peculiarities), and the choice of type can be used to provide some elementary structure for the file. The first type mentioned above will give easy access to individual bits; whereas the second provides twelve-bit bytes.

On the other hand, not everything reasonable will work. "**file of set of** 0 . . . 59," for example, is rejected by the compiler because it exceeds the maximum number of elements in a set (0 . . . 58 is allowed, but does not have the desired meaning). "**file of packed array** [1 . . . 15] **of** 0 . . . 255," which one might consider to indicate 15 bytes of eight bits packed into every two machine words (most 9-track tape files look like this) will not work, although it is proper Pascal. Pascal refuses to split an element of a packed array across a word boundary, and insists on leaving unused bits of padding in each word and using an extra word for the fifteenth byte. This completely defeats the purpose of the exercise. It may be said in defense of Pascal that its data structures were never *intended* to be used in this COBOL-like manner.

So-called 'connected' files, which are "connected" to time-sharing terminals, suffer from a one-line lag. Pascal makes the end-of-file test available to the user before he reads the next (possible non-existent) line. This is very reasonable. Unfortunately, Scope refuses to give end-of-file information until an attempt is made to read the possibly non-existent line. Pascal therefore reads an extra line ahead internally. This is not objectionable in batch, but it is intolerable during time-sharing. It would have been better to wait for the programmer to issue the end-of-file test before reading ahead internally.

[*Material Deleted*]

10 ESCAPE

Sometimes it is necessary for a programmer to escape from the programming language in order to code a small part of the program in another language. This is usually done

- in order to improve efficiency,
- in order to use subroutines already written in another language, or
- in order to gain access to system facilities not supported by the run-time system of the language.

It is clear that the practicality of a language implementation for large projects depends in part on the nature of the escape facilities, and on the frequency with which the escape facilities are necessary.

Such a method of escape is usually done by providing a mechanism for calling assembly language routines. Systems providing this usually advertise this as calling FORTRAN routines, in order to convince former FORTRAN users that they will not have to rewrite all their old subroutine libraries. An assembler language program then masquerades as a FORTRAN program by using the same linkage conventions.

Some compilers for high-level languages provide another scheme for escape. They permit the programmer to specify the machine instructions to be generated for each use of an operator or procedure when he declares the operator or procedure. This method is especially good for operations that can be implemented by a few machine instructions in line.

We also have the following questions:

- Does the implementation use normal operating system interfaces for calling other subroutines? Does the operating system suggest any normal subroutine-linkage convention? If not, one can hardly blame the language.
- Can the programmer establish communication with the operating system concerning matters not or poorly built into the implementation?
- Does the language support the standard operating system overlay mechanism?

10.1 Pascal

Pascal makes it possible to call subprograms written in FORTRAN. Such a FORTRAN subprogram must have a procedure declaration in the Pascal program, except that the procedure body is replaced by the reserved word "*Fortran.*" It is of course possible to write the called subroutine in any language that supports FORTRAN linkage conventions, including assembly language.

Unfortunately, there are some restrictions. If the FORTRAN subroutine expects a function or subroutine as parameter, then it must be provided with a FORTRAN function or subroutine as paramater. It is not possible to provide a Pascal function; Pascal and FORTRAN have different linkage conventions, and neither is willing to provide the necessary interface for procedure parameters. One cannot even get around this by writing the alien procedure in assembly language; the Pascal compiler performs a compile-time check to enforce the restriction.

If one has a FORTRAN routine which accepts an array of adjustable dimensions, as in

NIKLAUS WIRTH

Federal Institute of Technology (ETH), Zurich, Switzerland

Programming Languages: What to Demand and How to Assess Them

1 INTRODUCTION

The cost of computing power offered by modern hardware is about 1,000 times cheaper than it was 25 years ago. As a consequence, computer methods are applied to much more complicated and sophisticated problems. The result is the manufacture of very complex and large programs. In this phenomenon of Software Inflation, operating systems took the lead, but there are indications that many application orientated programs, including data management systems, are bound to become at least as large and complicated.

In their struggle to build such complex systems, in their continual fight against logical mistakes and unforeseen difficulties, against unexpected growth of code and unreached performance figures, against cost overrun and deadlines, engineers are groping for more adequate methods and tools. They range from management and programming principles to testing techniques and programming languages. The important role of programming languages in the design of large systems is now being recognized (Brooks, 1975). In fact, they are indispensible. As a consequence, interest in better programming languages is being revived, and industrial, governmental, and military circles are establishing committees to design such languages. The programmer and engineer is confronted with the urgent question: what should we ask of these languages, and what can we expect from them?

This paper will deal primarily with programming languages. But I am tempted to convey some observations from the hardware front that reveal a strong analogy to happenings in the area of language development.

After the first generation of computers had evolved into some truly large-scale machines, a second generation emerged, the so-called minicomputers. By that time, the larger machines were already programmed primarily in "higher-level" languages, such as FORTRAN. But the minicomputers threw programmers back into the dark age of assembly coding and bit pushing, consequently offsetting much of the cost savings in hardware by increasing cost in program preparation and upkeep. The reason for this regress was not so much the fact that the minicomputers' stores were too small to hold a compiler, but that their structure, order code, and architecture were determined in such an excruciatingly intelligent way that an automatic compiler was at a decided disadvantage compared to the cunning machine code programmer. Now we witness the emergence of the third generation of computers, the so-called microprocessors. The same phenomenon is repeating itself. Minicomputers have advanced to the state where most people realize that hand-coding is an arduous, hazardous, and costly business, and therefore prefer to use even mediocre compilers on their minis. So the old art of trickery is transferred to microprocessors, advertised, taught, and sold under a new heading: microprogramming. Again, the primary reason for this movement is the unnecessary and undesirable complexity that microprocessor designers mould into their chips during their flights of fancy. The first commercially available microprocessor is indeed of appalling baroqueness. Naturally, competitors try to outdo this very complexity, with the result that successors will in all probability be worse. Perhaps pocket calculators will repeat this story a third time.

Why don't manufacturers produce powerful but simple processors? Simply because complexity has proven to be a sure winner in attracting customers that are easily impressed by sophisticated gadgets. They haven't sufficiently realized that the additional performance of a complex design is usually much more than offset by its intransparency or even unreliability, difficulty of documentation, likelihood of misapplication, and cost in maintenance. But we shall probably have to wait for a long time, until simplicity will work as a sales argument. To be sure, "simple" must not be equated with "simple-minded," or "unsophisticated," but rather with "systematic" and "uncompromising." A simple design requires much more thought, experience, and sound judgement, the lack of which is so easily disguised in complexity. And here we hit the source of our dilemma: a simple design that requires more development labour than a complex design isn't very attractive to a trade-secret orientated organization in a profit-orientated society.

2 LANGUAGES TO INSTRUCT OR TO CONSTRUCT MACHINES?

The same phenomenon is chiefly responsible for a similar development in programming languages. Here, the temptation to accumulate facilities for specialized tasks is overwhelming, and the difficulties in finding generally useful, practical, yet systematic and mathematically appealing concepts are even greater. They require wide experience, ranging from familiarity with diversified application areas, through intimate knowledge of programming techniques, to insight in the area of hardware design. Simplicity appears as even less glamorous, and the possibilities to mend and cover up defects or inconsistencies are unparalleled. The cost is enormous, when these cover-up activities have reached their limits. These costs, however, are usually carried by the customer rather than the designer.

In addition to the general gross underestimation of the difficulties of good language design, there appears to be a lack of understanding of its purpose. Dijkstra once remarked that most programmers adhere to the old-fashioned view that *the purpose of our programs is to instruct our machines*, whereas the modern programmer knows that *the purpose of our machines is to execute the programs* which represent our abstract machines. I consider both views as legitimate, depending on the circumstance. A considerable step in the right direction will be taken, when designers *and* programmers become actively conscious of these two views and their fundamental difference. Unfortunately, so far very few have been aware of them. Let me therefore dwell somewhat longer on this point.

It has by now become widely accepted that the primary goal of programming languages is to allow the programmer to formulate his thoughts in terms of abstractions suitable to his problem rather than in terms of facilities offered by his hardware. Yet we encounter the phenomenon that most programmers, although using higher-level languages, know the representation of their program and data in terms of computer code to a surprising level of detail. The result is that their programs often make active use of this hardware-oriented knowledge and cannot be understood without it. One is tempted to conclude that these programmers have not recognized the true objective of their language: To allow the precise, formal specification of abstract machines.

However the languages must also take their part of the blame. Most programmers today start their career by learning a higher level language, for example FORTRAN. After a few attempts at program testing, the programmer finds out that knowledge of the computer's architecture, instruction code, and—above all—its data representation is a necessary ingredient of this profession. For, if something "unexpected" happens, the computer replies not in the programmer's language (i.e., in FORTRAN) but in terms of its own, which consists of cryptic words and octal or hexadecimal numbers. This leads the novice into the "real world" of computing, and he realizes that the constructs properly described in his manual are but a small subset of what the computer can actually do. For example:

1. Logical values are represented like numbers, and space can be saved by packing many of them into one "word." Selection of individual bits can be achieved by appropriate arithmetic, since the language doesn't really know whether the data represents a set of logical values or a single number.

2. An array element with index 0 can be simulated by declaring a simple variable one line ahead of the array which starts with index 1. The zero index element can then for example be used as a sentinel in a linear search through the array.

3. The control variable in a DO statement after termination has a value which is equal to the DO-limit plus 1 (if the step is (as usual) unity).

4. A modulo operation on an integer variable by a power of 2 can be programmed by an .AND. operation (if the integer is positive!).

5. 10 characters are packed into one word and can be extracted by suitable arithmetic and .AND. operations. For instance, two such 10-tuples can be compared by a single subtraction (and the result is correct, if both operands start with a letter or a digit less than 5!).

In all these cases, the main culprit is the language that does not provide suitable constructs to represent in a proper abstract way those features that the computer itself possesses. It is only natural that language designers therefore aim at introducing these facilities in newer languages. This leads to the introduction of a richer set of data structures, strings, sequences, etc., but unfortunately we also find features that are patently machine-orientated rather than corresponding to any well understood mathematical abstractions and objects. For example:

1. The label list (called switch), permitting an indexed jump, and the label variable permitting "assigned go to."

2. The address, reference, or pointer to variables and points in the program, and the use of ordinary arithmetic operations to manipulate them.

3. The interrupt as an event or "on-condition."

4. The bit-string as a set of logical values, denoted by octal numbers.

5. The equivalence statement permitting the sharing of store for different sets of variables (supposedly used during disjoint intervals of the computation).

Now what could be wrong with these features? It is the fact that they neither help the programmer to think in terms of structures suitable to his problem, nor

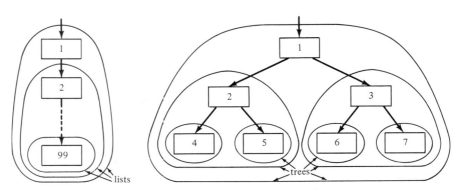

Figure 1   Lists and trees as recursive structures

enable a compiler to double-check the legality of the program statements within a well-defined framework of abstraction. Instead, they merely represent structures suitable to the machine disguised in the costume of a high-level language, and they leave the task of finding appropriate applications to the programmer. Hence, the advantage of using a language with these features over using assembly code is only marginal. Perhaps it increases a programmer's productivity, if measured in lines of code per day. But the more important task of increasing a programmer's ability to find structures most appropriate to the original problem, to find inherently effective solutions, and to design reliable programs, is affected to a much lesser degree.

In order to illustrate this subtle but important point let me offer you the following language constructs as alternatives to those criticized.

1. Instead of a label list and an indexed **goto** statement, introduce a selective statement. It not only eliminates the need for explicit labels and jumps, but makes the choice of precisely one of several statements much more obvious.

```
switch S = L1, L2, L3, L4;
goto S[i + 1];                         case i of
L1: statement-0; goto L5;                 0: statement-0;
L2: statement-1; goto L5;                 1: statement-1;
L3: statement-2; goto L5;                 2: statement-2;
L4: statement-3; goto L5;                 3: statement-3
L5: . . .                              end
```

In the above pieces of programs, one of four satements is to be executed, namely statement-0 in the case of variable i having the value 0, statement-1 in case $i=1$, etc. This is concisely and naturally expressed by a case statement (Hoare, 1964a). Instead, the ALGOL-60 program at the left uses a **goto** statement referring to a switch declaration, in analogy to an indexed branch instruction in assembler code.

2. If pointers are to serve to construct lists and trees, a facility for defining recursive data structures might well replace them and express the intended data structure more naturally. For example (see Figure 1):

```
type list=(node: integer; tail: list)
type tree=(node: integer; left, right: tree)
```

If more general structures, including rings, are to be made available, or if the main objective is data sharing, then pointers should at least be restricted to the role they must play, namely to refer to other objects. All notions that suggest that a pointer is represented by an integer denoting a storage address must be avoided. If a language supports the notion of data types, each pointer should be restricted to point to one type of object only. This permits an inexpensive compile-time check to prevent many common and costly errors in the use of pointers (Hoare, 1964b). For example:

```
DECLARE                                         type treenode =
   1 TREE-NODE CONTROLLED (CURRENT)              ↑record  key:  integer;
      2 KEY FIXED BINARY,                           left, right: treenode
      2 (LEFT, RIGHT) POINTER                     end;
   1 LIST-NODE CONTROLLED (CURRENT)            listnode =
      2 KEY 1 FIXED BINARY,                       ↑record key: integer;
      2 (NEXT, TREE) POINTER,                       next: listnode;
   ROOT POINTER STATIC                             tree: treenode
                                                 end;

                                               var root: listnode
```

The above pieces of program, expressed in PL/I at the left and Pascal at the right, allow to generate a data structure consisting of a ring of listnodes which are the roots of binary trees (see Figure 2). The danger of the PL/I formulation lies in the circumstance that treenodes may be inserted inadvertently in place of listnodes and vice versa, and that a reference to one kind of node is possible under the misbelief that it is a node of the other kind. Such an error cannot even be detected at the time of node generation. In the Pascal version, this kind of confusion would already be detected at compile-time, because of the distinction of pointers to listnodes from pointers to treenodes.

3. An interrupt is a highly machine-oriented concept that allows a single processor to participate in the execution of several concurrent processes. A language should either be devoted to the formulation of strictly sequential algorithms, in which case the interrupt has no place as a concept, or it is designed to express the concurrency of several sequential processes. In this case a suitable form of synchronization operations must be found, but again the interrupt as a concept is inappropriate, because it refers to a processor (machine) instead of a process (conceptual unit of the abstract algorithm).

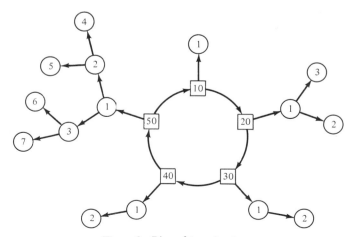

Figure 2 Ring of tree structures

4. The bitstring or word, if used as a set of logical values could well be represented as a Boolean array with indices ranging from 1 to w (where w is the wordlength of the computer). However, the denotation of constants of this type is usually by octal or hexadecimal numbers, which are conceptually foreign to the notion of logical values. A more natural concept that can very well be implemented by bitstrings is the **set** (of integers between 1 and w).

```
bits b              var s: set
b: = 132B;          s: = {2,4,5,7}
if b[4] then        if 4 in s then
b1 and b2           s1 * s2 (set intersection)
```

5. The dangers of a facility like the Equivalence statement to share store lie not so much in the conceptual realm as in the pitfalls of its application. It is too easy to forget the fact that the different sets of variables should be mutually exclusive in time. Hence, a facility that does not necessarily advertise shared use of store, but instead implicitly allocates and frees store as needed, would be preferable by far. This is precisely the effect achieved by the facility of variable declarations local to procedures of ALGOL 60. It enables a compiler to guarantee that inadvertant use of the variable under the wrong name is impossible.

```
COMMON A,B
EQUIVALENCE A,B
SUBROUTINE S1( )        procedure P1( );
    ... A ...              var a: T1;
END                     begin ... a ... end;
SUBROUTINE S2( )        procedure P2( );
    ... B ...              var b: T2;
END                     begin ... b ... end
```

I believe that there will be no real progress until programmers learn to distinguish clearly between a language (definition) and its implementation in terms of compiler and computer. The former must be understood without knowledge of the latter. And we can only expect programmers to understand this vital distinction, if language designers take the lead, and when implementors and manual writers follow that lead.

3 CRITERIA FOR JUDGING A LANGUAGE AND ITS DOCUMENTATION

Hence, we conclude that the first criterion that any future programming language must satisfy, and that prospective customers must ask for, is *a complete definition without reference to compiler or computer*. Such a definition will inherently be of a rather mathematical nature.

To many hardcore programmers, this demand perhaps sounds academic and (nearly) impossible. I certainly have not claimed that it is easy! I only claim that it is a necessary condition for genuine progress. I even have considerable sympathy for objections and reservations. Given a particular problem and confronted with one's installed hardware, one is often close to the point of despair when trying to maintain these high aspirations. It is therefore precisely the criterion where most language designers—often unconsciously—compromise and fail.

One may argue legitimately that there will always remain certain aspects of hardware that will be particular if not peculiar and that *must* be utilized and programmed as well (evidently enforcing the "old view" upon the programmer). We mainly think of interfaces to peripheral equipment, input/output devices, on-line sensors, or machinery to be controlled. But even in this area we must aim at a much higher standard of functional definition. Until this is widely achieved, language designers are well-advised to provide a facility to delineate modules within which certain device dependent language features are admitted and protected from access from elsewhere in a program. Such a facility, if well designed, would obviate the hitherto common practice of using several languages of different "levels" in designing a large system. This is a point of considerable practical importance, because interfacing between different languages (and operating systems) is precisely the occasion that most frequently forces programmers to step down to the "bit pattern level" as the only common ground of all implementations.

Hence, I recommend that a future language must provide a *modularization facility which introduces and encapsulates an abstract concept.* Such concepts can then be built out of concepts defined in lower level modules, and will express composite objects and actions on higher levels. This modularization facility is instrumental in keeping the size of a language—measured in terms of the number of data types, operators, control structures, etc.—within reasonable bounds. Without it, the temptation to include an additional feature each time a new application comes to mind is enormous. It can hardly be resisted, if there is no provision for expressing it in a closed and protected form within the language.

This leads us to another criterion for judging future language proposals: their *size*. We have witnessed the traumatic effects of languages of extreme size, whose descriptions comprise hundreds of pages of specialized and diffuse terminology with the disguised purpose to disguise confusion. A journey through the world of programming language manuals is indeed a sobering experience. The failure to distinguish between language definition and compiler description, between the meaning of language constructs and restrictions imposed by an implementation, between essential and incidental, has already been mentioned. But I must point out a common deficiency of even more fundamental nature: poor mastery of (natural) language. This phenomenon is unfortunately very widespread not only in manuals but also in the prolific computer science literature. It is not my intention to recommend the practice of embellishing imprecise thoughts with artful language, but I advise any author to straighten out his thoughts until simple words suffice to express them. In programming, we are dealing with complicated issues, and the more complicated an issue, the simpler must be the language to describe it. Sloppy use of language—be it English, German, FORTRAN, or PL/I—is an unmistakable symptom of inadequacy.

Hence, our next demand addressed to future language designers is *conciseness and clarity of description,* and *sound use of language.* To give a concrete figure, the definition of a language, comprising its syntax specifying the set of well-formed sentences, and its semantics defining the meaning of these sentences, should not extend over more than 50 pages. This primary document should be accompanied by separate documents describing implementations, their limitations, effectiveness, and their reactions to ill-formed programs. The total length of these documents should be not more than 25 pages, and they *must be written in good style, devoid of ill-defined technical jargon.* Anything else is unacceptable, regardless of the high-level committees sponsoring the product, the pressing economic reasons, the urging of politicians to promote international co-operation, governmental blessing, or even commercial advertisement campaigns. On the contrary, the appearance of such décor must be taken as a call for extra vigilance.

4 TECHNICAL CRITERIA FOR JUDGING A LANGUAGE IMPLEMENTATION

My insistence on separating the language, its syntax, and its semantics as an abstract entity on the one side, and its implementation as a concrete tool on the other side, should not be interpreted as emphasis of the abstract at the expense of technical realities. We cannot close our eyes to the fact that programs are developed exclusively either to be executed by computers or as academic exercises. Hence to most people a language is at most as good as its compiler. My point is that we should not waste our time evaluating a compiler until we have closely examined the language. However, if a language has shown to be conceptually sound, what are the criteria to judge a compiler? Let me list the most important ones.

The *compiler must be totally reliable.* This requirement is threefold. First, it implies that every program is checked against *every single rule of the language,* that no formally incorrect program be allowed to pass without an indication. Second, it implies that any correct program is translated correctly. All efforts of systematic design, program verification, etc., rely on total compiler correctness. Third, no incorrect program can be allowed to cause the compiler to crash. These are very stringent conditions not only for the compiler engineer, but also for the language designer. For, under this rule the hardships of the former grow exponentially with the generosity of the latter. Consider, for example, the case where a language definition contains the rule that there may be no procedures exerting so-called side-effects on non-local variables. Then we ask that a compiler be able to detect such side-effects.

In spite of its exhaustive checking facilities, a compiler must *compile at reasonable speed.* This is particularly important when constructing large programs, such as operating systems and compilers themselves. The figure of one second per page of source program is a reasonable figure for a medium-size computer. An efficient compiler makes all desire for so-called interactive or incremental compilation disappear, and reduces the need for separate compilability of program parts significantly. If part compilation is provided, then the compiler must be able to maintain full checks for all allowed interfaces, be they parameters (type compatibility) or global variables. Otherwise part compilation is a mixed blessing.

The next requirement of a good compiler is that it generate *efficient code.* This does not mean that every single odd facility of the hardware has to be utilized at all cost. But it implies the selection of reasonably obvious code, and in particular the lack of virtually any kind of run-time support routines. A most crucial point is an effective code for procedure calls.

A related requirement is that the *execution cost* of the code be *reasonably predictable*. There must be no circumstances where a language construct suddenly becomes drastically more expensive, if used in a certain special context. The programmer should have the possibility to understand the approximate costs of all language constructs. The same holds for the storage space consumed by code and—even more important—for data. For example, an implementation where the efficiency of access to indexed variables depends on the lower index bound being 0 or not, is rather undesirable. So is a system where the storage requirements of the two rectangular arrays.

> a1: **array** [1:2, 1:1000] **of** integer
> a2: **array** [1:1000, 1:2] **of** integer

are very different.

The *compiler* itself should also be *reasonably compact*. Bulky compilers are usually inefficient, too, particularly because loading is costly and inconvenient, and because the job priority will be lower—assuming a fair scheduling policy—if a large store is requested. This point is even more essential in interactive environments, where a system's swapping activity is greatly increased by colossal compilers.

Once again, let me emphasize the feedback on language design: these requirements postulate nothing less than that the designer must be intimately familiar with all techniques and details of implementation.

A compiler must provide a *simple and effective interface to the environment*, its file system, and/or its input and output devices. This places the requirement on the language design that it should reflect such objects in a decent way. The compiler and its code should not impose any additional overhead through such an interface, as for example extra buffering of transmitted data.

All preceding requirements concern the programmer directly. There are additional ones stemming from considerations of compiler maintenance problems. One is that the *compiler be written in its own language* (always assuming that we are concerned with a general-purpose programming language). A compiler written completely in a high-level language is immeasurably easier and safer to adapt to changing environments and demands. Only such a description enables you to pinpoint possible mistakes in a short time and to correct them immediately. Moreover, it is the best guarantee that the implementor has taken care to produce a good compiler; not only because sloppy work becomes much more subject to scrutiny by customers, but also because an effort to generate efficient and compact code immediately pays off in increased performance of the compiler itself.

If a language and its compiler are both of sufficient quality to define and process themselves, it also becomes economical to abandon the concept of "binary program libraries" and to collect and retain programs in their source form alone.

All these requirements more or less directly influence the design of a language itself. They all suggest a great deal of restraint of the designer against his flights of fancy. The most important argument for this point comes from the compiler engineer; *the development cost of a compiler* should stand in a proper relationship to the advantages gained by the use of the language. *This holds also for individual language features.* Hence, the language designer must be aware of the additional amount of effort needed to implement a feature under the presence of various other features. Very often such costs cannot be indicated without consideration of context.

For example:

1. The cost of implementation of dynamic arrays is negligible, if arrays cannot occur as components of other structures. If they can, the problem is very much more complex.
2. Packed data structures are relatively straightforward to implement, if all structures are static, i.e., if all their characteristics are constant and known at compile-time. The difficulties multiply, if dynamic structures are allowed, or if merely a static packed structure can be passed as a parameter to a sub-routine, in which its size is unknown.
3. Implementation of sequential files becomes drastically more complex, if the file elements are allowed to vary in type (size), whereas this freedom has little effect on the complexity of compiling arrays.

Hence, a proper design is characterized equally by what is omitted as by what is included.

5 CAN THESE CRITERIA BE MET?

I have suggested a number of criteria by which to judge present and future language designs and implementations of them. I admit that they are rather stringent. It is important to examine them critically and, if one has agreed with them, to uphold them, even if perhaps one has to abandon some of one's pet ideas on features that a language should contain.

Postulating stiff criteria is, however, an easy matter, and practicing programmers have learned to be suspicious of academics who preach high-spirited ideals. So perhaps I owe a proof that it is indeed possible to achieve these postulated merits by a single language. I am prepared to do so by providing a few figures and facts about the programming language *Pascal*. I offer this language only as a yardstick, in full awareness that Pascal is not the ultimate wisdom in language design, definition, and documentation. After all, a yardstick that cannot be surpassed would ill serve as an encouragement for future efforts.

First, a brief sketch of the language: Pascal offers a set of program structuring facilities supporting the concepts of structured programming. It includes well-known forms of conditional, selective, and repetitive statements. Its sub-routines can all be activated recursively, and there are several kinds of parameters: expressions (by value), variables (by reference), procedures, and functions. Variables are declared to be of a fixed type. There are the standard types integer, real, Boolean, and character. In addition, new types can be defined within the language. A scalar type is defined by enumerating its possible values, a structured type is defined by indicating its structuring scheme and the type(s) of its components. There are four basic structuring schemes: arrays, records, sets, and (sequential) files. In addition, dynamic structures of any pattern can be constructed with the aid of pointers, with comprehensive and inexpensive checks of the validity of their use. The language is defined by a concise report of 28 pages (Jensen and Wirth, 1974; Wirth, 1971a) and an attempt has been made to define its semantics by rigorous axioms (Hoare and Wirth, 1973).

Second, a brief sketch of the compiler (developed at ETH for the CDC 6000 computer family): It performs a complete check of syntax and type compatibility rules. Errors are accurately pinpointed and care is taken to avoid spurious messages. Great care is taken to generate effective code. For example:

1. Registers are used in a highly efficient way.
2. Address computation of components of structured variables is performed at compile time wherever possible.
3. Multiplications and divisions by powers of 2 are implemented as shifts.

Language rules that cannot be checked at compile-time are verified at runtime. This includes checking of index bounds, of case expressions, of assignment compatibility to subrange variables, etc. Upon detection of an illegal operation, a symbolic post-mortem dump is provided, listing currently accessible variables by name and current value.

The compiler supports the data facility of Pascal. On a computer with large wordlength, this can well lead to savings of storage by sizeable factors (up to 60 on the CDC system). The compiler itself profits by this, although the routines to implement packed data representations are extensive and complicated.

Moreover, the compiler provides a smooth interface to the resident file system. Files used in a program and existing before and/or after execution are clearly listed as parameters in a program heading. The compiler generates standard relocatable code and allows linkage with separately compiled procedures.

The single-pass compiler requires 20,000 words (=160,000 bytes) for code and data to compile small programs, and 23,000 words to recompile itself. (By comparison, the standard FORTRAN compiler requires 20,000 words.) The efficiency of the compiled code is indicated by a few sample programs in the Appendix. The average compilation speed is 110 lines of source code per second (measured when compiling the compiler). Compiling, loading, and executing the null-program takes 0.3 seconds. These figures have been obtained on a CDC 6400 computer (roughly equivalent to IBM 370/155 or Univac 1106).

The entire compiler is programmed exclusively in Pascal itself (Wirth, 1971c). There is no assembly code interspersed in the Pascal text. Every program is supported by a small run-time routine package that provides the interface to the computer's peripheral processors and the operating system. This nucleus is programmed in assembly code and occupies just 500 words. Conversion routines for numeric input and output (including floating-point conversion) are also described fully in Pascal.

The compiler itself is about 7,000 lines long. Hence, it takes only 63 seconds of processor time (on a CDC 6400) to recompile the compiler. By comparison, a cross-reference generator, also programmed entirely in Pascal, takes 30 seconds to produce an alphabetically ordered cross-reference table of the compiler program.

The latest compiler (again for the CDC 6400) was developed by a single expert programmer in 16 (full-time equivalent) months (Ammann, 1974, 1975). This figure excludes work on the small support package and the I/O conversion routines. It was developed according to rigid discipline and the top-down, stepwise refinement technique (Wirth, 1971b). Its remarkably high reliability is primarily due to its systematic design and the use of a suitable language for coding it.

Last but not least, the language Pascal was designed *seven years* ago. The first compiler was operational in late 1970. Since then the language has undergone extensive use and scrutiny (Habermann, 1973; Lecarme and Desjardins, 1975). Sufficient practical experience is available to make an objective assessment of its utility (Wirth, 1975), many other compilers have been or are being developed on other computers (Friesland et al., 1974; Welsh and Quinn, 1972), and Pascal has already spurred further developments in the direction of multiprogramming (Brinch Hansen, 1975).

So much about Pascal. It should suffice to convince that the afore postulated criteria are more than wishful thinking, but objectives that *can* be achieved, because they already *have* been achieved to a fair degree. My primary conclusion is that Pascal is a language which already approaches the system complexity, beyond which lies the land of diminishing returns. One should therefore be rather critical about new language proposals that usually start from scratch and rapidly build up to even greater complexity. I have provided this information and these figures in order that future languages—no matter where they come from—may be objectively compared, by the customers who will have to pay for them.

ACKNOWLEDGMENT

The author is grateful to C. A. R. Hoare for his many helpful comments and suggestions.

APPENDIX: PASCAL TEST PROGRAMS

The purpose of the following sample programs is to convey an impression of the character of the programming language Pascal, and to provide some performance figures for comparative studies. These figures were obtained on a CDC 6400 computer with the SCOPE 3.4 operating system. The statements "writeln(clock)" indicate the points where the time was taken.

Generate a Table of Powers of 2

This program computes the exact values of 2**k and 2**(−k) for k=1 . . . n, and
prints them in the form

2	1	.5
4	2	.25
8	3	.125
16	4	.0625
32	5	.03125
64	6	.015625

. . . .

```
program powersoftwo (output);
const m = 30; n = 90; {m> = n*log(2)}
var exp,i,j,k: integer;
    c,r,t: integer;
    d: array [0. .m] of integer; {positive powers}
    f: array [1. .n] of integer; {negative powers}
begin k : = 0; r : = 1; d[0] : = 1;
    writeln(clock);
    for exp : = 1 to n do
    begin {compute and print 2**exp} c : = 0;
      for i : = 0 to k do
      begin t : = 2*d[i] + c;
        if t > = 10 then
          begin d[i] : = t−10; c : = 1
          end
        else
          begin d[i] : = t; c : = 0
          end
      end;
      if c > 0 then
        begin k : = k + 1; d[k] : = 1
        end;
      for i : = m downto k do write (' ');
      for i : = k downto 0 do write (d[i]:1);
      write (exp:5,' .');
      {compute and print 2**(−exp)}
      for j : = 1 to exp− 1 do
      begin r : = 10*r + f[j];
        f[j] : = r div 2; r : = r − 2*f[j]; write (f[j]:1)
      end;
      f[exp] : = 5; writeln('5'); r : = 0
    end;
    writeln(clock)
end.
```

This program uses integer arithmetic exclusively. Execution time for computing the powers of 2 (n = 90) was measured as 916 (813) msec. The figure in parentheses is obtained when run-time index bound checks are disabled.

Palindromic Squares

A number is a palindrome, if it reads the same from both ends. Find all integers between 1 and 10000 whose squares are palindromes! For example: sqr(11) = 121, sqr(22) = 484, sqr(2002) = 4008004.

```
program palindromes(output);
    var i,j,k,n,r,s: integer;
        p: boolean;
        d: array [1. .10] of integer;
begin n : = 0; writeln(clock);
    repeat n : = n + 1; s : = n*n; k : = 0;
    repeat k : = k + 1; r : = s div 10;
        d[k] : = s − 10*r; s : = r
    until s = 0;
    i : = 1; j : = k;
    repeat p : = d[i] = d[j];
        i : = i + 1; j : = j − 1
    until (i>=j) or not p;
    if p then writeln(n,n*n)
    until n = 10000;
    writeln(clock)
end.
```

Execution time was measured as 3466 (2695) msec.

Quicksort

This program sorts an array of 10000 integers according to the method called Quicksort (Hoare, 1962). It uses a recursive procedure. The maximum depth of recursion is ln(10000).

```
program quicksort(output);
    const n = 10000;
    var i,z: integer;
        a: array [1. .n] of integer;
    procedure sort(k,r: integer);
        var i,j,x,w: integer;
    begin {quicksort with recursion on both partitions}
        i: = k; j: = r; x: = a[(i + j) div 23];
        repeat
            while a[i] < x do i : = i +1;
```

```
      while x < a[j] do j : = j - 1;
      if i < = j then
         begin w : = a[i]; a [i] : = a[j]; a[j] : = w;
            i : = i + 1; j : = j - 1
         end
      until i > j;
      if k < j then sort(k,j);
      if i < r then sort(i,r)
   end {sort};
begin z : = 1729; {generate random sequence}
   for i : = 1 to n do
      begin z : = (131071*z) mod 2147483647; a[i] : = z
      end;
   writeln(clock);
   sort(1,n);
   writeln(clock)
end.
```

Execution time: 4098 (2861) msec.

Count Characters in a File

The following program copies a text (file of characters) and counts the transmitted
blanks, letters, digits, special symbols, and lines. It also inserts a printer control
character at the beginning of each line.

```
program countcharacters(input,output);
   var ch: char;
      c0,c1,c2,c3,c4: integer; {counters}
begin writeln(clock); linelimit(output, -1);
   c0 : = 0; c1 : = 0; c2 : = 0; c3 : = 0; c4 : = 0;
   while not eof(input) do
   begin write(' '); c0 : = c0 + 1;
      while not eoln(input) do
      begin read(ch); write(ch);
         if ch = ' ' then c1 : = c1 + 1 else
         if ch in ['a'..'z'] then c2 : = c2 + 1 else
         if ch in ['0'..'9'] then c3 : = c3 + 1 else c4 : = c4 + 1
   end;
   readln; writeln
   end;
   writeln(clock);
   writeln(c0, ' lines');
   writeln(c1, ' blanks');
   writeln(c2, ' letters');
```

```
      writeln(c3, ' digits');
      writeln(c4, ' special characters');
      writeln(clock)
   end.
```

Execution time was measured as 4345 msec for a file with 1794 lines, 23441 blanks, 27331 letters, 1705 digits, and 9516 special characters. This results in an average of 0.068 msec per character, or 14680 characters per second.

Input and Output of Numbers

The next sample program generates a file *f* of 25000 real numbers, and computes their sum *s*. Then the file is reset and read, and a checksum is computed.

```
      program numericio(f,output);
         const n = 25000; d = 0.12345;
         var i: integer; x,s: real;
            f: file of real;
      begin writeln(clock);
         x : = 1.0; s : = 0; rewrite(f);
         for i : = 1 to n do
            begin write(f,x); s : = s + x; x : = x + d
            end;
         writeln(clock, s);
         reset(f); s : = 0;
         while not eof(f) do
            begin read(f,x); s : = s + x
            end;
         writeln(clock, s)
      end.
```

It took 1230 msec to generate the file, and 980 msec to read it. This corresponds to 49 μsec to write, and 39 μsec to read per number.

The amount of time increases drastically, if a decimal representation of the numbers on the file is requested. This is easily accomplished, namely by declaring the file to consist of characters instead of real numbers:

   f: **file of** char

In this case, the read and write statements include a conversion operation from decimal to binary and vice-versa. Generating the file then takes 28185 msec, reading takes 30313 msec. This corresponds to an increase by a factor of 23 in writing and 31 in reading. (Each number is represented by 22 characters on the file).

BIBLIOGRAPHY

Papers that appear in this book are marked with an asterisk.

ADDYMAN, A. M., et al., "A Draft Description of Pascal," *Software—Practice and Experience*, 9, **5**, 381–424 (1979).

ADDYMAN, A. M., "A Drafted Proposal for Pascal," *SIGPLAN Notices*, 15, **4**, 1–66 (April 1980).

ALBRECHT, P. F., P. E. GARRISON, S. L. GRAHAM, B. H. HYERLE, P. I. AND B. KRIEG-BROEKNER, "Source-to-Source Translation: Ada to Pascal and Pascal to Ada," *SIGPLAN Notices, 15,* **11,** 183–193 (1980).

AMERICAN NATIONAL STANDARDS INSTITUTE, INC., "Military Standard: Ada Programming Language," ANSI/MIL-STD-1815A, 1983.

AMERICAN NATIONAL STANDARDS INSTITUTE, INC., "IEEE Standard Pascal Computer Programming Language," ANSI/IEEE 770 X3.97, 1983.

AMERICAN STANDARDS ASSOCIATION INC., X3.9 1966 American National Standard FORTRAN (1966).

AMERICAN STANDARDS ASSOCIATION INC., X3.9 1978 American National Standard FORTRAN (1978).

AMERICAN STANDARDS ASSOCIATION INC., X3.23–1974 American National Standard COBOL (1974).

AMMANN, U., "The Method of Structured Programming Applied to the Development of a Compiler," in *International Computing Symposium 1973*, A. Günther et al., eds., North Holland (1974).

AMMANN, U., "Die Entwicklung eines Pascal-Compilers nach der Methode des strukturierten Programmierens," ETH-Diss. 54–56 (1975).

262

*ANDERSON, B., "Type Syntax in the Language C: An Object Lesson in Syntactic Innovation," *SIGPLAN Notices, 15,* **3,** 21–27, (March 1980).

ANDERSON, G. E., AND K. C. SHUMATE, "Selecting a Programming Language, Compiler and Support Environment—Method and Example," *IEEE Computer* (August 1982).

BARNES, J. P. G. "An Overview of Ada," *Software—Practice and Experience, 10,* 851–887 (1980).

BARNES, J. P. G., *Programming in Ada.* Addison-Wesley Publishing Co., Reading, MA. (1982).

Bell System Technical Journal, 57, **6,** part 2 (1978). Entire issue devoted to UNIX.

BARRON, D. W., et al., "The Main Features of CPL," *The Computer Journal, 6,* **2,** 134–43 (1963).

BELL TELEPHONE LABORATORIES, *The Bell System Technical Journal,* American Telephone and Telegraph Co. (1978).

BERSOFF, E. H., V. D. HENDERSON, AND S. G. SIEGEL, "Software Configuration Management: A Tutorial," *IEEE Computer Magazine, 12,* **1,** 6–13 (1979).

BIRTWISTLE, DAHL, MYHRHAUG, NYGAARD, "SIMULA *Begin,*" Studentlitteratur, Lund (1974).

BLUM, E. K., "Programming Parallel Numerical Algorithms in Ada," in *The Relationship between Numerical Computation and Programming Languages,* edited by J. K. Reid, pp. 297–304, North-Holland, Amsterdam (1982).

BOEHM, B. W., J. R. BROWN, H. KASPAR, M. LIPOW, G. J. MACLEOD, AND M. J. MERRITT, *Characteristics of Software Quality,* North-Holland, Amsterdam, 1978.

*BOOM, H. J., AND E. DE JONG, "A Critical Comparison of Several Programming Language Implementations," *Software-Practice and Experience, 10,* **6,** 435–73 (June 1980).

BOWLES, K. L., *Problem solving using PASCAL,* Springer-Verlag, New York (1977).

BRINCH HANSEN, P., *The Architecture of Concurrent Programs,* Prentice-Hall, Englewood Cliffs, NJ (1977).

BRINCH HANSEN, P., "The Programming Language Concurrent Pascal," *IEEE Trans. on Software Engineering, 1,* **2,** 199–227 (1975).

BRINCH HANSEN, P., "A Programming Methodology for Operating System Design," in *Information Processing 74,* Rosenfeld, J. L., ed. North-Holland, Amsterdam (1974).

BROOKS, F. P., JR., "The Mythical Man-Month," in *Essays on Software Engineering,* Addison-Wesley, Reading, MA (1975).

BROOKS, R., "Using a Behavioral Theory of Program Comprehension in Software Engineering," *Proceedings of the Third International Conference on Software Engineering,* IEEE, 196–201 (1978).

BSI, *Draft Standard Specification for the Computer Programming Language Pascal,* Document 79/60528 DC. (1979).

CARDOZO, P., *"TUNIS-2: a UNIX-Like Portable Operating System,"* Master's thesis, University of Toronto. Department of Computer Science (1980).

CARLSON, W. E., et al., "Introducing Ada," in *Proceedings of the 1980 Annual Conference,* Association for Computing Machinery, 263–71 (1980).

COHEN, N. C., "Parallel Quicksort: An Exploration of Concurrent Programming in Ada," *Ada Letters, II,* **2** (September–October 1982).

COMER, D., "MAP: A Pascal Macro Preprocessor for Large Program Development," *Software-Practice and Experience*, 9, 203–209 (1979).

CONRADI, R., "Further Critical Comments on the Programming Language Pascal, Particularly as a System Programming Language," *SIGPLAN Notices*, 11, 8–25 (1976).

COOPER, D., *Standard Pascal User Reference Manual*, W. W. Norton & Company, New York (1983).

DAHL, O., et al., *Simula 67: Common Base Language.* Norwegian Computing Center, University of Oslo (1967).

DAHL, O., E. W. DIJKSTRA, AND C. A. R. HOARE, *Structured Programming*, Academic Press, New York (1972).

DE MORGAN, R. M., I. D. HILL, AND B. A. WICHMANN, "A Supplement to the ALGOL 60 Revised Report," *The Computer Journal*, 19, 3, 276–288 (1976a).

DE MORGAN, R. M., I. D. HILL, AND B. A. WICHMANN, "Modified report on Algorithmic Language ALGOL 60," *The Computer Journal*, 19, 4, 364–379 (1976b).

DEREMER, F. AND H. H. KRON, "Programming-in-the-Large Versus Programming-in-the-Small." *IEEE Transactions on Software Engineering*, SE-2, 80–86 (June 1976).

DESJARDINS, P., "A Pascal Compiler for the Xerox Sigma 6," *SIGPLAN Notices*, 8, 6, 34–36 (1973).

DIJKSTRA, E. W., *A Discipline of Programming*, Prentice-Hall, Englewood Cliffs, NJ (1976).

DIJKSTRA, E. W., "On the GREEN Language Submitted to DoD," *SIGPLAN Notices*, 13, 10 (October 1978).

DIJKSTRA, E. W., "GOTO Statements Considered Harmful," *Comm. ACM*, 11, 147–148 (March 1968).

DIJKSTRA, E. W., "Hierarchical Ordering of Sequential Processes," *Acta Informatica*, 1, 115–138 (1971).

DIJKSTRA, E. W., "The Humble Programmer," *Comm. ACM*, 15, 859–866 (1972a).

DIJKSTRA, E. W., "Notes on structured programming," in O. J. Dahl, E. W. Dijkstra, and C. A. R. Hoare, *Structured Programming*, Academic Press, New York (1972).

DIJKSTRA, E. W., "A Short Introduction to the Art of Programming. "Department of Mathematics, Technische Hogeschool Eindhoven, EWD-316 (1971).

*FEUER, A., AND N. GEHANI, "A Comparison of the Programming Languages C and Pascal," *ACM Computing Surveys*, 14, 1 (March 1982).

FISHER, G., "AdaTEC Chairperson's Letter," *Ada Letters*, II, 5, 1–2 (March–April 1983).

FLON, LAWRENCE, "On Research into Structured Programming," *ACM SIGPLAN Notices*, 10, 10, 16–17 (1975).

FRIESLAND, G. et al., "A Pascal Compiler Bootstrapped on a DEC/System 10," *Lecture Notes in Computer Science*, 7, 101–113, Springer-Verlag, New York (1974).

GANNON, J. D., "An Experimental Evaluation of Data Type Conventions," *CACM*, 20, 8 (August 1977).

GANNON, J. D., AND J. J. HORNING, "Language Design for Programming Reliability," *IEEE Transactions on Software Engineering*, SE-1, 2, 179–91 (June 1975).

GEHANI, N., *Ada: An Advanced Introduction.* Prentice-Hall, Englewood Cliffs, NJ (1983).

GEHANI, N. H., "Ada's Derived Types and Units of Measure," submitted for publication (1983b).

GEHANI, N. H., AND T. A. CARGILL. "Concurrent Programming in the Ada Language: The Polling Bias," to be published in *Software—Practice and Experience.*

GEHANI, N. H., AND C. S. WETHERELL, "Levels of Concurrency," in preparation (1983c).

GEHANI, N. H., "Units of Measure as a Data Attribute," *Comput. Lang.,* **2,** 93–111 (1977).

GEHANI, N. H., AND C. S. WETHERELL, Unpublished notes (1980).

GESCHKE, C. M., JAMES H. MORRIS JR., AND EDWIN H. SATTERTHWAITE. "Early Experience with Mesa," *Communications of the ACM, 20,* **8,** 540–553 (1977).

GOODENOUGH, J. B., "The Ada Compiler Validation Capability," in *Proceedings of the ACM-SIGPLAN Symposium on the Ada Programming Language, SIGPLAN Notices, 15,* **11,** 1–8 (Nov 1980).

GOODENOUGH, J. B., *A Study of High Level Language Features: Detailed Feature Analysis,* SOFTECH Inc., Waltham, Massachusetts (1976).

GRIES, D., AND N. GEHANI, "Some Ideas on Data Types in High-Level Languages," *Communications of the ACM, 20,* **6** (June 1977).

*HABERMANN, A. N., "Critical Comments on the Programming Language Pascal," *Acta Informatica, 3,* 47–57 (1973).

HAMMARLING, S. J., AND B. A. WICHMANN, "Numerical Packages in Ada." IFIP TC2 Conference (August 1981).

HIGMAN, B., *A Comparative Study of Programming Languages,* Macdonald, London/American Elsevier, New York (1967).

HOARE, C. A. R., "Case Expressions," *ALGOL Bulletin,* 18.3.7, 20–22 (1964a).

HOARE, C. A. R., "Communicating Sequential Processes." *CACM, 21,* **8,** 666–677 (August 1978).

HOARE, C. A. R., "Data Reliability," *ACM SIGPLAN Notices, 10,* 528–533 (June 1975).

HOARE, C. A. R., "The Emperor's Old Clothes." 1980 ACM Turing Award Lecture in *CACM, 24,* **2,** 75–83 (February 1981).

HOARE, C. A. R., "Hints on Programming Language Design," *ACM SIGACT/SIGPLAN Symp. Principles of Programming Languages* (Boston, Mass., Oct. 1973), ACM, New York.

HOARE, C. A. R., "Monitors: An Operating System Structuring Concept," Computer Science Department, Stanford University, CS-401 (November 1973). Also published in *Comm. ACM* 17, 549–557 (1974b).

HOARE, C. A. R., "A Note on the *for* Statement," *BIT, 12,* 334–341 (1972).

HOARE, C. A. R., "Notes on Data Structuring," in Dahl, O.-J., *Structured Programming,* Academic Press, London (1972).

HOARE, C. A. R., "Proof of a Structured Program: The Sieve of Eratosthenes." *Computer J., 15,* 321–325 (1974a).

HOARE, C. A. R., "Quicksort," *Computer Journal, 5,* **1,** 13–15 (1962).

HOARE, C. A. R., "Record Handling," in *Programming Languages,* F. Genuys, ed., Academic Press, London and New York (1964b).

HOARE, C. A. R., "Recursive Data Structures," Computer Science Department, Stanford University, CS-400 (October 1973a).

HOARE, C. A. R., "Set Manipulation," *ALGOL Bulletin 27,* 29–37 (Dec. 1967).

HOARE, C. A. R., "Towards a Theory of Parallel Programming," *Programming Methodology* edited by D. Gries, Springer-Verlag, New York (1978).

HOARE, C. A. R., AND N. WIRTH, "An Axiomatic Definition of the Programming Language Pascal," *Acta Informatica*, *2*, 335–355 (1973).

HOLT, R. C., "Teaching the Fatal Disease (or) Introductory Computer Programming Using PL/I," *SIGPLAN Notices*, *8*, **5**, 8–23 (1973).

HONEYWELL-CIIBULL, *Formal Definition of the Ada Programming Language* (November 1980).

HORNING, J. J., "Effects of Programming Languages on Reliability," *Computing Systems Reliability*, edited by T. Anderson and B. Randell, Cambridge University Press, London (1979).

HOROWITZ, E., *Fundamentals of Programming Languages*, Computer Science Press, New York (1983).

IBM Corporation, General Information Manual: FORTRAN," *Document No. F28–8074–1* (1961).

IBM Corporation, "PL/I Language Specifications," Form C28–6571.

IBM Corporation, "PL/I (F) Reference Manual," Form C28–8201.

ICHBIAH, J. D. et al., "Rationale for the Design of the Ada Programming Language," *SIGPLAN Notices*, *14*, **6** (June 1979).

IGARASHI, S., R. L. LONDON, D. C. LUCKHAM, "Automatic Program Verification: A Logical Basis and Its Implementation," CS Report 73–365, Stanford University (May 1973).

JENSEN, K., AND N. WIRTH, *PASCAL User Manual and Report*, 2nd ed. Springer-Verlag, New York (1978).

JOHNSON, S. C., "A Portable Compiler: Theory and Practice," *Fifth Annual ACM Symp. Principles of Programming Languages* (Tucson, Arizona, Jan. 23–25), ACM, New York, pp. 97–104 (1978).

JOHNSON, S. C., "Lint, a C Program Checker," in *UNIX Programmer's Manual, 7th ed.*, Bell Telephone Laboratories, Inc. (1979).

JOHNSON, S. C., AND B. W. KERNIGHAN, "The Programming Language B," Comp. Sci. Tech. Rep. No. 8, Bell Laboratories (January 1973).

JOHNSON, S. C., AND D. M. RITCHIE, "Portability of C Programs and the UNIX System," *The Bell System Technical Journal*, *57*, 2021–2048 (1978).

JOY, W. N., S. L. GRAHAM, AND C. B. HALEY, "Berkeley Pascal User's Manual version 1.1," Dep. Electrical Engineering and Computer Science, Univ. of California, Berkeley (1980).

KERNIGHAN, B. W., AND M. D. MCILROY, (eds.), *UNIX Programmer's manual, 7th ed.*, Bell Laboratories, Murray Hill, NJ (1979).

KERNIGHAN, B., AND P. J. PLAUGER, *The Elements of Programming Style*, McGraw-Hill, New York (1974).

KERNIGHAN, B. W., AND P. J. PLAUGER, *Software Tools*, Addison-Wesley, Reading, MA (1976).

KERNIGHAN, B. W., AND P. J. PLAUGER, *Software Tools in Pascal*, Addison-Wesley, Reading, MA (1981).

KERNIGHAN, B. W., AND D. M. RITCHIE, *The C Programming Language*, Prentice-Hall, Englewood Cliffs, NJ (1978).

KIEBURTZ, R. B., W. BARBASH AND C. R. HILL, "A Type-checking Program Linkage System for Pascal," *Proceedings of the Third International Conference on Software Engineering*, IEEE, 23–28 (1978).

KOSARAJU, R., "Analysis of Structured Programs," *J. Computer and System Sciences*, *9*, **3**, 232–255 (1974).

KNUTH, D. E., *The Art of Computer Programming*, Vol. 1 (ch. 2). Addison-Wesley, Reading, MA (1968).

KNUTH, D. E., "An Empirical Study of FORTRAN Programs," *Software-Practice and Experience*, *1*, 105–133 (1971).

KNUTH, D. E., "Structured Programming with GOTO Statements," *Computing Surveys*, *6*, 261 (1974).

KUKI, H., "Mathematical Function Subprograms for Basic System Libraries—Objectives, Constraints, and Trade-off," *Mathematical Software* (ed. J. R. Rice), Academic Press, New York (1971).

LAMPSON, B. W., J. J. HORNING, R. L. LONDON, J. G. MITCHELL, AND G. L. POPEK, "Report on the Programming Language Euclid," *ACM SIGPLAN Notices*, *12*, **2**, ii + 79 (1977).

LEAVENWORTH, B. (ED), "Control Structures in Programming Languages. The goto Controversy." *SIGPLAN Notices*, *7*, **11**, 53–91 (1972).

LECARME, O., BOCHMANN, G. V., "A (truly) Usable and Portable Compiler Writing System," in ROSENFELD, J. L. (ed), *Information Processing 74*, North-Holland, Amsterdam (1974).

*LECARME, O., AND P. DESJARDINS, "More Comments on the Programming Language Pascal," *Acta Informatica*, *4*, 231–43 (1975).

LECARME, O., AND P. DESJARDINS, "Reply to a paper by A. N. Habermann on the programming language PASCAL," *SIGPLAN Notices*, *9*, 21–27 (Oct. 1974).

LEDGARD, H. F., AND M. MARCOTTY, "A Genealogy of Control Structures," *Communications of the ACM*, *18*, **11**, 629–639 (1975).

LISKOV, B., "Discussion," in J. H. Williams and D. A. Fisher (eds.), *Design and Implementation of Programming Languages*, Springer-Verlag, New York (Oct. 1976), p. 25.

LISKOV, B., A. SNYDER, R. ATKINSON, AND C. SCHAFFERT, "Abstraction Mechanisms in CLU," *Communications of ACM*, *20*, **8**, 564–576 (1977).

LISKOV, B., AND S. N. ZILLES, "Programming with Abstract Data Types," *SIGPLAN Notices*, *9*, **4**, 50–59 (April 1974).

MARMIER, E., "A Program Verifier for Pascal," *Information Processing 74* (IFIP Congress 1974), North-Holland, Amsterdam 1974.

MATETI, P., "Enumerated Types and Efficient Access of Array Elements," in preparation (1979a).

*MATETI, P., "Pascal versus C: A Subjective Comparison," *Language Design and Programming Methodology Symposium*, Springer-Verlag, Sydney, Australia (1979).

MATETI, P., "Specifications of a Macro Preprocessor for Pascal: A CS340 Project," University of Melbourne, Australia (1979b).

McILROY, M. D., E. N. PINSON AND B. A. TAGUE, "Foreword (to the special issue)," *The Bell System Technical Journal*, *57*, **6**, 1899–1904 (1978).

MOFFAT, D. V., "A Categorized Pascal Bibliography," *SIGPLAN Notices*, *15*, **10**, 63–75 (Oct 1980).

MORRIS, J. H., "Types are not Sets," *Conference Record ACM Symposium on Principles of Programming Languages*, Boston, MA, 120–124 (1973).

NAUR, P. (ed), "Revised Report on the Algorithmic Language ALGOL 60," *Comm. ACM,* *6,* 1–17 (1963).

NICHOLLS, J. E., *The Design and Structure of Programming Languages,* Addison-Wesley, Reading, MA (1975).

NUTT, G. J., "A Comparison of Pascal and FORTRAN as Introductory Programming Languages," *ACM SIGPLAN Notices,* 13, **2,** 57–62 (1978).

PARNAS, D. L., "On the Criteria to be Used in Decomposing Systems into Modules," *Commun. ACM,* 15, **12,** 1053–1058 (1972).

PASCAL NEWS. *News Letters of the Pascal Users Group.* A. Mickel (ed.), University of Minnesota (1970).

PLAUGER, P. J., "A Review of Kernighan and Ritchie 1978," *Computing Reviews,* 2–4 (1979).

PRATT, V., "Five Paradigm Shifts in Programming Language Design and their Realization in Viron, a Dataflow Programming Environment," Dept. of Computer Science Tech. Report STAN-CS-82-951, Stanford University, Stanford, CA (December 1982).

RICHARDS, M., "BCPL: A Tool for Compiler Writing and Systems Programming," *Proc. AFIPS SJCC,* 34, 557–566 (1969).

RITCHIE, D. M., "C Reference Manual," *Documents for Use with the Unix Time-Sharing System,* 5th ed. Bell Telephone Laboratories (1974).

*RITCHIE, D. M., S. C. JOHNSON, M. E. LESK, AND B. W. KERNIGHAN, "The C Programming Language," *The Bell System Technical Journal,* 57, **6,** part 2, 1991–2019 (July–August 1978).

RITCHIE, D. M., AND K. THOMPSON, "The UNIX Time-Sharing System," *Comm. ACM,* 17, **7,** 365–375 (and revised in *Bell Syst. Tech. J.,* 57, **6,** part 2, 1905–1929).

ROBERTS, E. S., E. M. CLARKE, A. EVANS, JR., C. R. MORGAN, "Task Management in Ada: A Critical Evaluation for Real-Time Multiprocessors, "*Software: Practice and Experience,* 11, **10,** 1019–52 (Oct. 1981).

SAMMET, J. E., "Roster of Programming Languages for 1976–1977," *ACM SIGPLAN Notices,* 13, **11,** 56–85 (1978).

SCHWARTZ, J. T., "On programming—Interim Report of the SETL Project," Courant Institute of Mathematical Sciences, New York (June 1975).

SCHWARTZ R. L., AND P. M. MELLIAR-SMITH, "On the Suitability of Ada for Artificial Intelligence Applications," SRI International, Menlo Park, CA (July 1980).

"Second Draft Proposal of the ISO Pascal Standard (January 1981)," *Pascal News* 20 (1981).

SETHI, R., "A Case Study in Specifying the Semantics of a Programming Language," *Seventh Annual ACM Symp. Principles of Programming Languages* (Las Vegas, Nevada, Jan. 28–30), New York, 117–130 (1980).

*SHAW, M., G. T. ALMES, J. M. NEWCOMER, B. K. REID, AND W. A. WULF, "A Comparison of Programming Languages for Software Engineering," *Software—Practice and Experience,* 11, 1–52 (1981).

SHAW, M., P. HILFINGER, W. A. WULF, "Tartan—Language Design for the Ironman Requirement: Reference Manual," *SIGPLAN Notices,* 13 9, 36–75 (September 1978).

SHAW, M., W. A. WULF, "Global Variables Considered Harmful," *SIGPLAN Notices,* 8, **2,** 28–34 (1973).

SPRINGER, A., "A Comparison of Language C and Pascal," IBM Technical Report G320–2128, Cambridge Scientific Center (August 1979).

STOTTS, P. D., JR., "A Comparative Survey of Concurrent Programming Languages," *SIGPLAN Notices*, *17*, **9,** 76–87 (1982).

SYKES, J. M., "Languages: the User's View of the Computer," in Boon, C. (ed.) *High Level Languages*, International Computer State of the Art Report 7, Infotech Information Ltd (1972).

TANENBAUM, A. S., "A Comparison of Pascal and ALGOL 68," *Computer Journal, 21,* **4** (1977).

U.S. AIR FORCE, *JOVIAL J73/1 Specifications*, Rome Air Development Center, Air Force Systems Command, Griffis Air Force Base, New York (1976a).

U.S. AIR FORCE, "Military standard Jovial(J3)," *MIL-STD-1588* (*USAF*) (1976b).

U.S. DEPARTMENT OF DEFENSE, "CODASYL, Initial Specifications for a Common Business Oriented Language" (1960).

U.S. DEPARTMENT OF DEFENSE, "Department of Defense Requirements for High-Order Computer Programming Languages: Ironman" (1977).

U.S. DEPARTMENT OF DEFENSE, "Preliminary Ada Reference Manual," *SIGPLAN Notices, 14,* **6,** part A (June 1979a).

U.S. DEPARTMENT OF DEFENSE, "Rationale for the Design of the Ada Programming Language," *SIGPLAN Notices, 14 ,* **6,** part B (June 1979b).

U.S. DEPARTMENT OF DEFENSE, *Reference Manual for the Ada Programming Language* (July 1980).

U.S. DEPARTMENT OF DEFENSE, *Reference Manual for the Ada Programming Language* (July 1982).

U.S. DEPARTMENT OF DEFENSE, *Reference Manual for the Ada Programming Language* (January 1983).

U.S. DEPARTMENT OF DEFENSE, *Requirements for Ada Programming Support Environment*, STONEMAN (February 1980).

U.S. DEPARTMENT OF DEFENSE, "Steelman—Requirements for High Order Computer Programming Languages," in *Tutorial*: *Programming Language Design*, ed. by A. I. Wasserman, IEEE Computer Society Press, 298–315 (1978).

VAN WIJNGAARDEN, A. et al., "Report on the Algorithmic Language ALGOL 68," *Numer. Math, 14,* 79–218 (1969).

WALKER, J., et al., *Praxis Language Reference Manual*, BBN Report 4582. Bolt Beranek and Newman Inc. (1981).

WEINBERG, G., *The Psychology of Computer Programming*, Van Nostrand Reinhold, New York (1971).

WEGNER, P., "Emperors, Generals and Programmers: Reflections on the Ada Controversy," ACM Forum, *CACM, 25,* **1,** 80–81 (January 1982).

WEGNER, P., "On the Unification of Data and Program Abstraction in Ada." Conference Record, *Tenth Annual ACM Symposium on Principles of Programming Languages*, Austin, TX, 256–264 (January 1983).

WEISSMAN, C. "Psychological Complexity of Computer Programs: An Initial Experiment," *Computer Systems Research Group Technical Report*, University of Toronto (1973).

WELSH, J., AND D. W. BUSTARD, "Pascal-Plus—Another Language for Modular Multiprogramming," *Australian Computer Science Communications, 1,* **1,** 49–62 (1979).

WELSH, J., AND C. QUINN, "A Pascal Compiler for the ICL 1900 Series Computers," *Software—Practice and Experience, 2,* 73–77 (1972).

WELSH, J., W. J. SNEERINGER AND C. A. R. HOARE, "Ambiguities and Insecurities in Pascal," *Software—Practice and Experience, 7,* 685–696 (1977).

WETHERELL, C. S., Private Communication. (February 28 and March 18, 1983).

WICHMANN, B. A., "Ada—the way ahead," *Computer Weekly,* 6–7 (November 6, 1980).

WICHMANN, B. A., "ALGOL 60 Compilation and Assessment," *APIC Studies in Data Processing, 10,* (1970).

*WICHMANN, B. A., "A Comparison of Pascal and Ada," *Computer Journal* (May 1980).

WICHMANN, B. A., "Some Performance Aspects of System Implementation Languages," *Constructing Quality Software,* P. G. Hibbard/S. A. Schuman (eds.), IFIP, North-Holland, Amsterdam, 46–62 (1978).

WICHMANN, B. A., *Tutorial material on the real data-types in Ada.* US Army Contract Number DAJA37–80–M–0342, National Physical Laboratory, Teddington Middlesex TW11 OLW, UK (1981).

*WIRTH, N., "An Assessment of the Programming Language Pascal," *IEEE Transactions on Software Engineering, SE-1,* **2,** 192–98 (June 1975).

WIRTH, N., "An Assessment of the Programming Language Pascal," *Proceedings International Conference on Reliable Software, SIGPLAN Notices, 10,* **6,** 23–30 (1975).

WIRTH, N., "The Design of a Pascal Compiler," *Software—Practice and Experience, 1,* 309–333 (1971).

WIRTH, N., "Modula: A Language for Modular Multiprogramming," *Software—Practice and Experience, 7,* 3–35 (1977a).

WIRTH, N., "On the Design of Programming Languages," *Information Processing 1974,* J. L. Rosenfeld (ed.), North-Holland, Amsterdam, 386–393 (1974).

WIRTH, N., *On* "Pascal Code Generation, and the CDC 6600 Computer," Report STAN-CS–72–257, Computer Science Department, School of Humanities and Sciences, Stanford University.

WIRTH, N., "Program Development by Stepwise Refinement," *Comm. ACM, 14,* **4,** 221–227 (1971b).

*WIRTH, N., "Programming Languages: What to Demand and How to Assess Them," *Software Engineering,* ed. by R. H. Perrott, Academic Press, New York, 155–173 (1977b).

WIRTH, N., "The Programming Language Pascal," *Acta Informatica, 1,* 35–63, Springer-Verlag, New York (1971).

WIRTH, N., "From Programming Techniques to Programming Methods," in Günther, Levrat, Lipps (eds.), *International Computing Symposium 1973,* North Holland, Amsterdam (1974b).

WIRTH, N., *Systematic Programming—An Introduction,* Prentice-Hall, Englewood Cliffs, NJ (1973).

WIRTH, N., AND C. A. R. HOARE. "A Contribution to the Development of ALGOL," *Commun. ACM, 9,* **6,** 413–431 (June 1966).

WORTMAN, B., AND J. R. CORDY, "Early Experiences with Euclid," in *5th International Conference on Software Engineering,* IEEE Computer Society Press, 27–32 (1981).

WULF, W. A., R. L. LONDON, AND M. SHAW, "An Introduction to the Construction and Verification of Alphard Programs," *IEEE Transactions on Software Engineering*, *2*, 253–265 (1976).

WULF, W. A., D. E. RUSSELL, AND A. N. HABERMANN, "BLISS: A Language for Systems Programming," *Communications of the ACM*, *14*, **12** (1971).

WULF, W. A., AND M. SHAW, "Global Variable Considered Harmful," *SIGPLAN Notices*, *8*, **2**, 28–34 (February 1973).

YOUNG, S. J., "Trends in the Design of Real Time Languages," *The Australian Computer Bulletin*, *4*, **5**, 5–7 (June 1980). Reprinted from the March 80 issue of Computer Bulletin.

ZUCKERMAN, S. L. "Problems with the Multitasking Facilities in the Ada Programming Language," Technical Note, Defense Communications Engineering Center, Reston, VA (1981).